AMERICA'S
SPECIAL FORCES

AMERICA'S
SPECIAL FORCES

The organization, men, weapons,
and the actions of the
United States Special Operations Forces

RAY BONDS

PUBLISHED BY
SALAMANDER BOOKS LIMITED
LONDON

A SALAMANDER BOOK

Published by Salamander Books Ltd.
8 Blenheim Court
Brewery Road
London N7 9NT
United Kingdom

© Salamander Books Ltd., 2001

A member of the Chrysalis Group plc

ISBN 1 84065 193 8

CREDITS

Designers: Interprep Ltd
Reproduction: Media Print (UK) Limited
Printed and bound in Spain

THE AUTHOR

Ray Bonds has been a defense journalist, editor, and publisher during a career
spanning over thirty-five years, covering periods and activities as wide-ranging
as the U.S. Civil War, anti-ballistic missile systems, stealth warfare, and modern
military intelligence gathering. He has written and edited scores of well-
respected titles on the world's major armed forces, their battles, weapons, and
organization, with a specialism in the armed services of the United States. His
works have included well-thumbed books on the shelves of official military
education centers throughout the United States, Europe, and Asia, and have
included the important trilogy *The U.S. War Machine, The Soviet War Machine,*
and *The Chinese War Machine.*

ACKNOWLEDGMENTS

The author and publishers would like to thank the following people and institutions for their valuable
assistance in providing information and illustrations used in this book:

George B. Grimes, Deputy Public Affairs Officer, U.S. Special Operations Command, MacDill Air Force
Base, Florida; Walt Sokalski and Ben Abel, U.S. Army Special Operations Command Public Affairs
office; Joan Prichard, U.S. Air Force Special Operations Command, Hurlburt Field, Florida;
Commander Jeff Alderson, and Mrs. Patricia O'Connor, U.S. Naval Special Warfare Command; Kathy
Vinson, Still Media Representative, Defense Visual Information Center (DVIC), March ARB, California;
Captain Jaret Heil, U.S. Marine Corps; Sgt Mike Bornfriend, U.S. Marine Corps, 1st Recon Bn, 1st Plt,
1st Marine Div (Special Operations Equipment Webmaster); U.S. Air Force Photo Services, Bolling Air
Force Base; Office of the Assistant Secretary of Defense (Special Operations/Low Intensity Conflict),
Office of the deputy Assistant Secretary of Defense for Special Operations Policy and Support, The
Pentagon, Washington, D.C.

CONTENTS

INTRODUCTION

U.S. Special Operations Forces: The Way Ahead

General Peter J. Schoomaker,
former Commander, U.S. Special Operations Command*

Having emerged from the Cold War as a uniquely postured superpower, America's armed forces stand at the threshold of a new millennium – peering into a seething cauldron of global activity.

As we venture into an uncertain future, threats to U.S. interests are developing new dimensions. We are being increasingly challenged by regional instability, transnational dangers, asymmetric threats and the likelihood of unpredictable events – threats that are not easily addressed by simple force-on-force calculations.

To meet these challenges, we must leverage the best capabilities and potential of our armed forces. This will be a difficult undertaking. We will have to make hard choices to achieve the trade-offs that will bring the best balance, most capability and greatest interoperability for the least cost. America's Special Operations Forces (SOF) have an important and growing role in addressing many of these challenges, and effectively satisfying the cost-benefit criteria.

Since being created by the Cohen-Nunn Amendment to the DoD Authorization Act of 1987, the U.S. Special Operations Command (USSOCOM) has provided highly trained, rapidly deployable and regionally focused SOF in support of global requirements from the National Command Authorities, the geographic commanders in chief, and our American ambassadors and their country teams.

During 1997, SOF deployed to 144 countries around the world, with an average of 4,760 SOF personnel deployed per week – a threefold increase in missions since 1991. SOF consists of over 46,000 people, active and reserve, who are organized into a variety of land, sea and aerospace forces including:

- U.S. Army Special Forces, the 75th Ranger Regiment, the 160th Special Operations Aviation Regiment (Airborne), psychological operations units and civil affairs units;
- U.S. Navy Sea-Air-Land forces (SEALs), special boat units and SEAL delivery units; and
- U.S. Air Force special operations squadrons (fixed and rotary wing), special tactics squadrons, a foreign internal defense squadron, and a combat weather squadron.

Although the acronym SOF is used to describe this community of world-class organizations, no one joins "SOF" per se. Instead, they join one of the units above, each of which is unique in its history, culture and contribution to the joint SOF team – and the United States is better served as a result of this diversity.

Above: The consummate "Global Warrior," Gen. Peter J. Schoomaker, for two years C-in-C of U.S. Special Operations Command prior to retirement in November 2000, has warned of new threats to U.S. national interests.

The legislation that created USSOCOM also specified certain SOF activities and assigned the Command specific authorities and responsibilities. These tasks, similar to those assigned to the Services, include:

- Manage a separate program and budget (Major Force Program 11: MFP-11) for SOF-unique requirements;
- Conduct research, development, and acquisition of SCF-peculiar items;
- Develop joint SOF doctrine, tactics, techniques and procedures;
- Conduct joint SOF-specialized courses of instruction;
- Train all assigned forces and ensure joint interoperability;
- Monitor the readiness of all assigned and forward deployed joint SOF;
- Monitor the professional development of SOF personnel of all services.

---

* Based on a statement presented to USSOCOM members by General Schoomaker prior to his retirement from the Command in October 2000.

The first two tasks give USSOCOM great flexibility in training, equipping and employing its forces.

The national military strategy of the United States requires its armed forces to advance national security by applying military power to help shape the international environment and respond to the full spectrum of crises, while also preparing now for an uncertain future. SOF support this "shape, respond, prepare now" strategy by providing an array of expanded options, strategic economy of force, "tailor to task" capabilities – and are particularly adept at countering transnational and asymmetrical threats.

SOF expand the options of the National Command Authority (NCA) and commanders-in-chief, particularly in crises that fall between wholly diplomatic initiatives and the overt use of large warfighting forces. Decision makers may choose SOF as an option because they provide the broadest range of capabilities that have direct applicability in an increasing number of missions, from major theater wars to smaller-scale contingencies to humanitarian assistance.

SOF allow decision makers the flexibility to tailor U.S. responses, lethal and nonlethal, to encompass this wide range of possibilities and reduce the risk of escalation associated with larger, more visible force deployments. Consequently, SOF may be the best choice for crises requiring immediate response or precise use of force, such as Operation Assured Response, the evacuation of 2,115 non-combatants from Liberia in 1996 with no loss of life.

SOF may be most effective in conducting economy of force operations, generating strategic advantage disproportionate to the resources they represent. For example, combat-ready Army Special Forces (SF) teams are routinely deployed around the world in support of peacetime engagement to prevent conflict and conserve resources.

By training host-nation forces to provide their own security, and using integrated civil affairs and psychological operations programs to strengthen government infrastructures, SF foster stability and help prevent local problems from developing into threats to international security. Should conflict arise, these "global scouts" can quickly transition to combat operations and spearhead decisive victory. As SOF engage in additional peacetime operations, it is important to remember that they are, first and foremost, warriors.

During conflict, SOF conduct operational and strategic missions that directly or indirectly support the joint force commander's campaign plan. Fully integrated into the joint campaign plan, SOF can attack high-value, time-sensitive targets throughout the battlespace to assist in rapidly achieving land, sea, air and space dominance. SOF also conduct information operations, train indigenous forces, assist conventional force management of civilians on the battlefield, and provide advisory and liaison capabilities to rapidly integrate coalition partners and leverage their unique qualities to enhance the capabilities of the entire force.

During post-conflict situations, SOF's training skills, coupled with civil affairs and psychological operations expertise, help speed the transition to normalcy, thereby allowing conventional forces to redeploy quickly. SOF use these same skills during peace operations, such as occurred in Haiti and Bosnia, to defuse volatile situations, provide "ground truth" to commanders and assist in the development of post-hostilities controls.

SOF are rapidly adaptable to a broad and constantly varying range of tasks and conditions. This organizational agility allows SOF to quickly concentrate synergistic effects from widely

Above: High on the list of U.S. Special Operations Forces' priorities is to prevent the spread of weapons of mass destruction (WMD), such as this Iraqi SCUD missile targeted during the Gulf War of 1991.

dispersed locations and assist joint force commanders in achieving decisive results without the need for time-consuming and risky massing of people and equipment. Even under the most austere conditions, SOF can conduct 24-hour, multidimensional operations to penetrate denied or sensitive areas and resolve terrorist activity, pre-empt the threat posed by weapons of mass destruction (WMD), or strike key targets with precision and discrimination.

Although a potent military force, SOF can often accomplish their mission without resorting to the use of force. SOF training skills combined with language proficiency, cultural awareness, regional orientation and an understanding of the political context of their missions make SOF unique in the U.S. military – true "warrior-diplomats." Moreover, this broad array of versatile capabilities allows SOF to "tailor to task" and operate effectively in any situation or environment.

SOF use this expertise to assist our American ambassadors and the geographic C-in-Cs in influencing situations favorably toward U.S. national interests through recurring interaction with current and potential allies.

During FY [fiscal year] 1997, SOF conducted 17 crisis response operations, 194 counterdrug missions, and humanitarian demining operations in 11 countries. In addition to these real-world requirements, SOF maintained a robust exercise schedule, participating in 224 combined exercises for training in 91 countries around the world. This proactive peacetime engagement allows SOF to help host nations meet their legitimate defense needs while encouraging regional cooperation, maintaining U.S. access, and visibly demonstrating the role of a professional military in a democratic society.

SOF's ability to help mold the international environment, rather than merely responding to it, is USSOCOM's most important day-to-day contribution to the U.S. national security and represents its "steady state" for the future.

U.S. conventional military dominance encourages future adversaries and competitors – ranging from established nations to non-state groups, such as terrorists, insurgents and new and unpredictable extremists – to avoid direct military confrontation with the United States. Instead, they will use asymmetric means such as WMD, information warfare, terrorism, taking the fight to urban areas, or the application of technological or operational surprise to offset our conventional advantages and achieve their goals – even posing a direct threat to the U.S. homeland. Moreover, an adversary already engaged in conventional warfare with the U.S. could still employ these means to gain temporary or localized battlespace parity or asymmetrical advantage.

The asymmetric challenge with the gravest potential facing the U.S. today is the threat posed by the global proliferation of WMD and their means of delivery. In recognition of the significant dangers associated with WMD, the Department of Defense assigned SOF some specific responsibilities in May 1995 in support of the broader interagency task of preventing the proliferation of WMD.

Today, counterproliferation (CP) has been given top operational priority at USSOCOM. CP includes actions taken to locate, identify, seize, destroy, render safe or transport WMD. USSOCOM is pursuing several approaches to address the WMD threat, including working with the geographic C-in-Cs to determine how best to bring SOF's capabilities to bear in support of theater CP objectives. The Command continues to refine its tactics, techniques and procedures in order to allow engagement of the full range of WMD targets including nuclear, biological and chemical weapons, improvised devices, means of delivery and supporting infrastructure.

Another serious asymmetric reality is information-based conflict. The power of information is growing exponentially and the increasing dependence of the U.S. and its adversaries on information presents many vulnerabilities and opportunities. In the past, information operations were the "punctuation" on the grammar of conflict – enhancing the impact of the military, diplomatic and economic effort. Today, the military often augments the other elements of national power to "punctuate" information operations – adding support, emphasis and authority.

The "Information Age" has also opened up a wide range of new opportunities, seemingly endless possibilities and significant vulnerabilities for SOF. Accordingly, USSOCOM is examining new ways to enhance its capabilities to ensure uninterrupted information exchange, reduce an adversary's ability to use information and influence situations to support mission accomplishment. These capabilities range from passive defense to psychological operations to precision strike operations against key information nodes.

The revolutionary capabilities offered by "Information Age" technologies are forcing us away from traditional assumptions about SOF organization and even the conduct of operations. For example, future psychological operations will employ a "CNN Central" approach – deploying small teams that can reach back to a supporting network of expertise and disseminate information quickly over satellites, the Internet, television, radio and other media.

Meanwhile, the explosive growth of commercial information technologies has made it possible for terrorist organizations, crime syndicates and drug cartels to organize, plan and coordinate activities from multiple locations around the world. With ties to rogue states, corrupt public officials and business organizations, these transnational entities can target many important public infrastructures (financial institutions, air traffic control systems, energy grids, telecommunications networks), U.S. military forces and American citizens.

One consequence of this increased connectivity will be the creation of "distributed" threats and conflicts that will make national boundaries irrelevant. Given this threat evolution, U.S. SOF will operate with increasing autonomy within the commander's intent – relying on distributed C2 (command and control), technology templating, and information avenues of approach to locate and neutralize widely dispersed targets with both cyber and kinetic weapons. Maintaining OPSEC (operations security) and employing deception will be critical

Above: The principles, psychology, and weapons of terrorism, along with anti-terrorist tactics, are described during a course on the "Dynamics of International Terrorism" run by the Air Force Special Operations School.

as U.S. SOF's own digitized signatures multiply.

Clearly, those who can exploit rapid advances in information and information-related technologies stand to gain significant advantages, and the most momentous changes in this sector are yet to come. But technology alone is not the answer. We must also capture the true "art" of information operations – the techniques typified in the "reality manipulation" employed daily by the marketing and advertising behemoths of Hollywood and Madison Avenue.

The capabilities required to counter WMD, conduct information operations and deal with other transnational and asymmetric threats are extremely resource-intensive and in some cases dependent upon the continued development of revolutionary technologies.

Equally important is the development and continued adaptation of definitive U.S. policy for addressing these and other emerging threats. These efforts will be critical to ensuring that SOF have the resources and increasingly sophisticated capabilities required to dominate any form of conflict. Considerable progress has already been made in each of these areas. Much, however, remains to be done.

USSOCOM faces an operational environment characterized by accelerating geopolitical change, rapid technological advancement, evolving threats, constrained resources and potential new roles. These factors require innovative thinking and new ways to shape change if the Command is to provide the widest array of options in protecting America's interests. And the truth is, "business as usual" will not provide the capabilities needed to deal with the transnational and asymmetric opponents of tomorrow.

A rapidly changing world deals ruthlessly with organizations that do not change – and USSOCOM is no exception. Guided by a comprehensive, enduring vision and supporting goals, it must constantly reshape itself to remain a relevant and useful member of the joint (military) team. This reality means that USSOCOM must embrace and institutionalize the process of change in a disciplined manner that allows it to move closer to its vision. During this journey, only its core values are permanent and non-negotiable. Everything else – its organization, force structure, platforms, equipment and missions – must continuously evolve to meet the needs of the United States and seize the opportunities brought about by change.

To be relevant in the future, USSOCOM must continue its

transformation, while maintaining the readiness required to shape and respond to the world today. The Command needs to anticipate trends and future scenarios, conditioning itself to not be surprised by surprise and the rapidity of change and the dynamics that follow. As new threats arise, the Command must decide which of its current capabilities to retain or modify, which new ones to develop, and which old ones to discard.

SOF must focus on emerging threats that either exceed the capabilities of conventional forces or can be dealt with better by small, highly specialized units. SOF must carefully assess those threats and, as appropriate, provide an effective solution through strategic planning, resourcing, acquisition and operational support initiatives. As important, SOF must identify those missions no longer relevant for SOF and recommend shifting these missions to conventional forces in order to better focus resources on critical special operations activities.

SOF must be a full-spectrum, multimission force – providing a comprehensive set of capabilities to the United States. This means that SOF must swiftly adapt to diverse and evolving threats from less technologically advanced adversaries to peer competitors. SOF must continue to operate effectively in joint, combined and interagency environments, yet must transcend these traditional parameters to fuse all of America's political, military, economic, intellectual, technical and cultural strengths into a comprehensive approach to future challenges. This will allow SOF to tap into such diverse areas as commercial information technologies, utilization of space, biomedicine, environmental science, robotics, organizational design and commercial research and development.

The 21st century SOF warrior – selectively recruited and assessed, mature, superbly trained and led – will remain the key to success in special operations. These warriors must be proficient in core competencies, training for certainty while educating for uncertainty. SOF must be capable of conducting strategic operations in tactical environment, combining a warrior ethos with language proficiency, cultural awareness, political sensitivity, and the ability to use "Information Age" technology.

SOF must also have the intellectual agility to conceptualize creative, useful solutions to ambiguous problems and provide a coherent set of choices to the supported C-in-C or joint force commander – more often like Sun Tzu, less like Clausewitz. This means training and educating people how to think, not just what to think.

SOF must examine every advantage that technological genius can supply and selectively exploit those few required for success. SOF cannot afford purely materiel fixes to every future problem; therefore, SOF must leverage those critical technologies that give a decided advantage.

SOF must be quick to capitalize on emerging technologies with the potential for significantly enhancing the human dimension, especially low-observable/masking technologies, smarter weapons, long-range precision capability and information technologies.

Merging technology with the human dimension will improve the SOF warrior's survivability, lethality, mobility and ability to access and use all relevant information sources.

The benefits of technological change cannot be fully realized until they are incorporated into new organizational forms. SOF organizational innovation is as important as innovation in weapon systems. Replacing technology without replacing old structures will not work. Most importantly, it must be remembered that the purpose of technology is to equip the man, not simply to man the equipment.

SOF people are at the heart of all special operations; platforms and equipment merely help them accomplish the mission. The fingers on SOF's future triggers still must be controlled by willing warriors of courage, compassion and judgment – individuals of character with strong legal, moral and ethical foundation – organized into dynamic and agile joint SOF teams.

As USSOCOM moves into the 21st century, it is evolving to meet future challenges and sustain the relative capability advantage that it enjoys today. USSOCOM is already considering new and innovative methods of assessing and developing people, is debating possible changes in doctrine, roles, missions and force structure, is preparing an investment plan for modernization and streamlined acquisition, and is examining new operational concepts for the conduct of special operations in future environments. USSOCOM headquarters is leading this change by transitioning from a traditional military staff to an "Information Age" staff that is matrix-shaped around core functions, more flexible and better postured to resource and support global SOF requirements.

It cannot be known with certainty who the foes will be or precisely what demands will be placed on SOF in the future. However, in a time of both uncertainty and opportunity, USSOCOM will continue to provide the United States with the means to protect its interests and promote a peace that benefits America and the democratic ideals that it cherishes.

Right: **More important than the power and sophistication of Special Operations Forces' weapons and equipment are the courage, intelligence, and judgment of their personnel – the "global warriors" trained for a multitude of missions.**

PART ONE

THE HISTORY OF AMERICA'S SPECIAL OPERATIONS FORCES

THE HISTORY OF AMERICA'S SPECIAL OPERATIONS FORCES

The United States has a long and rich history of military special operations, predating the Revolutionary War. In every conflict since that war, the United States has employed special operations tactics and strategies to exploit an enemy's vulnerabilities. These operations have always been carried out by specially trained people with a remarkable inventory of skills.

The first truly integrated modern special operations organization was not formed until 10 April 1952 when the US Army established the Psychological Warfare Center at Fort Bragg, NC. Notably, psychological warfare in the Army at the time also consisted of unconventional warfare – a legacy of the special operations of the Office of Strategic Services (OSS) headed by Gen. "Wild Bill" Donovan during World War II.

The Special Forces were resuscitated in the early 1950s, with the Army's 10th Special Forces Group being activated at Fort Bragg on 20 June 1952, followed by 77th Special Forces Group on 25 September 1953. (The numbering appears to have been entirely at random.) These were followed by 1st Special Forces Group, which was raised on 24 June 1957 in Okinawa. During that year, this group

sent a small team to train 58 men of the South Vietnamese Army at Nha Trang, beginning a long association between US Special Forces and the Republic of Vietnam. Next, 5th Special Forces Group was raised on 21 September 1961, initially at Fort Bragg, but later it moved to Vietnam and became responsible for all Special Forces activities in that country.

President John F. Kennedy was fascinated with the Special Forces and visited Fort Bragg, where he authorized the wearing of the distinctive and symbolic headdress – the green beret – in 1961. Also as a result of the Kennedy visit was the deployment of the first Special Forces troops to South Vietnam in November 1961.

The original idea was that the Special Forces would wage guerrilla operations against regular enemy troops in conventional war. It soon became clear, however, that in Vietnam the enemy himself was a guerrilla, forcing the Special Forces to revise their basic concepts. One of the principal programs was the raising and training of Civilian Irregular Defense Groups (CIDG), with more than 80 CIDG camps being set up in the years 1961-65.

The Special Forces operated throughout South Vietnam in a variety of roles, some of which have yet to be revealed. They had more extensive dealings with the ARVN (South Vietnamese Army) – and particularly with the Montagnard, or mountain people – than any other element of the U.S. forces. They received awards for heroism and for dedication to duty far out of proportion to their numbers. Despite this, their relationship with some elements of the U.S. chain-of-command was not always easy, with mistrust and suspicion sometimes interfering with their operations, an all too frequent problem for any elite force, and one that dogged the United States special operations forces in later years.

The last Army Special Forces soldier left South Vietnam in March 1971, and there followed a period of general decline in Special Operations Forces (SOF) during the 1970s. SOF capabilities deteriorated throughout the post-Vietnam era, a time marked by considerable distrust between SOF and the conventional military and by significant funding cuts for special operations.

Below: Army Col. Arthur D. "Bull" Simons, leader of the special forces mission to rescue PoWs in North Vietnam, explains what went wrong.

This period culminated with an event that struck a blow to American prestige and helped erode the public's confidence in the U.S. government at that time — the failed mission to rescue 53 American hostages held in Iran. At a desolate site in Iran known as "Desert One," tragedy occurred minutes after the "mission abort" decision had been sanctioned by Defense Secretary Harold Brown and President Carter on 24 April 1980. Two aircraft involved in the operation collided on the ground and eight SOF men died.

The Desert One disaster, however, led the Defense Department to appoint an investigative panel, chaired by the former Chief of Naval Operations, Admiral James L. Holloway. The Holloway Commission's findings caused the Defense Department to create a counter-terrorist joint task force and the Special Operations Advisory Panel.

Desert One served to strengthen the resolve of some within the Department of Defense to reform SOF. Army Chief of Staff General Edward C. "Shy" Meyer called for a further restructuring of special operations capabilities. Although unsuccessful at the joint level, Meyer nevertheless went on to consolidate Army SOF units under the new 1st Special Operations Command in 1982, a significant step to improve Army SOF.

By 1983, there was a small but growing sense in Congress of the need for military reforms. In June, the Senate Armed Services Committee (SASC), under the chairmanship of Senator Barry Goldwater, began a two-year-long study of the Defense Department which included an examination of SOF. Two events in October 1983 further demonstrated the need for change: the terrorist bombing attack in Lebanon and the invasion of Grenada. The loss of 237 Marine lives to terrorism, combined with command and control problems that occurred during the Grenada invasion, refocused Congressional attention on the growing threat of low-intensity conflict and on the issue of joint interoperability.

With concern mounting on Capitol Hill, the Department of Defense created the Joint Special Operations Agency on 1 January 1984; this agency, however, had neither operational nor command authority over any SOF. The Joint Special Operations Agency thus did little to improve SOF readiness, capabilities, or policies — hardly what Congress had in mind as a systemic fix for SOF's problems. Within the Defense Department, there were a few staunch SOF supporters. Noel Koch, Principal Deputy Assistant Secretary of Defense for International Security Affairs, and his deputy, Lynn Rylander, both advocated SOF reforms.

At the same time, a few visionaries on Capitol Hill were determined to overhaul SOF. They included Senators Sam Nunn and William Cohen, both members of the Armed Services Committee, and Representative Dan Daniel, the chairman of the Readiness Subcommittee of the House Armed Services Committee. Congressman Daniel had become convinced that the U.S. military establishment was not interested in special operations, that the country's capability in this area was second rate, and that SOF operational command and control was an endemic problem. Senators Nunn and Cohen also felt strongly that the Department of Defense was not preparing adequately for future threats. Senator Nunn expressed a growing frustration with the Services' practice

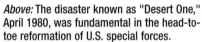

Above: **The disaster known as "Desert One," April 1980, was fundamental in the head-to-toe reformation of U.S. special forces.**

of reallocating monies appropriated for SOF modernization to non-SOF programs. Senator Cohen agreed that the U.S. needed a clearer organizational focus and chain of command for special operations to deal with low-intensity conflicts.

In October 1985, the Senate Armed Services Committee published the results of its two-year review of the U.S. military structure, entitled "Defense Organization: The Need for Change." Mr. James R. Locher III,

Below: **Senators Nunn (left) and Cohen fought to have Congress pass laws governing the organization and activities of U.S. Special Operations Forces.**

Above: **Rangers move out from Salines Airport during first day operations in Grenada, 1983, where SOF elements were misused by conventional forces.**

the principal author of this study, also examined past special operations and speculated on the most likely future threats. This influential document led to the Goldwater-Nichols Defense Reorganization Act of 1986.

By Spring 1986, SOF advocates had introduced reform bills in both houses of Congress. On 15 May, Senator Cohen introduced the Senate bill, co-sponsored by Senator Nunn and others, which called for a joint military organization for SOF and the establishment of an office in the Defense Department to ensure adequate funding and policy emphasis for low-intensity conflict and special operations. Representative Daniel's proposal went even further – he wanted a national special operations agency headed by a civilian who would bypass the Joint Chiefs and report directly to the Secretary of Defense; this would keep Joint Chiefs and the Services out of the SOF budget process.

Congress held hearings on the two bills in the summer of 1986. Admiral William J. Crowe, Jr., Chairman of the Joint Chiefs of Staff, led the Pentagon's opposition to the bills. He proposed, as an alternative, a new special operations forces command led by a three-star general. This proposal was not well received on Capitol Hill – Congress wanted a four-star general in charge to give SOF more clout. A number of retired military officers and others testified in favor of the need for reform.

By most accounts, retired Army Major General Richard Scholtes gave the most compelling reasons for change. Scholtes, who commanded the joint special operations task force in Grenada, explained how conventional force leaders misused SOF during the operation, not allowing them to use their unique capabilities, which resulted in high SOF casualties. After his formal testimony, Scholtes met privately with a small number of Senators to elaborate on the problems that they had encountered in Grenada.

Both the House and Senate passed SOF reform bills, and these went to conference committee for reconciliation. Senate and House conferees forged a compromise. The bill called for a unified combatant command headed by a four-star general for all SOF, an Assistant Secretary of Defense for Special Operations and Low-Intensity Conflict, a coordinating board for low-intensity conflict within the National Security Council, and a new Major Force Program (MFP-11) specifically for SOF (the so-called "SOF checkbook"). The House had conceded on the issue of a new civilian-led agency, but insisted on including MFP-11 to protect SOF funding. The final bill, attached as a rider to the 1987 Defense Authorization Act, amended the Goldwater-

Below: **75th Rangers Pfc Romick receives medals for wounds and performance in Grenada. Better use of SOF could have reduced casualties.**

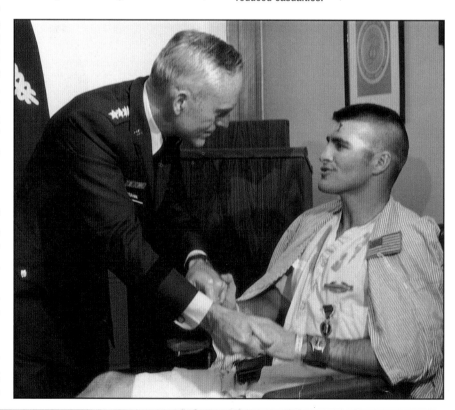

Above: U.S. Readiness Command had to make way for the new U.S. Special Operations Command (USSOCOM) when this was formed in 1987.

Nichols Act and was signed into law.

For the first time, Congress had mandated that the President create a unified combatant command. Congress clearly intended to force the Department of Defense and the Administration to face up to the realities of past failures and emerging threats. The Department of Defense and the Administration were responsible for implementing the law, and Congress subsequently

Below: General James J. Lindsay, former commander of U.S. Readiness Command, was the first C-in-C of USSOCOM, serving for more than three years.

had to pass two additional bills to ensure proper implementation.

The legislation promised to improve SOF in several respects. Once implemented, MFP-11 provided SOF with control over its own resources, better enabling it to modernize the force. Additionally, the law fostered interservice cooperation: a single commander for all SOF promoted interoperability among the forces assigned to the same command. The establishment of a four-star Commander in Chief and an Assistant Secretary of Defense for Special Operations and Low Intensity Conflict [ASD (SO/LIC)] eventually gave SOF a voice in the highest councils of the Defense Department.

The establishment of United States Special Operations Command (USSOCOM)

Above: All elements of the U.S. special forces (except those of the Marine Corps) were brought into USSOCOM, approved for activation 13 April 1987.

provided its own measure of excitement. A quick solution to manning and basing a brand new unified command was to abolish an existing command. United States Readiness Command (USREDCOM), an often misunderstood product of an earlier age, did not appear to have a viable mission in the post Goldwater-Nichols era. Also, its Commander in Chief, General James Lindsay, had had some special operations experience. On 23 January 1987, the Joint Chiefs of Staff recommended to the Secretary of Defense that USREDCOM be disestablished to provide billets and facilities for USSOCOM.

President Ronald Regan approved the establishment of the new Command on 13 April 1987. The Department of Defense activated USSOCOM on 16 April 1987 and nominated General Lindsay to the first Commander in Chief (USCINCSOC). The Senate accepted him without debate.

USSOCOM had its activation ceremony on 1 June 1987. Guest speakers included William H. Taft IV, Deputy Secretary of Defense, and Admiral William J. Crowe, Jr., two men who had opposed the Nunn-Cohen amendment. Admiral Crowe's speech at the ceremony advised General Lindsay to integrate the new Command into the mainstream military: "First, break down the wall that has more or less come between special operations forces and the other parts of our military, the wall that some people will try to build higher. Second, educate the rest of the military – spread a recognition and understanding of what you do, why you do it, and how important it is that you do it. Last, integrate your efforts into the full spectrum of our military capabilities." Putting this advice into action,

17

General Lindsay knew, would pose significant challenges (a "sporty" course, he called it), considering the opposition the Defense Department had shown.

USSOCOM Commanders

There have been six CINCSOCs since 1987 – Generals James J. Lindsay (16 April 1987-27 June 1990), Carl W. Stiner (27 June 1990-20 May 1993), Wayne A. Downing (20 May 1993-29 February 1996), Henry H. Shelton (29 February 1996 to 25 September 1997), Peter J. Schoomaker (5 November 1997 to 27 October 2000), and Charles Holland (from November 2000 to the present). Each CINCSOC has faced unique challenges and opportunities, but one constant throughout this period has been change and new challenges for the U.S. military. The demise of the Soviet Union, the downsizing of the U.S. military, the appearance of new aggressor states, heightened regional instabilities and the proliferation of weapons of mass destruction, have all led to an increased use of SOF by the conventional U.S. military, ambassadors, and other government agencies.

Mission and Organization

USSOCOM's mission, as delineated in the 1987 JCS Manual 71–87, was to prepare SOF to carry out assigned missions and, if directed by the President or Secretary of Defense, to plan for and conduct special operations. Mission responsibilities were outlined as:

- Develop SOF doctrine, tactics, techniques and procedures.
- Conduct specialized courses of instruction for all SOF.
- Train assigned forces and ensure interoperability of equipment and forces.
- Monitor the preparedness of SOF assigned to other unified commands.

Below: In 1998, Gen. Schoomaker radically reorganized USSOCOM's headquarters to concentrate on strategic and operational priorities.

- Monitor the promotions, assignments, retention, training and professional development of all SOF personnel.
- Consolidate and submit program and budget proposals for Major Force Program 11 (MFP-11).
- Develop and acquire special operations-peculiar equipment, material, supplies, and services.

These last two tasks, managing MFP-11, and developing and acquiring special operations-peculiar items, made USSOCOM unique among the unified commands. These responsibilities – dubbed "service-like" – had heretofore been performed exclusively by the Services. Congress had given the Command extraordinary authority over SOF force structure, equipping and resourcing.

The USSOCOM's first C-in-C, General Lindsay, organized the Command along the lines of a typical unified command "J directorate" structure, with two modifications: he assigned MFP-11 and acquisition responsibilities to the J-8 (Resources) directorate, and created a new J-9 directorate, responsible for Psychological Operations (PSYOP) and Civil

Above: Damage to the U.S. embassy in Beirut, Lebanon, 1983, highlighted an increasing threat, that of global terrorism, that USSOCOM would have to combat.

Affairs (CA) support on 15 June 1988.

The Command's mission statement evolved with the changing geopolitical environment. With the fall of the Soviet Union and the rise of regional instability, SOF's capabilities were in ever greater demand. To reflect this increased operational tempo, which called for a large SOF involvement in peace-keeping and humanitarian operations, General Downing modified the command's mission statement in 1993. The revised wording read: *"Prepare SOF to successfully conduct world-wide special operations, civil affairs, and psychological operations in peace and war in support of the regional combatant commanders, American ambassadors and their country teams, and other government agencies."*

USSOCOM also added counter-proliferation and information operations-command and control warfare to its list of principal missions, and expanded the counter-terrorism mission to include defensive measures (antiterrorism).

General Shelton continued to refine the Command's mission statement, goals, and vision in order to serve SOF's customers more effectively. In December 1996, he approved a slightly revised mission statement: *"Provide Special Operations Forces to the National Command Authorities, regional Combatant Commanders, and American ambassadors and their country teams for successful conduct of worldwide special operations, civil affairs, and psychological operations during peace and war."*

After General Shelton became the Chairman of the Joint Chiefs of Staff on 1

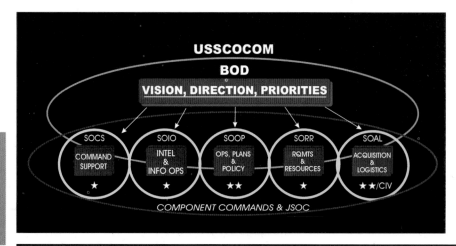

Above: Focused and fighting fit, this Ranger represents one of several special operation units within the Army's 1st SOCOM assigned to USSOCOM.

October 1997, the new CINCSOC, General Schoomaker, elected to retain this mission statement. He did, however, articulate a new vision for USSOCOM: *"Be the most capable and relevant Special Operations Forces in existence – living personal and professional standards of excellence to which all others aspire.".*

Though the Command's mission statement remained constant, the same could not be said for how General Schoomaker viewed the headquarters' organization. His predecessor had initiated a review of the organization in hopes of aligning similar functions, streamlining procedures, and redirecting human resources. As a former component commander, General Schoomaker perceived that the headquarters did not adequately focus on the Command's critical functions, which he defined as resourcing SOF. He therefore boldly scrapped the traditional J-staff alignment and incorporated like or complementary functions into five "centers of excellence." A general officer, flag officer, or senior executive service civilian led each center. The reorganization enabled CINCSOC to concentrate on strategic and operational priorities.

The Operations, Plans and Policy Center (SOOP) combined functions from the J3 and J5 directorates. Merging combat simulations and requirements (J7) with programming and comptroller functions (J8) resulted in the Center for Force Structure, Requirements, Resources, and Strategic Assessments (SORR). The Intelligence and Information Operations Center (SOIO) included command, control, communications, computers and information systems (J6); the intelligence

directorate (J2); and information operations (J3). The Acquisition Center (AC) and logistics directorate (J4) formed the Center of Acquisition and Logistics (SOAL). Finally, the Command Support Center (SOCS) included the personnel directorate (J1) and the special staff offices. This headquarters reorganization promised to strengthen the resourcing functions of USSOCOM – and ultimately, support to SOF, the theater C-in-Cs, and American ambassadors.

USSOCOM Forces

The activation of USSOCOM required the assignment of components and forces, a task not without controversy. The law establishing USSOCOM said: *"Unless otherwise directed by the Secretary of Defense, all active and reserve special operations forces of all armed forces stationed in the United States shall be assigned to the Special Operations Command."* Caspar Weinberger, at that time Secretary of Defense, initially assigned USSO-

COM three component commands and most of their forces. He assigned USSOCOM the 23rd Air Force located at Hurlburt Field, Florida; the Naval Special Warfare Command, headquartered at NAB Coronado, San Diego, California; and the Army's 1st SOCOM, at Ft. Bragg, North Carolina. Weinberger assigned the Joint Special Operations Command (JSOC) on 14 August 1987, after USSOCOM had become operational. Later, JSOC became a sub-unified command of USSOCOM.

At the time of its assignment, 1st SOCOM had charge of all the US Army's special operation units. Its mission was to prepare, provide, and sustain Army SOF to conduct foreign internal defense, unconventional warfare, special intelligence, psychological operations, strike operations, and related special operations. The 1st SOCOM forces included 1st, 5th, 7th and 10th Special Forces Group (Airborne); 4th Psychological Operations Group; 96th Civil Affairs; 75th Ranger Regiment; 160th Special Operations Aviation Group (Airborne); numerous Reserve and National Guard units; and the John F. Kennedy Special Warfare Center and School.

Not all of these units were immediately transferred to USSOCOM, however. Secretary Weinberger withheld the Active Duty and Reserve Psychological Operations and Civil Affairs units, pending a special review. Earlier in 1987, the Office of the Secretary of Defense had proposed creating a separate sub-unified command for PSYOP and CA forces. Like other SOF units PSYOP and CA had suffered severe cutbacks during the 1970s and 1980s, and some proponents feared that they would not fare much better under USSOCOM. General Lindsay opposed the plan, arguing that the

Below: A psychological operations (PSYOP) broadcast mission being coordinated from a 193rd Special Operations group EC-130E Volant Solo.

Created by the Navy on 16 April 1987, the Naval Special Warfare Command had only the Naval Special Warfare Center (the training command) assigned to it. Naval Special Warfare Groups I and II (and their SEALs and Special Boat Units) were not assigned because the Navy argued that these organizations and their forces belonged to the Pacific and Atlantic fleets, respectively, and, therefore, were not available for assignment to USSOCOM. Secretary of the Navy James Webb and Navy leadership felt the assignment of the special warfare assets to USSOCOM would detract from their close relationship with the fleets.

General Lindsay maintained that the special warfare forces rightfully belonged to USSOCOM since they were based in the United States. He reasoned that the Naval Special Warfare Groups' relationships to the fleets were no different from a Special Forces Group's assignment to a particular theater, and he wanted to integrate Naval Special Warfare units with other SOF. On 23 October 1987, Secretary Weinberger ruled in favor of USSOCOM. Accordingly, operational control of the SEALs, Special Boat Units, and Naval Special Warfare Groups passed to the Naval Special Warfare Command on 1 March 1988 and that command assumed administrative control for these units on 1 October 1988.

Command could use its authority to safeguard these SOF assets, and Admiral Crowe, the Chairman of the Joint Chiefs of Staff, agreed with him. On 15 October 1987, Secretary Weinberger assigned all Army and Air Force Active and Reserve Component PSYOP and CA units to USSOCOM.

Secretary Weinberger's actions, however, did not settle the PSYOP and CA issue completely. During General Stiner's tenure, another long-standing issue in assignment of

PSYOP and CA was addressed. Reserve and National Guard leaders argued that these forces were assigned to USSOCOM only in wartime, upon mobilization. General Stiner pushed through an initiative that the Secretary of Defense approved in March 1993, designating PSYOP and CA as SOF. This decision enabled USSOCOM to command and control these units in peacetime as well, which greatly improved the Command's ability to fund, train, equip and organize these forces.

The 23rd Air Force was a unique organization with two separate but interrelated missions; it was both a numbered air force assigned to the Military Airlift Command (MAC) and, as USSOCOM's Air Force component, it supported SOF from all the Services. Secretary Weinberger assigned only the 23rd's special operations functions and units to USSOCOM, including its Reserve and National Guard units and the Air Force Special Operations School. MAC retained oversight responsibility for the 23rd's other mission areas (such as aeromedical airlift, rescue and weather reconnaissance, and operational support airlift missions). Since General Lindsay expected all components to be major command equivalents, this arrangement created problems.

From the outset, USSOCOM had wanted the 23rd "purified" of its non-SOF elements. MAC went along with this request. General Lindsay's paramount concern remained: he still had to coordinate with MAC to effect

Right: One of two MH-47 Chinooks from the 3/160th Special Operations Aviation Regiment (SOAR) offloading from a MAC C-5A Galaxy.

changes at the 23rd. The current organizational arrangement thwarted his efforts to build the command that Congress had mandated. The solution, he decided, was to elevate the 23rd to a major air command. General Larry Welsh, the Air Force Chief of Staff, agreed and on 22 May 1990 redesignated the 23rd AF as the Air Force Special Operations Command (AFSOC).

Budget and POM Development

The creation of MFP-11 was an important priority for both General Lindsay and Congress. Although the Nunn-Cohen Amendment had created MFP-11 to reform SOF funding, the wording of the law permitted varying interpretations, and some Defense Department officials argued that the new Command should not submit its own Program Objective Memorandum (POM). General Lindsay and Ambassador Whitehouse, the ASD (SO/LIC), argued just the opposite and worked extremely hard to win approval of a POM and budget for the Command.

This debate lingered until September 1988, when Senators Nunn and Cohen clarified Congressional intent, saying that the sponsors of the law "fully intended that the commander of the Special Operations Command would have sole responsibility for the preparation of the POM." Congress enacted Public Law 100–456 that same month, which directed USCINCSOC to submit a POM directly to the Secretary of Defense.

On 24 January 1989, the Assistant Secretary of Defense, William H. Taft IV, signed a memorandum giving UNCINCSOC budgetary authority over MFP-11. Soon afterwards, the Office of the Secretary of Defense gave USSOCOM control of selected MFP-11 programs effective 1 October 1990 and total MFP-11 responsibility in October 1991. For the first time, a C-in-C was granted authority for a budget and POM.

The Command needed to create a new Planning, Programming, and Budgeting System (PPBS) process to structure a POM and budget for all SOF. Even with a Congressional mandate, the Command found it difficult to establish MFP-11. Because of a staff shortfall, the Command took a measured approach to assuming these tasks. The POM was the first step, with the initial one completed and submitted in 1988 through the Department of the Air Force. Based on Secretary Taft's directive, the Command assumed budget execution authority by October 1990. In 1991 the Command began

to submit fully supported POMs: this was the first time USSOCOM researched SOF mission requirements and developed the analysis for the POM justification instead of "crosswalking" requirements which the individual Services had developed in previous years. The establishment of MFP-11 set up a more focused resource process and ensured a balanced view of special operations requirements and programs.

General Downing directed the creation of the Strategic Planning Process to allocate the Command's resources in the most effective ways. This prioritization and allocation process continued under Generals Shelton and Schoomaker. The latter directed that there would be significant changes in how the

Command allocated its increasingly constrained resources.

First, to end the competition for scarce dollars, General Schoomaker melded the headquarters and components into one team. This meant that the priorities decided upon by CINCSOC and his component commanders (the so-called Board of Directors or "BOD") would be executed without changes being made by subordinate commands. Second, charged by the C-in-C to ensure "fidelity" in the resourcing process, the Center for Force Structure, Requirements, Resources and Strategic Assessments developed procedures to monitor how the budget was executed in accordance with BOD decisions. In this way, General Schoomaker aligned the dollars to the Command's most important acquisition programs.

Systems Acquisitions and Force Modernization

A primary rationale for establishing the Command was the Services' failure to modernize SOF systems. Keen Congressional interest in this area continued after the Command was activated, and a 17 November 1987 conference report criticized the Defense Department for the lack of progress in procuring "SOF-peculiar equipment." Congress enacted an additional piece of legislation on 4 December 1987 which authorized CINCSOC to function as a "Head of Agency" for SOF acquisition programs, an authority normally reserved for the Service Secretaries.

The Command took another major step forward when the Deputy Secretary of Defense approved establishment of the Special Operations Research, Development, and Acquisition Center (SORDAC) on 10 December 1990. By early 1991, SORDAC had started performing its acquisition functions and operated within the Resources Directorate (J-8). In 1992, General Stiner consolidated the Command's acquisition and contracting management functions in a new directorate under a Deputy for Acquisition, who was named the Command's Acquisition

Below: An AC-130U Spooky II Gunship serving with AFSOC, which is tasked to deliver special operations combat air power anytime, anywhere.

Executive and Senior Procurement Executive. To discharge its acquisition responsibilities, the Command concentrated on fielding systems meeting component requirements. Emphasizing a streamlined acquisition process, the Command's procurement strategy was to modify existing weapons or buy "non-developmental" (off the shelf technology) systems – an approach which permitted quick, economical improvements to operational capabilities.

Since 1987, USSOCOM has fielded a number of modified or new systems affecting nearly every aspect of special operations. Some of the more notable were the MC-130H Combat Talon II long-range insertion aircraft and the SOCRATES automated intelligence handling system, both used in Operation Desert Storm, and the Cyclone-class patrol coastal ships, used in Operations Support Democracy and Uphold Democracy. Other significant acquisitions included the MH-47E Chinook, a medium-range helicopter designed to conduct insertion operations under all weather conditions; the AC-130U Spectre gunship, used for close air support and reconnaissance; and the Mark V Special Operations Craft, a high performance combatant boat capable of being transported over land and aboard C-5 aircraft. In 1997, the Acquisition Center's Naval Special Warfare Rigid Inflatable Boat (NSW-RIB) Program provided a long-sought capability for a high speed SEAL insertion and extraction craft..

Moreover, USSOCOM's acquisition capability was used a number of times during

contingencies to provide SOF with the latest technology or to accelerate modifications. During Desert Storm, for example, the Command modified Chinooks with aircraft survivability equipment before they deployed to the Iraqi area of operations. USSOCOM procured specialized cold-weather gear for SOF deploying to Bosnia during Joint Endeavour.

In 1998 General Schoomaker designated a few key acquisition programs as "flagship systems," so called because they were deemed essential to the future of SOF. In an era of tightly constrained budgets, funding for these strategic programs would be preserved, even at the expense of other acquisitions. The CV-22 aircraft program and the Advanced SEAL Delivery System were among the first flagship programs.

OPTEMPO and Quality People

There has been a steady increase in SOF deployment since USSOCOM's inception, measured in both personnel deployments and in the number of countries visited. At varying times during the 1990s, certain "high demand/low density" specialties within Special Operations, Psychological Operations, and Civil Affairs forces endured repeated, long deployments. Concerns arose within the Department of Defense about the long term impact these absences were having on retention and readiness. During fiscal year 1993, USSOCOM averaged 2,036 personnel deployed away from home station per week;

by fiscal year 1996 the average had more than doubled, climbing to 4,613. In fiscal year 1999, the number had climbed to 5,141. What caused this dramatic increase?

The fall of the Soviet Union and the end of the Cold War resulted in (to use General Lindsay's term) a more "violent peace" – regional destabilization, a new round of terrorism, and an increased availability of weapons of mass destruction (WMD). The changed military threat made SOF's capabilities more relevant to the National Military Strategy.

Why were SOF used so often as an instrument of national policy? SOF were versatile, ready and uniquely capable of operating in all politico-military environments, skilled at peacetime training, foreign international defense, and nation assistance operations, as well as during full-blown conventional warfare. SOF's versatility was particularly useful in areas where political constraints prevented using conventional forces. In combat situations SOF were "force multipliers," conducting special reconnaissance, direct action, and coalition support, while in peacetime they deployed to every continent and conducted training, supported the theater C-in-Cs' strategy, and did things that conventional forces were not capable of doing.

Additionally, the theater C-in-Cs and their staffs better understood SOF's capabilities. This increased awareness was due to USSOCOM's efforts to involve the other C-in-Cs in planning and joint mission area analyses, and to support their Special Operations Commands with MFP-11 funding and personnel. Moreover, SOF were the theater commanders' force of choice for such diverse operations as counterdrug and demining training, foreign internal defense, medical exercises, non-combatant evacuations, or handling emergency situations like Operation Pacific Haven in 1996, when CA and PSYOP forces helped Kurdish refugees prepare to emigrate to the U.S. As the number of peacekeeping missions and small-scale contingencies grew, so also did the need for SOF support.

Each CINCSOC identified as a basic requirement the recruitment and retention of people who could meet the rigorous warfighting standards of special operations and also adapt to the role of warrior-diplomat. Special operators were most likely to deploy to remote locations where, by virtue of being among the first, and often the only, U.S. troops a host nation's military and political leaders might see, their military mission took on diplomatic responsibilities. When in combat, SOF went deep behind enemy lines – for example, providing special reconnaissance, or conducting "tip of the spear" H-Hour strike missions.

General Downing distilled the need for quality people into the SOF "Truths":

- Humans are more important than hardware.
- Quality is better than quantity.
- Special Operations Forces cannot be mass-produced.

- SOF cannot be created after emergencies.

Both Generals Shelton and Schoomaker embraced the SOF "Truths." To ensure that the force remained professional, General Schoomaker made training and education – "trained for certainty, while being educated for uncertainty" – one of his hallmarks. SOF often encountered ambiguous circumstances while conducting peacetime operations, circumstances that could have a potential impact on strategic issues. The unique conditions SOF operated under required not only flexibility and mature judgment, but also uncompromising integrity.

General Schoomaker cited the maturity and personal qualities of SOF, coupled with their widespread presence around the world, as reasons why SOF served as "Global Scouts." During crises, by virtue of their cultural awareness, regional familiarity, ability to respond quickly, or simply due to their presence nearby, SOF were called upon to support American interests. Some examples of SOF Global Scouts missions were the recovery of American casualties from Croatia after Secretary of Commerce Brown's CT-43A crashed into a mountainside in 1996, assistance in evacuating U.S. citizens from Sierra Leone in 1997, and SOF aircraft and crews bringing aid to Vietnam flood victims in 1999.

Below: **A Halter Marine Mark V combatant craft offloading from a USAF C-5A. It has a five-man crew and can carry sixteen SEALs.**

MAJOR OPERATIONS: 1987 TO THE PRESENT

Since 1987, Special Operations Forces have participated in a wide range of military operations – from peacetime engagement to a major theater war. The U.S. Special Operations Command has worked steadily to enhance SOF support to the theater commanders in chief and the American ambassadors. Providing this support was not always easy, since it involved carrying out military operations in different ways and in some cases theater commanders in chief had to be convinced that SOF offered specialized capabilities to them. USSOCOM had just been established when SOF faced an operational challenge in the Persian Gulf, what the commander in chief of U.S. Central Command called guerrilla warfare on the high seas.

PERSIAN GULF
Operation Earnest Will (1987-1989)
During Operation Earnest Will, the United States ensured that neutral oil tankers and other merchant ships could safely transit the Persian Gulf during the Iran-Iraq War. Iranian attacks on tankers prompted Kuwait to ask the United States in December 1986 to register 11 Kuwaiti tankers as American ships so that they could be escorted by the US Navy. President Reagan agreed to the Kuwaiti request on 10 March 1987, hoping it would deter Iranian attacks. Operation Earnest Will was planned by U.S. Central Command (CENTCOM) under General George B. Crist.

The protection offered by U.S. naval vessels, however, did not stop Iran, which used mines and small boats to harass the convoys steaming to and from Kuwait. To stop these attacks, the U.S. needed surveillance and patrol forces in the northern Persian Gulf and bases for these patrol forces. SOF, including Army helicopters and Navy SEALs and Special Boat Units, had the best trained personnel and most capable equipment for monitoring hostile activity, particularly at night when the Iranians conducted their missions. The Army's special operations helicopter crews trained to fly and fight at night. These helicopters were difficult to spot on radar and were relatively quiet, allowing them to get close to a target. Shallow-draft naval special warfare patrol boats could ply waters that had not been swept for mines.

In late July 1987, Rear Admiral Harold J. Bernsen, commander of the Middle East Force, requested naval special warfare assets. Six Mark III Patrol Boats, other Special Boat assets, and two SEAL platoons deployed

in August. At the same time, two MH-6 and four AH-6 Army special operations helicopters and thirty-nine men received orders to head for the region in a deployment called Operation Prime Chance I.

The Middle East Force decided to convert two oil servicing barges, *Hercules* and *Wimbrown VII*, into mobile sea bases. Besides obviating the need to ask for land bases, the mobile sea bases allowed SOF in the northern Persian Gulf to thwart clandestine Iranian mining and small boat attacks. Each mobile sea base housed ten small boats, three helicopters, sufficient fuel, ammunition, equipment, and workshops to support their operations, and more than 150 men. In October the mobile sea bases became operational.

In the interim, SOF operated from various surface vessels. On 8 August, the helicopters, designated SEABATs, escorted the third Earnest Will convoy and looked for signs of Iranian mine laying. The patrol boats began escort missions on 9 September. It was not long before SOF showed what they could do. On the evening of 21 September, one MH-6 and two AH-6 helicopters took off from the frigate *Jarrett* (FFG-33) to track an Iranian ship, the *Iran Ajr*. The helicopters observed the *Iran Ajr* extinguish its lights and begin laying mines. Receiving permission to attack, the helicopters fired guns and rockets, stopping

the ship. As the *Iran Ajr*'s crew began to push mines over the side, the helicopters resumed firing until the crew abandoned ship.

RADM Bernsen then ordered the SEAL platoon from the *Guadalcanal* to board the *Iran Ajr*. Two patrol boats provided security. Shortly after first light, the SEALs boarded the ship and found nine mines and various arming mechanisms. The patrol boats rescued ten Iranians in a lifeboat and thirteen in life vests floating nearby. Documents found aboard the ship showed where the Iranians had laid mines, implicating Iran in mining international waters. The *Iran Ajr* was sunk in deep water on 26 September.

The mobile sea bases entered service in early October in the northern Persian Gulf. From these bases, U.S. patrol craft and helicopters could then monitor Iranian patrol craft in the northern Gulf and deter their attacks. Within a few days, patrol boat and AH/MH-6 helicopter personnel had determined the Iranian pattern of activity – the Iranians hid during the day near oil and gas separation platforms in Iranian waters and at night they headed toward the Middle Shoals Buoy, a

Below: On 21 September 1987, during Operation Earnest Will in the Persian Gulf, the *Iran Ajr,* caught laying mines, was attacked by Army special operations helicopters and boarded by SEALs.

navigation aid for the tankers.

With this knowledge, SOF sent three of their helicopters and two patrol craft toward the buoy on the night of 8 October. The AH/MH-6 helicopters arrived first and were fired upon by three Iranian boats anchored near the buoy. After a short but intense firefight, the helicopters sank all three boats. The U.S. patrol boats moved in and picked up five Iranian survivors who were subsequently repatriated to Iran.

SOF next saw action on 19 October, three days after an Iranian Silkworm missile hit the reflagged tanker *Sea Isle City* near the oil terminal outside Kuwait City. Seventeen crewmen and the American captain were injured in the missile attack. In Operation Nimble Archer, four Navy destroyers shelled the two oil platforms in the Rostam oil field on 19 October. After the shelling, a SEAL platoon and a demolition unit planted explosive charges on one of the platforms to destroy it. The SEALs next boarded and searched a third platform two miles away. Documents and radios were taken for intelligence purposes.

After Nimble Archer, *Hercules* and *Wimbrown V11* continued to operate near Karan Island, within 15 miles of each other, and sent patrol boats and helicopters on regular patrols. In November 1987, two MH-60 Blackhawk helicopters arrived to provide

Below: Army and Navy SOF used the barge *Hercules* as an operating base.

Bottom: An Iranian Boghammar sunk by Army SOF AH-6 helicopter fire.

nighttime combat search and rescue. As Earnest Will continued, SOF were rotated on a regular basis; eventually, some personnel rotated back to the Persian Gulf for second or even third tours. In 1988, the Army replaced the AH/MH-6 helicopters and crews with OH-58D Kiowa helicopters.

On 14 April 1988, approximately 65 miles east of Bahrain, the US Navy frigate *Samuel B. Roberts* (FFG-58) hit a mine, blowing a 30- by 23-foot hole in its hull. Ten sailors were injured. The United States struck back hard, attacking the Iranian frigate *Sabalan* and oil platforms in the Sirri and Sassan oil fields on 18 April during Operation Praying Mantis. After U.S. warships bombarded the Sirri platform and set it ablaze, a UH-60 with a SEAL platoon flew toward the platform but was unable to get close enough because of the roaring fire. Secondary explosions soon wrecked the platform.

Elsewhere, U.S. forces wreaked havoc on Iranian vessels, sinking two and damaging five others. In northern Persian Gulf, Iranian forces fired two Silkworm missiles at the mobile sea barges, but chaff fired by the frigate *Gary* decoyed the missiles. Later that day Iranian F-4 fighters and patrol boats approached the mobile sea bases, but fled when the *Gary* locked its fire control radars on them.

Thereafter, Iranian attacks on neutral ships dropped drastically. On 18 July, Iran accepted the United Nations ceasefire; on 20 August 1988, the Iran-Iraq War ended. On 16 July, the last AH-6 and MH-6 helicopters

departed from the theater. In December 1988, the *Wimbrown V11* entered a Bahraini shipyard for reconversion to civilian use. The final Earnest Will convoy was run that month. The US Navy had escorted 259 ships in 127 convoys since June 1987. The mobile sea base *Hercules* was not withdrawn until September 1989. The remaining SEALs, patrol boats, and helicopters then returned to the United States.

Special Operations Forces provided the critical skills necessary to help CENTCOM gain control of the northern Persian Gulf and counter Iran's small boats and minelayers. Their ability to work at night proved vital, since Iranian units used darkness to hide their actions. The most important lessons to come out of Operation Earnest Will were the need to have highly trained Special Operations Forces capable of responding rapidly to crises anywhere around the globe and the vital need for interoperability between conventional and special operations forces. Additionally, based on Earnest Will operational requirements, USSOCOM would acquire new weapons systems – the patrol coastal ships and the Mark V Special Operations Craft.

PANAMA
Operation Just Cause (1989-1990)

The U.S. invasion of Panama, known as Operation Just Cause, was an unusually delicate, violent, and complex operation. Its key objectives were the capture of Manuel Noriega and the establishment of a democratic government. The United States applied overwhelming combat power during the invasion, seeking to minimize loss of life and destruction of property, and to speed the transition to friendly relations. The U.S. troops had a long-standing relationship with the Panama Defense Forces (PDF). American SOF personnel, having been based in Panama, were acutely aware of the delicate nature of the mission and were instrumental in achieving U.S. objectives.

During Operation Just Cause, the special operations component of Joint Task Force South (the overall invasion force) was the Joint Special Operations Task Force (JSOTF), commanded by Major General Wayne A. Downing. It was organized into smaller task forces: TF RED (the Army's 75th Ranger Regiment), TF BLACK (Army Special Forces), and TF WHITE (SEALs and Special Boat Unit assets). These task forces were supported by Psychological Operations and Civil Affairs units, Army Special Operations helicopters, and USAF air commando units.

The Opening Mission
The JSOTF's principal H-Hour missions were the capture of Noriega and the destruction of

Above: SOF were supported by M-113 APCs during their attack on the Panamanian Defense Forces' Comandancia (HQ) and prison.

the PDF's ability to fight. As it turned out, the U.S. forces did not know Noriega's location at H-Hour; accordingly the JSOTF focused on the H-Hour missions against the PDF. The attack on the Comandancia (the PDF's headquarters in Panama City) and the rescue of an American citizen from the adjoining prison (the Carcel Modelo) were the responsibility of a joint task force that included SOF ground elements, SOF helicopters and AC-130 gunships, and TF GATOR (M-113 armored personnel carriers and soldiers from the 4th Battalion, 6th Infantry (Mechanized)). Because of indications that H-Hour had been compromised, the attack on the Comandancia began 15 minutes early, at 0045 on 20 December 1989.

TF GATOR was responsible for moving M-113s to blocking positions around the Comandancia and the prison, and then, in conjunction with the AC-130 and AH-6 gunships, attacking and leveling the PDF headquarters. Maneuvring to the blocking positions, they came under increasingly heavy sniper fire from PDF soldiers in buildings (including a 16-story high rise) on the west side of the Comandancia and prison complex. TF GATOR suffered some wounded and one killed while its forces were moving to their blocking positions. Near the target, TF GATOR encountered roadblocks; the M-113s squashed some roadblocks and went around others. The heavy enemy fire, coming from various directions, continued as the armored

personnel carriers began their assault on the Comandancia.

At 0045, the revised H-Hour, AC-130s and AH-6s started firing upon the Comandancia area. The PDF shot down the lead AH-6, but its crew managed a controlled crash in the Comandancia courtyard. They were in the wrong place at the wrong time, since the AC-130s were pounding the Comandancia. By keeping their wits about them, however, they evaded both enemy and friendly fire for over two hours, made it to the back wall (where they captured a PDF soldier), climbed the wall, and linked up with a TF GATOR blocking position.

By now buildings in the compound were ablaze, and the smoke obscured the area for the AC-130 firing. One TF GATOR element was fired upon by an AC-130, suffering 12 soldiers wounded. A second AC-130 volley about an hour later wounded nine more. At first, the soldiers believed that they had been attacked by PDF mortars, but during the second volley they realized it was coming from the AC-130 and called through the fire support network to end the shooting.

During the attack on the Comandancia, a rescue force had entered the prison and freed the American citizen. The helicopter carrying part of the rescue force and the former prisoner was shot down and crashed in an alley to the north of the prison. Everyone on board, except the former prisoner, was injured to one degree or another, but the rescuers reacted as they had trained, formed a defensive position, con-

tacted a TF GATOR blocking element, and were evacuated by M-113s.

TF GATOR kept the Comandancia isolated during the day of 20 December and continued to receive sporadic sniper fire. That afternoon, Company C, 3rd Battalion, 75th Ranger Regiment arrived from Omar Torrijos International Airport to clear the Comandancia. All of these forces then engaged in follow on missions.

Task Force RED

Task Force RED was the largest component of the Joint Special Operations Task Force. It consisted of the Army's 75th Ranger Regiment reinforced by contingents from the from the 4th Psychological Operations Group (PSYOP) and 96th Civil Affairs (CA) Battalion, and included Air Force Special Tactics teams and Marine Corps/Naval Gunfire liaison troops. Close air support aircraft included AH-6 attack helicopters from the 160th Special Operations Aviation Regiment, AC-130H gunships from the 1st Special Operations Wing and, from the conventional forces, AH-64 Apaches and F-117A fighter-bombers.

The task force was to perform two simultaneous airborne assaults at H-Hour (0100 on 20 December 1989). One contingent would parachute onto the Omar Torrijos International Airport/Tucumen military airport complex,

Above: After seizing the Torrijos/Tocumen airport, which enabled the 82nd Airborne Division to come into the country, the 75th Rangers cleared the Comandancia.

while another would drop onto Rio Hato airfield. Upon securing these objectives, TF RED would then link-up with conventional forces for follow-on combat operations.

The Assault on Torrijos Airport/Tocumen Airfield

Omar Torrijos International Airport was the main international airport serving Panama, and the adjoining Tocumen military airfield was the home base of the Panamanian Air Force. Capturing Torrijos/Tocumen was crucial to the Just Cause campaign plan because it would enable the 82nd Airborne Division to come into the country, while preventing the 2nd Panamanian Defense Force Company and the Panamanian Air Force from interfering with American operations. The Torrijos/Tocumen complex formed a target area approximately 3.75 miles long and 1.25 miles wide.

The TF RED commander, Colonel William F. "Buck" Kernan, gave the mission of capturing Torrijos/Tocumen to 1st Battalion, 75th Ranger Regiment, commanded by LTC Robert W. Wagner. The Rangers had a tight schedule to seize this complex – an 82nd Airborne Division brigade was supposed to jump onto the complex only 45 minutes after H-Hour to start follow-on missions. The three companies of 1st Battalion were augmented by Company

C, 3rd Battalion, 75th Ranger Regiment, PSYOP teams, a Civil Affairs team, two AH-6 attack helicopters, Air Force Special Tactics teams (combat controllers and pararescuemen), and an AC-130H gunship.

LTC Wagner's plan called for the helicopters and AC-130H to attack the PDF positions at H-Hour, just prior to the Ranger parachute assault. After parachuting in, Company A would seize the Panamanian Air Force compound and destroy the aircraft. Company C, reinforced with a platoon from Company B, would seize the 2nd PDF compound and destroy the PDF Company. The rest of Company B, reinforced with twelve gun jeeps and ten motorcycles, would clear both runways and establish blocking positions to prevent other PDF forces from interfering with the battalion's operations. Finally, Company C, 3rd Battalion, would clear the smaller buildings near the Torrijos terminal, isolate the terminal building, and then enter the terminal building and destroy PDF resistance there.

Prior to the attack, three combat controllers and one pararescueman placed navigation beacons near the end of the runway. The attack began at 0100, with the AC-130H and AH-6s opening fire on PDF positions on the airfield. The AH-6s eliminated three targets while the AC-130H fired on the PDF's 2nd Rifle Company's barracks and headquarters building. It should be remembered that TF GATOR and other units had attacked the Comandancia in Panama City 15 minutes

early, at 0045, which meant the PDF at Torrijos/Tocumen knew of the invasion prior to the Rangers' airdrop. At 0103, the first jumpers left their aircraft.

Company A received only sporadic fire and secured all of its objectives within two hours after capturing virtually the entire Panamanian Air Force on the ground. The company captured about 20 Panamanian Air Force personnel hiding in one of the hangars. Company B also landed on target and quickly secured its blocking positions. Like Company A, it received only sporadic enemy fire and took some prisoners. The biggest problem Company B had was with the Panamanian vehicles ignoring its warning signs and barricades and trying to run its blocking positions. Generally these vehicles turned around and fled after the Rangers fired warning shots, but one vehicle had to be disabled by shooting out its tires. One of the vehicles that fled from warning shots contained Manuel Noriega, who had been visiting the Cereme Military Recreation Center. Company C assaulted the barracks of the PDF's 2nd Company and received only ineffective enemy fire; they quickly cleared the area, killing one PDF soldier who had refused to surrender.

Company C, 3rd Battalion, 75th Ranger Regiment, was to secure the international air terminal, and this proved to be the only portion of the assault on Torrijos/Tocumen that was significantly more difficult than expected. First, one-fourth of the company landed in ten-foot-tall cunna grass to the west of the runway and took two hours to join the main body. The depleted Company C had no trouble securing its objectives outside the terminal building, however, and the troops were impressed with how the AH-6s had destroyed the guard house outside the terminal and killed the two guards there. The 3rd Platoon seized the fire station on the north side of the terminal and then received fire from the second floor of the terminal.

These Rangers entered the terminal from the north, where they encountered two surprises. First, two civilian flights had arrived just prior to H-Hour, and about 400 civilians were in the terminal. The other surprise was that the PDF troops defended the terminal more determinedly than anywhere else in the Torrijos/Tocumen complex.

When two Rangers searched one of the airport's huge men's rooms on the second floor, two PDF soldiers jumped out of a stall and shot one of the Rangers several times with a pistol. The other Ranger returned fire and, with the assistance of two more Rangers, dragged his wounded buddy out of the men's room. In the process, the Ranger pulling the wounded man was himself shot twice in the back of the head, but his kevlar helmet stopped both rounds. From outside the men's room door, the unhurt Rangers threw in grenades, but the men's room stalls protected the PDF soldiers. The Rangers then re-entered the men's room and waited for the PDF to show themselves. The Rangers got the better of the ensuing hand-to-hand struggle. One of the PDF soldiers was killed in the men's room while the other was knocked out of the window; he fell two stories and almost landed on a Ranger patrolling outside. When the PDF soldier tried to draw his pistol, the Ranger killed him.

Meanwhile, the 2nd Platoon entered the terminal from the south and started clearing the building, with one squad on each of the three main floors. Enemy soldiers opened fired on the third floor, but the Rangers' counterattack drove them from the terminal, and the rest of the third floor was cleared without incident.

The situation on the first floor was more difficult; about ten PDF troopers had taken two American girls hostage. When their escape route led them right into the Ranger security detail stationed outside the terminal, they fled back inside, where 2nd Platoon Rangers cornered them after several exchanges of fire. At 0500, after a tense two-and-a-half-hour standoff, the Rangers announced they were going to come in shooting. Rather than face an all-out assault, the holdouts then released their hostages and surrendered.

Later that morning, at about 1100, the 82nd Airborne Division assumed operational control of 1st Battalion, 75th Ranger Regiment, and began operations out of Torrijos/Tocumen. Likewise, Company C, 3rd Battalion, was put under the operational control of TF BAYONET to clear La Comandancia at 1500 on 20 December. The Rangers' extensive training in airfield seizure and building clearing, along with their detailed mission plan, were key factors in their successful seizure of the Torrijos/Tocumen complex with minimal collateral damage and casualties.

The Attack on Rio Hato Airfield

The Panamanian military base near the small village of Rio Hato was located 65 miles west of Panama City. It contained a large airfield and was home to two PDF companies: the 6th Rifle Company (Mechanized), equipped with 19 armored cars, and the 7th Rifle Company, an elite counterinsurgency force known to be loyal to Noriega. In addition, the base housed a PDF engineer platoon and PDF training schools. TF RED's mission was to destroy PDF forces and seize the airfield for follow on missions. The total number of PDF forces was estimated to exceed 500 men; these units, particularly the 7th Rifle Company, were expected to offer stiff opposition to the TF RED forces.

The Rio Hato military base ranged along the coastline of the Gulf of Panama, with the airfield runway nearly perpendicular to the shoreline. The barracks for the PDF's 6th and 7th Companies were on the runway's southwest side. There were a number of beach houses along a dirt lane to the south of the runway; Manual Noriega owned (and occasionally used) one of them. To the west of the runway, and above the 6th and 7th Companies' barracks, was the PDF school complex. A highway bisected the airfield.

The TF RED commander, Colonel Kernan, led the forces assaulting Rio Hato. These included the 2nd Ranger Battalion, the 3rd Ranger Battalion (minus one company, used in the Torrijos/Tocumen assault), and elements of the 4th Psychological Operations Group, Civil Affairs assets, Air Force Special Tactics teams, and Marine Corps Air/Naval Gunfire liaison troops. Aerial fire support was provided by two F-117A fighters, two AH-64 and four AH-6 helicopters, and one AC-130H gunship. The 2nd and 3rd Battalions split the responsibility for taking and holding ground: the 2nd was to parachute into the area along the southern edge of the runway and around the PDF barracks and engage the enemy, while the 3rd was to jump farther north, securing the area from counterattacks and clearing the runway.

Thirteen C-130 transports were cross-loaded with Rangers from both battalions. The aircraft were to approach from the south, with the 2nd Battalion soldiers parachuting first and the 3rd Battalion troops jumping second. The 2nd Battalion's Company A would assault and clear the PDF school complex. Company B, 2nd Battalion, would assault the PDF 7th Company from the east, and if it was still effective after destroying that unit (planners had anticipated 30 percent casualties), it would push westward and clear the PDF 6th Company area. If Company B suffered excessive casualties, Company C would take over the assault. If Company B did not need reinforcement, then Company C would seize Noriega's beach house.

Below: Rangers celebrate neutralizing a Panamanian Defense Forces .50 caliber machine gun guarding the stone entryway to the Rio Hato airfield.

Though the Rangers wanted the F-117As to hit the PDF barracks, the bombing targets had been changed to an area near the barracks in the hope of frightening, rather than killing, the PDF troops. The bombs landed on schedule, at H-Hour, although one missed its target and exploded harmlessly near the beach. The AH-6s and AC-130H aircraft immediately followed with attacks on their designated targets. Of particular importance, the AC-130H destroyed two anti-aircraft positions before the Rangers jumped.

In spite of the three-minute air attack, the Rangers jumped into effective anti-aircraft machine gun fire. Eleven of the aircraft carrying Rangers were struck, and one Ranger was hit by anti-aircraft fire while still in the aircraft. The jump, however, went on as scheduled at 0103. Those Rangers who had jumped into Grenada in 1983 judged the enemy fire to have been heavier at Rio Hato.

Once on the ground, the 2nd Battalion Rangers saw a lot of tracers, but were able to return fire and assemble without too much trouble. The PDF troops apparently had left their barracks upon learning that the U.S. troops were coming and had either set up defenses on and around the airfield, or fled. As planned, Company A assembled before the other units and moved up to clear the school complex.

As Company A was advancing on the school complex, Company B began its assault on the PDF 7th Company area. After using demolition charges to blow holes in the wall surrounding the compound, Company B moved in and set about clearing each building, room by room. Having cleared the 7th's

Below: **The 75th Rangers Regiment used this type of jeep during the assault on the Rio Hato airfield. Some Rangers parachuted into the attack.**

area without serious losses, Company B continued to push west and had begun clearing the PDF 6th Company area by dawn on 21 December. Company B's success freed Company C to assault Noriega's beach house area two hours after H-Hour, and the Rangers cleared the house by morning.

Company B finished clearing the 6th Company barracks area that morning as well and, with all of its initial assault objectives secured, continued to advance west into the small village inhabited by the families of the PDF troops. The Rangers detained for questioning all the adult males found there, assuming the vast majority were PDF troops in hiding.

The 3rd Battalion Rangers, who were loaded first in each of the 13 C-130s, jumped after the 2nd Battalion. By the time they jumped into the warm, humid night, the PDF knew they were coming. The 3rd's airborne assault included heavy "drops" of four jeeps and six motorcycles. Company A's motorcycles were to race north along the runway and screen the Americans from possible counterattacks, while the Company B jeep teams were to establish blocking positions and watch for possible PDF activities.

Taking out a Machine gun Post

When the Company A Rangers jumped, they scattered from south of the Pan American Highway to well north of it. This company's primary mission was to neutralize the .50 caliber machine gun positioned on the concrete and stone entryway leading to the Rio Hato airfield. By chance, the Company's executive officer and a few other Rangers landed within 30 feet of the entryway; they killed the PDF gunner as he was firing at the other Rangers parachuting to the ground and took possession of the fortified position.

Other Company A elements had begun to clear the NCO academy headquarters and classroom areas. The Rangers encountered more PDF soldiers than expected. In the words of LTC Joseph Hunt, 3rd Battalion commander, these PDF soldiers "gave them a good run for their money for about 30 minutes." As the Rangers aggressively cleared the NCO academy buildings, the Panamanian soldiers abandoned their resistance and fled from the advancing Rangers. Company A Rangers did capture about 167 cadets, who were unarmed, frightened, and eager to surrender. Within an hour of H-Hour, Company A had secured its objectives.

Company B, 3rd Battalion, severed the Pan American Highway on the east side of the airfield. There was more traffic on the highway than expected, and the blocking element fired warning shots at a few vehicles to force them to turn around. The largest Company B element concentrated on clearing the runway south of the highway so that aircraft could begin landing, and this proved more time-consuming than anticipated. The Rangers quickly removed such obstacles as barrels, barbed wire, and trucks, but needed extra time to pick up the hundreds of parachutes left behind by the airborne assault. Company B Rangers also took control of the air traffic control tower. Approximately an hour and a half into the operation, the Rangers finished clearing the runway, and C-130s began landing with more people and additional supplies.

The Rangers who were assigned to end PDF resistance north of the Pan American Highway encountered a surprising amount of opposition. Here, as night turned to dawn, some PDF soldiers conducted a deliberate withdrawal, fighting from building to building through a small built-up area. A Ranger element engaged the PDF and called for fire support from two AH-6 helicopter gunships. These fired on the buildings, but unbeknown to the pilots, an element of Rangers moved into a tree line to flank the PDF. As the gunships came around for a second pass, one pilot saw movement in the trees and, believing they were PDF soldiers, fired upon the Rangers, killing two and wounding four. The movement of the Rangers into the tree line had not been radioed to the AH-6 pilots.

Having secured the military complex on 20 December, the Rangers conducted follow-on missions out of Rio Hato for the next three days. At 2200 on 20 December, Company A, 2nd Battalion, left Rio Hato aboard special operations helicopters and, at 0230 on the 21st, took over security for the American embassy in Panama City. The same day, the Rangers participated in one of the early surrender missions – what became known as the

"Ma Bell" Campaign – when Col. Kernan brought the PDF leaders of the Penonome Prison and 6th Military Zone Headquarters to Rio Hato to discuss their forces' surrender. Later, with an AC-130H circling overhead, the 3rd Battalion's Company A accepted the surrender of the town's garrison; then the Rangers demonstrated a "dry run" assault on the prison, showing the Panamanians what would have happened to them if they had resisted. Word of this display of force and surrender quickly spread throughout the remaining PDF troops in the countryside. After relocating to Howard AFB, the Rangers, in conjunction with Special Forces soldiers, conducted the "Ma Bell" surrender of David, a major city in western Panama.

The Rangers also performed stability operations in areas around Panama City. In response to civil disturbances and continued PDF and Dignity Battalion (Noriega's paramilitary supporters) activities, the 2nd Battalion, 75th Rangers, set up operations in Area of Operations (AO) Diaz, an area containing the towns of Alcalde Diaz and Las Cumbres, on 27 December. With the assistance of PSYOP forces, they created a visible American presence by establishing checkpoints and blocking positions, and running "saturation" patrols and night ambushes. While in AO Diaz, the Rangers rounded up former PDF and Dignity Battalion members and seized several caches of weapons. The American presence of Rangers, PSYOP, and Civil Affairs soldiers stabilized the area and allowed the new government to reestablish control.

Task Force WHITE

On 19 December 1989, TF WHITE, the Naval Special Warfare component of the JSOTF, established operations at Rodman Naval Station on the west side of the Panama Canal. The task force consisted of five SEAL platoons, three patrol boats, four

Above: Speed of action epitomised the SEALs operations during Just Cause, in which they used a variety of fast armed vessels.

riverine patrol boats, and two light patrol boats (22-foot Boston Whalers), which were divided among four task units. Each task unit had its own H-Hour mission; Task Unit (TU) Papa, the largest unit, was to deny use of the Paitilla Airfield; TU Whiskey was to destroy a Panamanian patrol boat in Balboa Harbor; TU Charlie and TU Foxtrot were charged with securing, respectively, the Atlantic and Pacific entrances to the Panama Canal.

The Paitilla Airfield assault force, TU Papa, had a 62-man ground force comprised of three SEAL platoons (Bravo, Delta and Golf platoons), Air Force combat controllers to perform liaison with an AC-130H gunship, and a command, control, communications, and mortar element. A 26-man support team included surveillance forces, a signals intelligence team, a psychological operations team, and boat crews.

At 1930 on 19 December, fifteen combat rubber raiding craft, carrying the ground force, launched from the Howard AFB beach, eight miles from Paitilla, while two patrol boats left from Rodman Naval

Station. At 2330, with the rubber boats waiting off the airfield, two SEALs swam ashore to reconnoiter the landing site and mark the beach with a strobe light.

At 0045 on the 20th, coming ashore near the end of the runway, the ground force heard firing and explosions from the attack on the Comandancia. The element of surprise had been lost. The SEALs hurried up the trail, through a hole in the security fence, and formed into platoons near the southern end of the runway. Learning of a report that Noriega was about to arrive in a small plane, Delta platoon set an ambush halfway up the runway for a few minutes, before advancing toward the tower. The other two platoons, Golf and Bravo, had moved up the grass apron on the west side of the runway.

By 0105, the SEALs were in front of the three northernmost hangars. Panamanians guarded the middle hangar, which housed Noriega's jet, and the hangar to the north. Golf platoon was in the lead, with one of its squads moving toward the northern edge of the tarmac. After an exchange of demands between the Americans and guards, a SEAL opened fire on a PDF guard who had assumed a firing position. A short but fierce firefight ensued, and within a matter of a minute or two eight SEALs were wounded, five seriously. The Golf platoon commander radioed for assistance, reporting heavy casualties. The ground force commander ordered other platoons to reinforce these SEALs. Two SEAL reinforcements were wounded as they maneuvered to engage the PDF in the hangars. The combination of SEAL fire discipline and superior firepower

Left: SEALs used inflatable rubber boats like these to take combat swimmers close to shore, where they carried out reconnaissance and left landing markers.

Above: U.S. Special Operations Forces shot up Manuel Noriega's private plane to ensure he could not escape Panama via the Paitilla Airfield.

soon took effect, however, and after three firefights the remaining PDF defenders withdrew at about 0117.

The SEALs reported the airfield was secure at 0146, and a medevac helicopter finally arrived at 0205 to recover the wounded. By 0315, the SEALS had set up a more defendable perimeter on the southeast side of the airfield. The reaction platoon from Rodman arrived a few minutes later. An AC-130H gunship, unable to establish reliable communications with the ground force, was replaced by an AC-130A at 0324. At dawn a patrol conducted a reconnaissance of the hangars, while other SEALs dragged airplanes onto the runway to block its use. The relief force did not arrive until 1400 on the 21st, when five CH-47 helicopters delivered a Ranger company. The SEALs left aboard the same helicopters. A planned five-hour mission had turned into a 37-hour operation. Four SEALs had died and eight others were wounded.

Subsequent to their operations at Paitilla airfield, TU Papa conducted several search and seizure missions looking for arms caches and Noriega followers. The unit was disbanded on 1 January 1990, and members returned to the United States the next day.

TU Whiskey's H-Hour mission was to destroy the Panamanian patrol boat docked in Balboa Harbor by having SEALs place demolition charges on its hull. Around 2300 on 19 December, two combat rubber raider craft left Rodman Naval Station, cut across the canal, passing vessels, and tied up in a mangrove stand near the docks. The first craft took two

Right: An AFSOC AC-130H crewmember loads a 105mm round into one of its guns. Spectres worked well in support of other SOF forces in Panama.

SEALs closer to the pier, where they slipped overboard for the swim to the Panamanian patrol boat, *Presidente Poras.* The next swim pair entered the canal five minutes later. The SEALs used Draegar underwater breathing apparatus which left no trail of air bubbles.

Reaching the boat, the SEALs attached haversacks of explosives to the propeller shafts, set the detonators, and swam to their extraction point. At 0100, an explosion ripped a hole in the *Presidente Poras,* and it sank. As the SEALs swam, they passed near a firefight between American and Panamanian forces; despite the hazards, the SEALs returned safely. This mission marked the first successful combat swimmer demolition attack by U.S. forces. Following the Balboa Harbor mission, TU Whiskey participated in the seizure of Noriega's yacht on 20 December and the capture of the Balboa Yacht Club the next day. On 23 December, TU Whiskey members helped repel PDF forces trying to board the merchant ship *Emanuel B* in the Panama Canal. Its last mission called for it to seize Noriega's beach house on Culebra Island on 25 December. TU Whiskey redeployed back to the United States

on 2 January 1990.

TU Charlie, assigned to secure the Carribbean side of the Panama Canal, worked closely with TF Atlantic. The task unit had eight SEALs, twelve soldiers, two riverine patrol boats, and two Army mechanized landing craft. On the night of the invasion, TU Charlie blocked all ships from entering the Canal from the Caribbean side and patrolled the shipping channel near Colon, preventing the PDF from commandeering boats and protecting the Canal from sabotage.

After conducting patrols all night, at 0930 on 20 December TU Charlie received a report that about 30 PDF members had boarded a German merchant ship, *Asian Senator,* in Cristobal. Once at the pier, the SEALs saw men in civilian clothes running down the *Asian Senator's* prow and other men on the ship throwing weapons onto the pier for them. One of the mechanized landing craft and the two riverine patrol boats fired at the Panamanians on the ship, who, shaken by this firepower, surrendered.

The SEALs came under fire as they were searching the PDF prisoners. As the volume of fire grew, the SEALs evacuated the prisoners to their boats. During subsequent patrols of the harbor and coastline, TU Charlie occasionally exchanged fire with PDF on the shore. TU Charlie later detained and searched a Colombian vessel, which yielded a cargo of looted electronic equipment, but no drugs or PDF. On Christmas Eve, the SEALs searched thirty-one boats moored in the Panama Canal Yacht Club. TU Charlie was deactivated on 26 December.

TU Foxtrot, the fourth task unit, conducted maritime patrols along the Pacific Ocean approaches to the Panama Canal. At H-Hour, SEALs in three patrol boats guarded the waters around Howard AFB, and two riverine patrol boats covered the approaches to the Bridge of the Americas. SEALs in a cayuga canoe searched the small islands off Howard

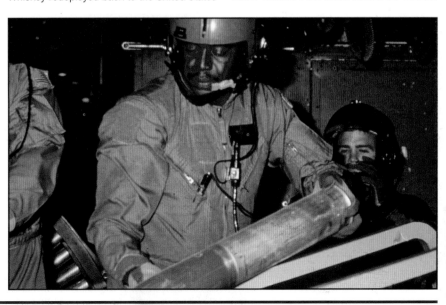

AFB for infiltrators. For the remainder of the night, the patrol boats searched and detained Panamanian fishing and pleasure boats found on the local waters.

On 21 December, the SEALs located and searched *Pass Porte Tout* and *Macho de Monde*, two of Noriega's sport yachts, capturing eighteen Panamanians and large quantities of small arms and ammunition. TU Foxtrot continued its maritime interdiction operations and, beginning on 26 December, it guarded the waters adjacent to the Papal Nunciature, the last refuge of Noriega. No incidents took place during this mission, and TU Foxtrot was disestablished on 2 January 1990.

Naval Special Warfare forces successfully executed all their missions during Operation Just Cause. Success did not come easily. Four SEALs died and eight more were wounded during the fight for Paitilla airfield, but TF WHITE accomplished its other missions without casualties. These operations underscored the value of forward-basing these units.

Task Force BLACK

TF BLACK was activated 18 December 1989 under the command of Colonel Robert C. "Jake" Jacobelly, who also served as commander of Special Operations Command SOUTH (SOCSOUTH). Before H-Hour, SOCSOUTH personnel and the headquarters unit of 3rd Battalion, 7th Special Forces Group (Airborne)[SFG(A)], moved to Albrook Air Force Base and together served as the TF BLACK headquarters and staff.

The 3rd Battalion, 7th SFG(A), commanded by LTC Roy R. Trumbull, formed the core of TF BLACK and was reinforced by Company A, 1st Battalion, 7th SFG(A), from Ft. Bragg. TF BLACK had use of five MH-60 helicopters from the 617th Special Operations Aviation Detachment and two UH-60 helicopters from the 1st Battalion, 228th Aviation Regiment. Air Force AC-130s from the 1st Special Operations Wing were available to provide fire support.

H-Hour Missions

At H-Hour, TF BLACK was to perform two reconnaissance and surveillance missions. The first, conducted by a Special Forces team from Company B, 3rd Battalion, 7th SFG(A), was to observe the PDF's Battalion 2000 at Fort Cimarron. By the time the team was in place, however, Battalion 2000 had already left the fort. The second mission involved watching the 1st PDF Company at Tinajitas. These Special Forces did not see or hear anything except for two mortar rounds being fired early in the morning.

Another reconnaissance mission was changed to direct action: seize and deny use of the Pacora River Bridge. The TF BLACK ele-

ment, commanded by Major Kevin M. Higgins, consisted of twenty-four men from Company A, 3rd Battalion, 7th SFG(A), and three helicopters. The bridge was the best place to prevent PDF Battalion 2000 from moving out of Fort Cimarron to Panama City. At ten minutes after midnight, small arms fire broke out at Albrook AFB while the troops were preparing to load onto their helicopters. Higgins and his troops dashed to the waiting aircraft and departed under fire.

As the helicopters neared the bridge, the lead helicopter pilot spotted a column of six PDF vehicles approaching. It was now 1245, the new H-Hour, and the mission had become a race between the SF troops and the PDF convoy to see who would take the bridge first. After the helicopters landed, Major Higgins yelled orders to his men to move up the steep slope and establish the ambush position by the road, but his men had already seized the initiative. The first man on the road looked straight into the headlights of the convoy's lead vehicle (which was already on the bridge) and fired a light anti-tank weapon. He missed his target, but the next two Special Forces soldiers did not. Then Special Forces gunners armed with squad automatic weapons (SAWs) opened up on the column with automatic weapons fire, and M203 gunners started firing grenades into the column.

With the column halted, the Air Force Combat Controller contacted an AC-130 and directed fire onto the PDF column. The AC-130 responded with devastating fire, forcing the PDF soldiers out of the trucks, and this circling aircraft provided vital intelligence on enemy movements. A second AC-130 was called in, providing additional firepower and surveillance, and the Special Operations Forces successfully repelled all PDF attempts to cross the bridge or the river.

At daybreak, the TF BLACK quick reaction force arrived to reinforce Higgins' element. Major Higgins and his troops controlled the bridge while the quick reaction force under Major Gilberto Perez cleared the east side of the river. They captured seventeen PDF members. The TF BLACK elements returned to Albrook AFB that evening.

The fourth TB BLACK H-Hour mission was to take Panamanian TV Channel 2 off the air. The mission was given to the Operational Detachment Alpha (ODA) 785, commanded by Captain John M. Custer and augmented by technical experts. At 0050 on 20 December, the eighteen-man team fast-roped from two helicopters near the TV broadcasting complex in the mountains northeast of Panama City. The PDF guards fled, the team took control of the complex, and the technical experts disabled the station. By 1500, the team had returned to base.

Post H-Hour Missions

The first three missions after H-Hour focused on stopping pro-Noriega radio broadcasts. After the invasion began, Radio Nacional's AM and FM stations had begun playing a recording of Manuel Noriega exhorting his followers to fight the Americans. Company C, 3rd Battalion, 7th SFG(A), commanded by Major David E. McCracken,, was given the mission to silence the radio broadcasts. Thirty-three Company C soldiers deployed in three helicopters and arrived at the Controlaria building, the location of the transmitter and antenna, at 1850 on 20 December.

The security element controlled traffic into and out of the target area. The assault teams

Below: SOF members' language skills were used to good effect in Operation Just Cause, helping to stabilize the civilian populace and gather intelligence.

fast-roped onto the roof. One element blew up the electronic junction boxes controlling the antenna, and the rest of the assault force made its way to the 7th floor where they blew the AM station off the air. The assault teams could not find the FM transmitters.

As soon as the force returned to Albrook AFB, they were briefed on their next target: the FM transmission antenna located on the outskirts of town. Maj. McCracken and his nineteen men launched about 2015 and, though conducted after dark with very little planning time, the mission went smoothly. By 2045, the Company C element had destroyed the FM antenna, silencing Radio Nacional.

On 21 December, ODA 785 went back to the TV transmission tower it had disabled the day before and replaced its damaged components. About this time, pro-Noriega forces began intermittent radio broadcasts from this area. On 24 December, the rest of Company B, 3rd Battalion, 7th SFG(A), arrived to reinforce their teammates and to search for the phantom radio station. The large number of Spanish speakers in the Company and their long experience in Panama helped them to gain the trust of the locals. On the 25th, local civilians led them to a cache site containing weapons, ammunition, and medical supplies. Following up on information received from Panamanians, a patrol found the PDF's radio transmission site and destroyed it on 29 December.

"Ma Bell" Missions

During the initial invasion, U.S. forces had captured Panama City, its airport, the areas near the Panama Canal, and Rio Hato, but in

Below: After surrendering to Special Operations Forces, former Panamanian dictator Manuel Noriega was handed over to Drug Enforcement Agency officials.

the countryside the PDF still had nominal control. PDF forces were scattered throughout the countryside in small garrisons ("cuartels"); no-one knew what these PDF forces would do, as each cuartel was on its own. The Americans could have easily crushed these posts, but this would have produced many casualties, destroyed Panamanian villages, and alienated the populace. The U.S. instead developed a strategy of capitulation missions, with American forces contacting the PDF enclaves and offering them the opportunity to surrender before being attacked. Complicating the situation, PDF officers on the "most wanted list" commanded some of the major cuartels.

The ideal capitulation scenario was for the PDF to remain in position and then surrender to the U.S. forces as they spread throughout the countryside. Once the PDF had surrendered, the Americans would separate PDF members into criminals and non-criminals. TF BLACK played a critical role in this capitulation effort, one of its most significant contributions to the success of Operation Just Cause.

Capitulation missions had not been included in the plans for Operation Just Cause, but from 22–31 December they dominated TF BLACK's activities. The typical method used was to attach a small Special Forces element (with Spanish speakers) to a larger force (either the 7th Infantry Division or the 75th Ranger Regiment) to coordinate the PDF capitulation. The Special Forces commander would call the cuartel commander on the telephone and tell him to put all of his weapons in the arms room, line up all of his men on the parade field, and surrender to the U.S. forces that would arrive shortly. Because of the heavy reliance on telephones, these missions were nicknamed

"Ma Bell" operations.

During this ten-day period, TF BLACK elements were instrumental in the surrender of fouteen cuartels – almost 2,000 troops and over 6,000 weapons – without a single American casualty. Several high-ranking cronies of Manuel Noriega who were on the "most wanted" list were also captured in Ma Bell operations.

After each cuartel capitulated, the task of rebuilding the town began. TF BLACK generally left small Special Forces elements in each town to support the rebuilding process and assist the U.S. conventional forces. The Special Forces soldiers' language skills, cultural awareness, and expertise in low intensity conflict proved invaluable in leading U.S. patrols, coordinating with local officials, gathering information on weapons caches, reestablishing Panamanian police forces, and performing a myriad of other tasks that sped the process of transforming Panama into a more democratic nation. These operations were a textbook example of how Special Forces should be used in low intensity conflict.

In the last days of December 1989 and the first days of January 1990, TF BLACK continued its transition from the combat missions of Operation Just Cause to the stabilization missions of Operation Promote Liberty. In order to accomplish its new missions, the Task Force was reinforced by the 2nd Battalion, 7th SFG(A), a Naval Special Warfare Unit, and an Air Force Special Operations Detachment. With the assignment of SOF units from the Air Force and Navy, TF BLACK became Joint Task Force BLACK. The commander and staff from the 7th SFG(A) also arrived to take command of the Army Special Operations Forces in Panama as a subordinate of the JTF BLACK commander. The additional Army Special Forces battalion gave JTF BLACK enough personnel to conduct stabilization operations throughout Panama. The Air Force Special Operations assets gave JTF BLACK the transportation to get troops into remote locations and support them once they were out there. The Naval Special Warfare Unit conducted patrols along the coast and rivers, investigated possible weapons cache sites, and assisted the Panamanians in re-establishing their maritime security force.

Noriega's Capture

The invasion culminated with Manuel Noriega's apprehension. Although the JSOTF had missed capturing him at H-Hour on 20 December, SOF targeted his known associates and hiding places in Panama. With few places to hide, Noriega sought refuge at the

Papal Nunciature on 24 December. JSOTF forces surrounded and isolated the Nunciature and, in conjunction with U.S. State Department and Vatican diplomats, began to negotiate Noriega's surrender. Over the next ten days, JSOTF units kept watch over the Nunciature and maintained order over the large crowds gathering nearby. On the evening of 3 January, shortly after 10,000 anti-Noriega demonstrators had ended a rally outside the Nunciature, the former Panamanian dictator walked out and surrendered to the JSOTF forces.

Just Cause: SOF Worth Proven

On 16 January 1990, Operation Just Cause officially ended, and JTF BLACK ceased to exist. Some JTF BLACK forces returned to the continental United States or to the control of U.S. Southern Command. The rest remained under the control of JTF BLACK headquarters, renamed Joint Special Operations Task Force Panama, and continued Promote Liberty operations. Throughout Panama, SOF continued the difficult and delicate task of restoring peace, security, and democratic government to Panama one village at a time.

Just Cause demonstrated just how far SOF had come since Desert One – not only with regard to internal enhancements to SOF capabilities and command and control structures, but also with regard to the manifest close integration of SOF and conventional forces. SOF were subordinate to the Joint Task Force South, so all SOF plans and operations were fully complementary the theatre campaign plan.

Just Cause clearly validated how SOF were trained, equipped, and organized. This operation showcased joint SOF capabilities, the high training standards of operators and staffs alike, their quality and professionalism and the value of interoperability procedures. Promote Liberty planning, and post-conflict strategy in general, still needed work. In particular, there were problems with integrating nation-building plans into the campaign plan, incorporating CA and PSYOP planning with operational planning, and mobilizing crucial Reserve Component CA and PSYOP forces.

IRAQ
Operations Desert Shield/Desert Storm (1990-1991)

Iraq invaded Kuwait a few hours before dawn on 2 August 1990, easily overrunning the Kuwaiti defense forces and massing along the Saudi Arabian border. While the Saudi forces established a thin defensive cordon along the border, the United States deployed air and ground forces to the Arabian Peninsula to deter further Iraqi aggression.

The United States Central Command (CENT-COM) had military responsibility for this area and prepared to reinforce the Saudi Arabian forces. Its special operations component, Special Operations Command Central (SOC-CENT), likewise prepared to deploy and conduct combat search and rescue operations and other assigned missions.

SOCCENT personnel deployed to Riyadh, Saudia Arabia, on 10 August 1990 and moved to King Fahd International Airport (KFIA) on 17 August. Its naval element, the Naval Special Warfare Task Group (NSWTG) arrived in Saudia Arabia on 10 August 1990 and received its second increment of personnel on 9 September 1990. Meanwhile SOCCENT's Air Force element, AFSOCCENT, established its headquarters at KFIA on 17 August 1990. In late August, the 5th Special Forces Group (Airborne) [5th SFG(A)] deployed two battalions to King Khalid Military City (KKMC) and retained the third at KFIA. Army aviation assets of the 160th Special Operations Aviation Regiment also deployed to KKMC.

Coalition warfare (warfighting with forces from more than one nation) was arguably the most important of all the SOCCENT missions. With Saudi concurrence, SOCCENT's first coalition warfare mission was given to NSWTG elements, which deployed to the Kuwait/Saudi Arabian border on 19 August 1990 to provide close air support and to serve as "trip wires" in case of an Iraqi invasion.

Above: One of the most important missions of Special Operations Command Central during the Gulf War was to work with Arab members of the Coalition.

The 5th SFG(A) began replacing the SEALs on 5 September 1990 and provided early warning, coalition warfare training, and communications for close air support.

The number and type of coalition warfare missions grew steadily throughout Desert Shield and Desert Storm. The Saudis requested more Special Forces teams to train them on the M-60A3 tank, artillery, vehicle maintenance, and other technical areas. Other allied forces, as they deployed to the Arabian Peninsula, wanted Special Forces to provide close air support and liaison with friendly forces. These increasing requirements for coalition warfare soon absorbed much of the 5th SFG(A).

SOF also trained Saudi naval forces in special warfare. Some Saudis had completed the BUD/S (Basic Underwater Demolition/ SEAL) training course in Coronado, California, and their commander had worked with SEALs during operation Earnest Will in the Persian Gulf. Instruction, which included combat swimming and leadership training, produced three Saudi SEAL teams. Other NSWTG personnel trained the Saudi high-speed boat operators as well as conventional Saudi naval forces.

Another NSWTG mission was to reconstitute the Kuwaiti Navy. Only two gunboats (*Al*

Above: CSAR operations were vital in the Gulf War. Main photo, an HH-60H takes off in the sand. Inset, Navy pilot Lt. Devon Jones is rescued by an MH-53J.

Sanbnouk and *Istigal*), some patrol craft, and a motorised coast guard barge (*Sawahil*) had escaped the Iraqis. In September the NSWTG began training Kuwaiti naval personnel; they used the *Sawahil* to train thirty-five Kuwaiti sailors in naval engineering, seamanship, and small weapons. To instruct the Kuwaitis in surface warfare, the NSWTG borrowed rated experts from the conventional U.S. Navy. Beginning in November, the *Sawahil* and its crew conducted joint training with NSWTG small boats and took part in a combat search and rescue exercise with the USS *Nicholas*. During Desert Storm, the *Sawahil* provided an operational platform for coalition forces, including NSWTG Special Boat Unit detachments, Kuwaiti patrol boats, and SEALs.

Coalition warfare training continued until the eve of the ground war. The Arab forces in the east and north faced formidable military obstacles along their projected areas of advance, including multiple Iraqi minefields, "fire trenches," and above-ground pipelines. A Special Forces team worked with a Saudi engineer battalion to plan for clearing invasion lanes through two Iraqi minefields and over an above-ground pipeline inside Kuwait. On 22 February, the Saudi engineers and U.S. Special Forces easily cleared six lanes

because the Iraqis, battered for over a month by allied air power, failed to cover the minefields with artillery fire. In the north, other SF teams worked with the Saudis and the Egyptians to create breaches in the minefields for the passage of their forces. On 25 February, the Egyptians drove into Kuwait against sporadic resistance. The Egyptian corps that the 5th SFG(A) teams supported served as the hinge for CENTCOM's huge turning movement. By the night of 26 February, the Egyptians and their SF advisors had reached their objectives near Kuwait City.

The 28 February cease fire marked the end of most SOCCENT coalition warfare activities. It had been a huge effort, requiring an entire Special Forces Group, SEALs, Special Boat Units, and support elements. SF teams accompanied 109 allied units, from battalion to corps, providing close air support and liaison between forces. SOF eventually trained some 30,000 coalition troops in forty-four subject areas.

Kuwaiti Reconstitution and Unconventional Warfare

American Special Forces units helped to reconstitute a number of Kuwaiti military forces, both conventional and unconventional. As a result of meetings between the SOCCENT commander, Colonel Jesse Johnson, and the Kuwaiti Armed Forces Chief of Staff, soldiers from the 5th SFG(A) began training

Kuwaiti soldiers in mid-September at KKMC. The initial mission was to form a Kuwaiti SF battalion and a commando brigade, but the training went so well that the mission grew to include four additional Kuwaiti infantry brigades. Eventually, SOF units trained a total of 6,357 Kuwaitis, who formed an SF battalion, a commando brigade, and the Al-Khulud, Al-Haq, Fatah, and Badr infantry brigades. The instruction included weapons training, tactics, staff procedures, close air support, anti-armor operations, and nuclear, chemical and biological defense.

Colonel Johnson also formed a Special Planning Group to conduct specialized unconventional warfare training for selected members of the Kuwaiti military. About a month before the start of the air war, seventeen Kuwaiti military personnel underwent a rigorous five-week training course, but when Desert Storm's air attack began on 16 January 1991, the Iraqis closed the border, limiting infiltration options. Out of necessity, training then concentrated on infiltration methods.

From 14 to 20 February 1991, SEALs trained thirteen Kuwaitis for a maritime infiltration onto a beach area south of Kuwait City. They conducted a dress rehearsal on 21 February 1991 and attempted infiltrating five of the Kuwaitis on the next day. SEAL swimmer scouts first reconnoitered the shoreline and then escorted the Kuwaitis to the pier. Unable to link up with the friendly forces, the Kuwaitis signaled for extraction and were picked up about 500 yards from the beach. The mission was aborted, and the SEALs and Kuwaitis returned safely. Postwar examination of the beach revealed undetected beach obstacles and heavier Iraqi troop dispositions than anticipated.

Combat Search and Rescue (CSAR)

During Desert Shield, SOCCENT established procedures for CSAR, a mission that planners expected would be of critical importance, given the projected losses of coalition aircraft. Before it would launch a CSAR mission, SOCCENT required a visual parachute sighting and a voice transmission from the downed pilot, as well as enemy threat analyses. SOCCENT conducted full scale CSAR exercises before the air war started. To support the CSAR mission, SOCCENT established forward operating bases near the Saudi border, close to the projected areas of operation.

The first successful CSAR operation of Desert Storm occurred on 21 January 1991. An Iraqi missile had shot down a Navy F-14, 60 miles northwest of Baghdad, and the pilot had evaded capture. At 0730, an MH-53J

Pave Low helicopter launched from Ar Ar in a fog so thick that even when flying at 100 feet the crew could not see the ground. They flew 130 miles into Iraq but could not contact the pilot – their coordinates for his location were nearly 50 miles off. The helicopter returned to Ar Ar to refuel and launched again at 1200. With better coordinates, the crew arrived at the pilot's location just as an Iraqi truck was descending upon him. The helicopter copilot directed the two A-10 fighter planes flying overhead to "smoke the truck." The A-10s destroyed the truck with cannon fire, and the helicopter picked up the pilot.

The next successful CSAR effort occurred on 23 January when a USAF F-16 pilot bailed out over the Gulf. A Navy SH-60B helicopter carrying two SEALs launched from the USS *Nicholas* and found the pilot six miles off the Kuwaiti coast. The SEALs jumped into the water, attaching a rescue harness to the pilot; the helicopter crew retrieved all three and returned to the *Nicholas* just 35 minutes after launching. The rescuers reported that the mission went "flawlessly" and described the pilot as "cold, but in good condition."

On 17 February 1991, an F-16 went down in southern Iraq 36 miles from the Kuwaiti border. Slightly injured, the pilot parachuted into a heavy concentration of Iraqi troops but still established contact with rescue forces. Two MH-60s from the 160th Special Operations Aviation Regiment launched from Rafha, plucked the pilot from the desert, and returned him directly to King Khalid Military City for medical treatment.

For a number of reasons, most downed aircrew members were not rescued. The aircrews needed better survival radios, and there were not always visual sightings of open parachutes. Many pilots landed in areas of heavy

Iraqi concentrations, and the Iraqis often beat the SOF rescuers to the downed airmen.

Special Reconnaissance (SR)

During Desert Shield Special Operations Forces conducted SR missions along the Iraqi border, providing CENTCOM with timely intelligence and an early warning capability. During the war, SOCCENT's SR efforts supported the ground offensive. SOCCENT forces conducted twelve SR missions during Desert Storm. One mission included fifteen separate near-shore boat operations that the NSWTG conducted in Kuwaiti waters between 30 January and 15 February as part of CENTCOM's deception plan. Another mission encompassed six searches for mines by SEALs in the northern Persian Gulf. Three SR missions continued the early warning network which the SEALs and 5th SFG(A) troops had established with Saudi and Kuwaiti forces during Desert Shield.

At the request of VII Corps, SF teams performed a "trafficability" survey on 18 February, analyzing the terrain and soil conditions along the Corps' planned invasion route into Iraq. Special operations helicopters inserted teams from the 3rd and 5th SFG(A)s into two sites. The teams included engineers who performed penetrometer tests on the soil, as well as combat crews, who used low-level light lenses to take still and video shots of the terrain, which proved to be the most valuable data collected. The teams executed the missions without incident.

The campaign plan for the ground war called for the XVIII Airborne Corps and VII Corps forces to drive deep into Iraq, flanking and then enveloping the strong Iraqi defenses in Kuwait and southern Iran. This movement would leave the flanks of both Corps vulnerable to counterattack. The Corps' commanders

Above: Army Ah-64 Apaches, led to their targets by MH-53J Pave Low helicopters, destroyed Iraqi radars prior to H-Hour, 0300 on 17 January 1991.

requested that SOCCENT provide SR teams to go deep inside Iraq, watch important lines of communication, and look for enemy movement toward the exposed flanks. G-Day was set for 24 February 1991.

Three missions provided ground reconnaissance of the main routes that Iraqi units could use to move into VII Corps' area of operations. Two of the missions successfully infiltrated on 23 February; they reported regularly on enemy activity until advance elements of the 1st Cavalry Division arrived on 27 February. The third team, inserted among Iraqi forces, had to be exfiltrated.

Special Forces launched three other SR missions on 23 February, these in support of the XVIII Airborne Corps. One team landed in the middle of a Bedouin encampment and called for an emergency exfiltration. After being picked up, they scouted the area for an alternative site and saw enemy activity everywhere. Coming under AAA and SAM attack, they aborted the mission. Another team went into the Euphrates River Valley to report on Iraqi military traffic moving along a major highway. During the insertion, one of the aircraft flew so low to avoid Iraqi radar that it tore loose its rear wheel on a sand dune.

By daylight the team was in place, having dug "hide" holes in a drainage canal about 300 yards northwest of Highway 7. To the horror of the hidden Americans, the surrounding fields came alive with people that morning, and they were soon spotted by some Iraqi children and an adult. A party of twenty-five armed villagers, joined by an Iraqi Army company, moved towards the team. Calling for close air

Above: BLU-82 "Daisy Cutter" bombs had a lethal impact on Iraqi forces. This one was destined to revenge the tragic loss of AC-130H Spectre "Spirit 03."

support and an emergency extraction, the SOF team destroyed their classified gear, engaged in a short but hot firefight with the Iraqis, and retreated to better fighting positions. Using their emergency radio, the team contacted close air support aircraft, which dropped cluster munitions and 2,000-pound bombs within 200 yards of the embattled team until nightfall. During one lull in the air strikes, two members of the team charged down the canal and eliminated an Iraqi element. After dark, the team moved 300 yards from the canal, where a helicopter extracted them without further opposition.

Another Special Reconnaissance mission sent two three-man teams to monitor an area between the Tigris and Euphrates rivers. Communications glitches prevented one team from reporting what they saw, and the team was picked up early on 27 February. The second team's reconnaissance site put it in the midst of Bedouin encampments, so team members established a hide site along a drainage canal. At daylight, they discovered that their "hide" site was near a major thoroughfare. Many Bedouins passed by without noticing them, but the team was compromised by a sharp-eyed little girl. The team fled with armed Bedouins in hot pursuit. Iraqi soldiers soon joined the firefight. The team held off the Iraqis for an hour and a half until F-16s appeared, followed by a 160th Special Operations Aviation Regiment Blackhawk helicopter. Although riddled by small arms fire, the helicopter made a dramatic daylight rescue of the team.

From 29 January until 16 February, NSWTG elements conducted nearshore and offshore reconnaissance missions in support of CENTCOM's deception strategy to fix Iraqi attention on a potential amphibious invasion by US Marines. The SR missions resulted in the collection of information, established a naval presence along with the Kuwaiti coast, and focused the attention of the Iraqi command on a possible maritime invasion. The deception effort culminated in a large-scale operation on the night of 23-24 February 1991, the eve of the ground offensive, which simulated a beach reconnaissance and clearing operation. The deception campaign prevented Iraqi units at the beaches from reinforcing those being attacked in the west.

Direct Action (DA) Missions

During Desert Storm, General H. Norman Schwarzkopf, CINCCENT, relied heavily on allied air power to hit targets which otherwise would have been SOF Direct Action (DA) missions. Even so, SOCCENT executed some critically important DA missions.

SOF's first and most important DA mission involved the destruction of two Iraqi early warning radar sites guarding the southwestern approaches to Iraq at the start of the Air War. Neutralizing these sites allowed allied aircraft to fly undetected toward the SCUD complexes in western Iraq. Colonel Jesse Johnson, the SOCCENT Commander, turned to AFSOCCENT, his Air Force component, to plan the operation. The concept called for MH-53 Pave Low helicopters to guide AH-64 Apaches to the targeted radar sites, which the Apaches would destroy. On 14 October, Colonel Johnson assured General Schwarzkopf that he and AFSOC-

CENT were 100 percent certain of success.

The Apache and Pave Low crews quickly worked out interoperability issues, and they conducted a full dress rehearsal in late December with the crews duplicating the formations, routes, bearings, times, and attack tactics. At 1500 on 16 January 1991, SOCCENT informed the Apache/Pave Low task force that the mission was a "go" for that night. H-Hour for the start of the air war was 0300 on 17 January with the opening helicopter strike beginning at 0238 hours. The task force consisted of White and Red teams, with two Pave Lows and four Apaches assigned to each one.

At 0058 on 17 January, the White Team lifted off from Al Jouf and headed toward the border, followed 15 minutes later by the Red Team. Flying less than 100 feet off the desert at 100 knots, the two teams avoided detection and safely reached the initial point, approximately 7.5 miles from the targets, where the Pave Lows dropped chemical lights and returned to the rendezvous point north of the border. The Apache pilots updated their navigational and targeting systems, flew toward their targets, and within seconds of the appointed time opened fire on the radar sites. All aircraft returned safely. Colonel Johnson then notified General Schwarzkopf of the mission's success. At the same time, combat control teams installed radar beacons along the Saudi-Kuwaiti-Iraqi borders to direct allied attack aircraft to the gaps in the early warning radar system. SOF had played a crucial role on the opening night of the air war.

AFSOCCENT conducted two other DA missions: dropping BLU-82 bombs and AC-130 fire missions. The BLU-82 "Daisy Cutters" were 15,000-pound bombs capable of destroying everything in a three mile radius on the flat desert terrain. Because of the anti-aircraft threat, AFSOCCENT planners determined that the bomb should be dropped from 16,000 to 21,000 feet. Accordingly, MC-130E Combat Talons flew five missions that dropped a total of eleven BLU-82s on minefields and Iraqi military positions. These huge bombs cleared wide routes through minefields, and their enormous blast either killed the enemy or acted as a potent psychological operations weapon.

AC-130s flew fire missions in support of ground forces, to attack the SCUD missile sites, and to engage Iraqi troops. Although these aircraft belonged to AFSOCCENT, they were under the operational control of Central Command's air component, CENTAF. This arrangement resulted in the AC-130s being used for inappropriate missions in medium threat areas. After an AC-130H was engaged by SAMs while on a SCUD-hunting mission, the AFSOCCENT commander was given mission oversight responsibility to ensure these SOF assets were used correctly.

On 31 January 1991, AFSOCCENT suffered the single worst air loss by any Coalition unit when an AC-130H Spectre gunship ("Spirit 03") was shot down while providing fire support to US Marines defending Khafji against an Iraqi attack. Three gunships were airborne that morning over the Marines, and the first two had destroyed numerous Iraqi armored personnel carriers. At 0600, "Spirit 03" was due to end its patrol when it received a call from the Marines, who wanted a missile

battery engaged. The crew of "Spirit 03" took out the battery, but as dark gave way to daylight a surface-to-air missile hit the aircraft. At 0635, the aircraft sent out a "mayday" distress call and then crashed into the Gulf. All fourteen crewmembers died.

During Desert Storm, British Special Forces carried out their own missions in western Iraq. One British mission – very close to Baghdad – included four American SOF personnel (three Special Forces and one Combat Controller), brought along to coordinate close air support. Their goal was to destroy a buried fiber optic cable supposedly used for SCUD command and control. The twenty Brits and four Americans were inserted by two helicopters on the night of 23 January slightly southwest of Baghdad. Digging teams found and cut several cables, but found no fiber optic cable. They then crammed 800 pounds of explosives into the hole and blew up what was left of the cables. After one and a half hours on the ground, the team returned safely to Al Jouf by helicopter.

Naval Special Warfare units had Direct Action missions in the Gulf. On 18 January 1991, when U.S. helicopters came under fire from seven oil platforms in the Durrah oil field, NSWTG elements counterattacked. SEALs boarded and cleared each of the seven platforms, capturing prisoners, weapons, and documents. Eight special boat unit personnel and thirty-two Kuwaiti Marines also seized Qaruh Island on 8 February, Maradim Island the next day, and Kubbar Island on 14 February – these operations

were the first reclamation of Kuwaiti territory. In the final hours of the war, NSWTG and Kuwaiti forces seized Bubiyan Island and captured its Iraqi defenders. SEALs also flew aboard Navy helicopters for both CSAR and countermine missions, during which they destroyed twenty-six moored or floating mines.

The Liberation of Kuwait: Operation Urban Freedom

SOCCENT assisted Kuwaiti forces in liberating their capital city and reestablishing Kuwaiti governmental authority. SOCCENT initiated Operation Urban Freedom when allied forces reached the outskirts of Kuwait City. SOCCENT deployed to Kuwait City International Airport on 27 February, along with 3rd SFG(A) teams and other personnel. Surprisingly, the Iraqis had abandoned the city, and the liberation forces met little organized opposition. As a precautionary measure, SOF units conducted a "take down" of the U.S. Embassy compound in Kuwait City. A ground convoy, composed of SEAL fast attack vehicles and 3rd SFG(A) soldiers, surrounded the compound while a Special Forces assault force fast-roped onto the roofs of buildings and searched for Iraqis and booby traps. None was found.

SCUD-hunting

Coalition forces had air superiority in the skies over Iraq and Kuwait from the war's first air strikes on 17 January 1991. Unable to do battle in the air, Saddam Hussein struck back with a clumsy, unsophisticated weapon – the SCUD missile – which he ordered to be launched at Israel. Tactically, the SCUD would not have a major impact, but its strategic effect was felt on 18 January, when seven SCUDs hit Israeli cities. If continued attacks brought Israel into the war, then the Coalition aligned against Saddam might crumble. General Schwarzkopf's insistence that the SCUD was not a significant military weapon did little to placate the Israelis or ease the pressure on the Bush Administration. By the end of the first week of war, over thirty SCUDs had been launched at targets in Israel and Saudi Arabia. The air campaign was not working fast enough to eradicate the mobile SCUD launchers.

By the end of January, the diplomatic pressure on the Bush Administration was such that General Colin Powell, Chairman of the Joint Chiefs of Staff, ordered General Schwarzkopf to use Special Operations Forces

Left: As many as four SOF teams were deep behind enemy lines by the time the ground war started, calling down fighter/attack strikes on SCUD missiles.

to hunt SCUDs and stop them from being fired at Israel. A Joint Special Operations Task Force (JSOTF), made up of special operations air and ground units, arrived in Saudi Arabia by 1 February. Operating from a base at Ar Ar in western Saudi Arabia, the JSOTF had a daunting mission: stop the SCUD attacks on Israel. Reconnaissance and surveillance teams would have to go hundreds of miles inside western Iraq and attack the SCUD infrastructure.

The first JSOTF cross-border mission, consisting of sixteen SOF personnel and two vehicles, occurred on 7 February. It set the pattern for subsequent cross-border operations. Armed Blackhawk helicopters, called defensive armed penetrators, accompanied the insertions. Once on the ground, the teams hid during the day and conducted reconnaissance at night. These SOF operations proved to be so successful – especially the Blackhawk attacks on SCUDs and SCUD-related targets – that General Schwarzkopf on 14 February approved augmenting the JSOTF with a reinforced Ranger company and more 160th Special Operations Aviation Regiment helicopters.

By the time the ground war started, the JSOTF was conducting a wide range of operations. As many as four SOF teams at the time were inside Iraq, conducting operations against the SCUD complexes. These teams called in F-15E, F-16, and A-10 sorties to strike the targets they found. On 26 February, SOF attacked a radio relay site: first, AH-6 attack helicopters peppered the radio relay compound with mini-gun and rocket fire; Rangers then secured the compound and set charges to destroy the 300-foot tall tower. The Blackhawks also conducted "Thunder Runs," which were Direct Action missions on SCUDs, their lines of communication, and other command and control facilities. The JSOTF also used "Gator" minefields to limit SCUD mobile launcher movement. Because of JSOTF operations, the number of SCUD launches fell dramatically, and their accuracy was greatly impaired.

PSYOP and CA Missions

Psychological Operations (PSYOP) and Civil Affairs (CA) units contributed significantly to the success in the Gulf War. The PSYOP campaign was directed toward individual units and soldiers, and stressed a single theme: the Coalition's quarrel was with Saddam Hussein and not with the Iraqi people or its army. In the early phases, the PSYOP themes emphasized "peace and brotherhood." It later evolved to

Right: **PSYOP and Civil Affairs (CA) missions were important during the Gulf War. Here CA soldiers distribute food and other supplies to displaced people.**

stronger themes, and finally turned to surrender appeals and threats.

Once begun, the PSYOP campaign (in conjunction with sustained air attacks) steadily eroded Iraqi military morale. Some 29 million leaflets were dropped from a variety of aircraft, with a few more distributed by artillery shells and balloons. Three AM and two FM ground stations transmitted "Voice of the Gulf" broadcasts for 72 days, which interspersed 3,200 news items and 189 PSYOP "messages" among sports and music programs. Resistance crumbled quickly when the Coalition ground forces attacked. A total 86,743 Iraqis were taken prisoner, and most of them were found to possess surrender leaflets when they capitulated.

The Combined Civil Affairs Task Force (CCATF) was created in February 1991 to provide emergency services for Kuwait City once it was liberated. Relief operations began on 28 February 1991 when the first convoy rolled into the city. The CCATF stayed in Kuwait for two months before turning the relief effort over to the Army Corps of Engineers. During that time it distributed 12.8 million liters of water, 12,500 tons of food, 1,250 tons of medicine, 750 vehicles and 245 electrical generators.

Flexibility best describes Special Operations Forces' contribution to the Desert Storm victory. Initially tasked with providing CSAR, SOCCENT steadily expanded its SOF missions as conventional commanders gained confidence in SOF's abilities and resources. The Coalition support mission became an important new SOF capability, used later in operations in Somalia and Bosnia; the new geopolitical environment had made SOF more relevant. The SCUD-hunting mission demonstrated SOF's ability to deploy rapidly and start operations with little delay, and to execute missions of the gravest national importance.

SOMALIA (1992–1995)

During the 1980s and early 1990s, unending violence in Somalia, East Africa, led to increasing international frustration as aid was seen to be getting into the hands of gunmen and failing to reach the starving Somali people. This was hardly surprising as Mogadishu port was held hostage by some 1,000 young gunmen belonging to five separate armed groups, each of which charged aid authorities "protection money" and then stole from the very convoys they were being paid to guard.

US Special Operations Forces first became involved in Somalia as part of Operation Provide Relief. In August 1992, soldiers of the 2nd Battalion, 5th Special Forces Group (Airborne), deployed to neighboring Kenya to provide security for relief flights en route from Kenya to Somalia. They formed an airborne reaction force, which included two desert mobility vehicles loaded inside C-130 aircraft. The C-130s circled over Somali airstrips during delivery of relief supplies. In addition, SOF medics and ground observers accompanied many relief flights into the airstrips throughout southern Somalia to conduct general area assessments. In many cases, they were the first U.S. soldiers in

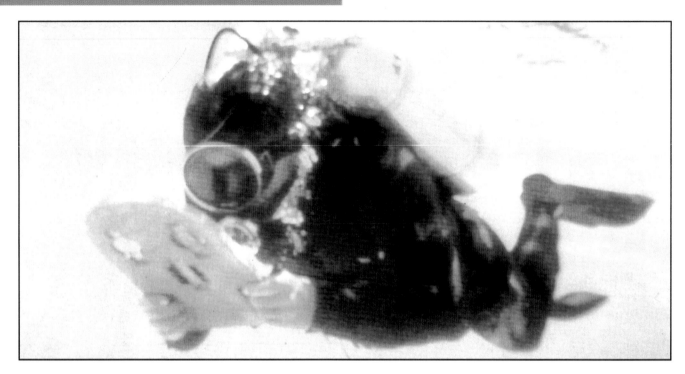

Somalia, arriving before U.S. forces who supported the expanded relief operations of Operation Restore Hope.

Operation Restore Hope

To support the United Nations relief effort, the Chairman of the Joint Chiefs of Staff, General Colin Powell, directed CENTCOM on 2 December 1992 to secure transportation facilities in Mogadishu. The operation was designated Restore Hope. An amphibious squadron, consisting of USS *Tripoli, Juneau*, and *Rushmore*, with a Marine Expeditionary Unit, a SEAL platoon, and a Special Boat Unit (SBU) detachment, arrived off the coast of Somalia shortly thereafter. To mount an amphibious landing to secure the Mogadishu airport, the Marines needed up-to-date charts for the beaches, which did not exist. The SEALs and SBU detachment conducted a hydrographic reconnaissance, the classic "frogman mission" dating from World War II, to chart the beaches.

The first mission occurred on the night of 6 December, when twelve SEALs conducted a hydrographic reconnaissance in the traditional method, swimming in a line toward shore, and taking depth soundings with weighted lines. Upon reaching waist-deep water, they each shifted to the right and swam back out, repeating the process. Meanwhile, another five SEALs swam ashore, and reconnoitered the beach. The two SEAL cartographers, measured the berm and noted the shore gradient and the presence of obstacles on the beach. The SEALs returned to the *Juneau* where they compiled charts, briefed the Marines, and prepared for their next night's mission.

On the night of 7 December, the SEALs swam into Mogadishu harbor, where they found suitable landing sites, assessed the area for threats, and ascertained that the port could support maritime prepositioned ship offloads. This was a tough mission: the SEALs swam against a strong current which left many of them overheated and exhausted, and they had to swim through raw sewerage in the harbor, which made them sick.

When the first SEALs hit the shore the following night, they were surprised to meet members of the news media. Thankfully, the first Marines came ashore soon thereafter, and the press corps redirected their attention to them, freeing the SEALs to proceed with their duties. Four SEALs thereupon conducted surf observations and initial terminal guidance for the Marines' landing craft.

On 17 December, the SEALs surveyed the port of Kismayu from the French frigate *Dupleix*. During this operation, Somali snipers fired at the SEALs, but no SEALs were hit. Later, the SEALs provided personal security for President George Bush during a visit to Somalia, and provided snipers to the Marines. Before leaving Somalia in February 1993, the SEALs also conducted joint training missions with Indian naval commandos.

A platoon from SEAL Team 2, with the Wasp Amphibious Ready Group, replaced the departed SEALs. On their first missions, these SEALs reconnoitered the Jubba River (which including dodging crocodiles) to gather intelligence on gun smuggling; based on this intelligence, Marines staged two raids on towns along the river. These SEALs performed operations in April and May: a predawn shore reconnaissance of Kismau; cleari   a potential beach landing site south of Mogadishu; reconnaissance missions in the Three Rivers region of Kismayu and at Koyaama Island; and

Above: Reminiscent of World War II frogman missions, Navy SEALs and Special Boat Unit personnel conducted hydrographic reconnaissance in Somalia.

a reconnaissance of Daanai beach in extremely rough seas.

Meanwhile, on 28 December 1992, the US Special Forces assets in Kenya moved to Somalia and joined Operation Restore Hope. On 12 January 1993, a Special Forces headquarters unit [FOB 52 (-)] deployed to Mogadishu as the Joint Special Operations Forces-Somalia (JSOFOR) that would command and control all special operations for Restore Hope. JSOFOR's mission was to make initial contact with indigenous factions and leaders; provide information for future relief and security operations. The Special Forces under JSOFOR supported the nine humanitarian relief sector commanders. Before redeploying in April, JSOFOR elements drove over 26,000 miles, captured 277 weapons, and destroyed over 45,320 pounds of ordnance. So successful were the Special Forces teams that the commander of UN operations in Somalia, LTG Bir (Turkey), considered them a "must have" asset.

The 96th CA Battalion (Airborne) deployed a CA Tactical Support Team and six CA Direct Support Teams which provided a liaison between Army and Marine commanders, local Somali committees, and representatives of over forty non-governmental organizations. CA personnel also staffed humanitarian operations centers throughout Somalia, from which they coordinated medical and engineer civic action projects.

The Joint PSYOP Task Force (JPOTF) supported unified operations by integrating PSYOP into all plans and operations, and by

Above: Rangers take cover and return fire in Mogadishu, where some of the urban firefights were the fiercest since the Vietnam War.

hiring more than thirty Somalis to help with the PSYOP newspaper *Rajo* ("Truth") and radio broadcasting. More than seven million copies of thirty-seven different leaflets and a dozen handbills and posters were printed and disseminated. PSYOP soldiers, including eight loudspeaker support teams from the 9th PSYOP Battalion, with native linguists and pre-recorded tapes, supported both the Marine 7th Regimental Combat Support Team and Army maneuver units.

As a complement to *Rajo*, the JPOTF established a radio station in the U.S. Embassy compound, which broadcast a 45-minute Somali language program twice a day. The station featured religious, news, entertainment, and music programs, and its broadcasts eventually reached every city and town in Somalia where UN forces were based.

Operation Restore Hope gave way to UN Operations Somalia in May 1993, after having brought an end to starvation and making the lives of Somali somewhat safer. But the overall success of US Special Operations Forces in Somalia will always be overshadowed by the events of 3-4 October 1993, when U.S. troops found themselves in the fiercest urban firefight since the Vietnam War.

UNOSOM II

On 5 June 1993, General Mohamed Farah Aideed's Somalia National Alliance forces ambushed and killed twenty-four Pakistani soldiers assigned to UN Operations Somalia (UNOSOM II). The next day, General Joseph P. Hoar, Commander in Chief, U.S. Central Command, asked the Joint Staff to send four AC-130 gunships to carry out air strikes against the Somalis. Four AFSOC gunships deployed on 7 June and remained until 14 July, flying a total of thirty-two interdiction, reconnaissance, and PSYOP missions in support of UNOSOM II. Eight of those missions were combat sorties flown over the streets of Mogadishu between 11-17 June.

As part of the initial strike against Aideed, three gunships flew over Mogadishu on 11 June and used their 105mm and 40mm cannons to demolish two weapons storage facilities, an armored tank compound, and Aideed's "Radio Mogadishu" propaganda station. The next day, two AC-130s obliterated a second radio station and a weapons factory. On 13, 14 and 17 June, ASFOC crews flew single AC-130 missions that concentrated on destroying weapons storage areas and vehicle compounds belonging to Aideed and his key supporters. During these missions, Air Force special tactics operators provided target guidance. The AC-130 missions and related ground operations together drove Aideed into hiding. The AC-130s redeployed in mid-July, and other Special Operations Forces later took up the hunt for Aideed.

Task Force Ranger

On 22 August 1993, Secretary of Defense Les Aspin directed the deployment of a Joint Special Operations Task Force (JSOTF) to Somalia in response to attacks made by Aideed supporters upon U.S. and UNOSOM forces and installations. The JSOTF, named Task Force (TF) Ranger, was directed to capture Aideed and his key lieutenants and turn them over to UNOSOM II forces. This was a challenging mission, for Aideed had gone underground in June, after several AC-130 air raids and UNOSOM II ground assaults on his strongholds.

The command and control structure of TF Ranger is of interest. Per the Goldwater-Nichols Defense Reorganization Act, the unified commander (in this case, General Hoar, Commander in Chief, U.S. Central Command) was entitled to organize his forces as he saw fit. General Hoar had the TF Ranger commander, Major General William Garrison, report to him directly. Thus, TF Ranger did not fall under the UNOSOM II commander, and at all times it remained under U.S. operational command and control. Major General Garrison did, however, coordinate TF Ranger operations with Major General Thomas M. Montgomery, the commander of the U.S. Forces Somalia.

By 28 August, the task force had arrived in country, was conducting training exercises, and was setting up the necessary liaison and communications networks. TF Ranger was made up of special operations ground forces, special operations helicopters, Air Force special tactics personnel, and SEALs. During August and September 1993, the task force conducted six missions into Mogadishu, all of which were tactical successes. They ran these missions both by day and night, and used both helicopters and ground vehicles to reach their targets. Although Aideed remained free, the cumulative effect of these missions limited his movements.

On 3 October, TF Ranger launched its seventh mission, this time into Aideed's stronghold to capture two of his key lieutenants. Helicopters carrying assault and blocking forces launched at 1532 from the TF Ranger compound at Mogadishu airport, with a ground convoy moving out three minutes later. By 1542, the ground forces had arrived at the target location, as the blocking force was setting up perimeter positions and the assault force was searching the compound for Aideed's supporters.

These forces came under increasingly heavy enemy fire, more intense than during previous raids. The assault team had captured twenty-four Somalis and was about to load them onto the convoy trucks when an MH-60 Blackhawk was hit by a rocket-propelled grenade (RPG) and crashed about three blocks from the target location. Almost immediately, one six-man element of the blocking force, as well as an MH-6 assault helicopter and an MH-60 carrying a 15-man combat search and rescue (CSAR) team, began rushing to the scene. The MH-6 crew got there first and amid a firefight evacuated two wounded soldiers to a military field hospital. Next, the six-man blocking element arrived, followed by the CSAR helicopter. As the last two members of the CSAR team were sliding down the fast ropes, their helicopter was also hit by an RPG, but somehow the pilot kept the helicopter steady while the two reached the ground safely, and he then nursed the helicopter back to the airport.

The situation only worsened. Ground fire struck two more MH-60s, with one crashing less than a mile to the south of the first downed helicopter. A Somali mob overran this second site, and, despite a heroic defense, killed everyone except the pilot, whom they took prisoner. Two defenders of this crash site, Master Sergeant Gary Gordon and Sergeant First Class Randall Shughart, were posthumously awarded the Medal of Honor. The other MH-60 was hit

Below: **MSG Gary Gordon and SFC Randall Shughart (bottom) lost their lives defending an MH-60 crash site. Both were awarded the Medal of Honor.**

broadside by an RPG, but the crew somehow coaxed it to the new port area where they carried out a controlled crash landing.

Meanwhile, after loading the detainees on the ground convoy trucks, the assault and blocking forces moved on foot to the first crash area, passing through heavy fire that wounded a number of solders, and occupied buildings south and southwest of the downed helicopter. They established defensive positions, laid down a suppressive fire to hold the Somalis at bay, treated their wounded, and worked to free the pilot's body from the wreckage of the first MH-60.

With the detainees loaded on trucks, the ground convoy force attempted to reach the first crash site from the north. Unable to find it amongst the narrow, winding alleyways, the convoy came under withering small arms and RPG fire. The convoy had to return to base after suffering numerous casualties, losing two 5-ton trucks, and sustaining substantial damage to the other vehicles. On the way back to base, this convoy encountered a second convoy that had left the airport in hopes of reach the second crash site.

The second group loaded casualties into its vehicles and escorted the first convoy back to base. About this time, the mission's quick reaction force (a company of the 10th Mountain Division in support of UNOSOM II) also tried to reach the second crash site. This force too was pinned by Somali fire and required the fire support of two AH-6 helicopters before it could break contact and make its way back to the base.

The TF Ranger soldiers at the first crash site were resupplied from a helicopter that evening. Reinforcements, consisting of Rangers, 10th Mountain Division soldiers, SEALs, and Malaysian armored personnel carriers, finally arrived at 0155 on 4 October. The

combined force worked until dawn to free the pilot's body, receiving RPG and small arms fire throughout the night.

All the casualties were loaded onto the armored personnel carriers, and the remainder of the force moved out on foot. With the armored personnel carriers providing rolling cover, the run-and-gun movement, known as the "Mogadishu mile," began at 0542. Somalis continued firing at the convoy, but the Rangers sustained only minor wounds. AH-6 gunships raked the cross streets with fire to support the movement. The main force of the convoy arrived at the Pakistani Stadium at 0630. Medical personnel gave emergency treatment to the wounded, and all personnel were prepared for movement to the hospital or the airfield.

Thus ended one of the bloodiest and fiercest urban firefights since the Vietnam War. A total of sixteen members of TF Ranger were killed on 3-4 October, and there were eighty-three wounded (the 10th Mountain Division suffered numerous wounded and one killed). Various estimates placed Somali casualties about 1,000. All told during their time in Somalia, TF Ranger experienced a total of seventeen killed in action and one hundred and six wounded. Task force members had to operate in an extremely difficult environment which required constant innovation, flexibility, and sound judgment. The task force had more than held its own against a vastly superior enemy that was battle-hardened from years of civil war and urban fighting. Nevertheless, their mission – that of capturing Aideed and his lieutenants – had not been accomplished.

Below: **A 160th Special Operations Aviation Regiment MH-6 "Little Bird," such as those used in the heavy urban fighting in Mogadishu.**

The Withdrawal From Somalia

In the aftermath of the 3-4 October battle, U.S. military presence in Somalia increased significantly. Two AC-130s deployed to Kenya and flew reconnaissance missions over Mogadishu. More Special Forces also deployed, as did a platoon from SEAL Team 2 and one from SEAL Team 8.

The SEALs provided security detachments to U.S. and UN troops by occupying sniper positions and guarding allied encampments, by flying on aircraft traveling between Somalia and the carrier battle groups off shore, and by providing VIP protection. Other SEALs aboard rigid inflatable boats provided harbor security for Marine Corps landing boats shuttling between ships offshore and Marine Corps encampments on the beach. Most U.S. forces pulled out of Somalia by 25 March 1994.

To assist the UN forces' withdrawal, the final amphibious ready group arrived off Somalia on 5 February 1995. During February and March 1995, the SEALs first conducted hydrographic reconnaissance missions on the beaches around Mogadishu to determine the best evacuation routes, and then performed initial terminal guidance for Marine landing craft and assault vehicles. The SEALs maintained security on the evacuation route, conducting anti-sniper patrols on the beach flanks and around the harbor. Operation United Shield, the withdrawal from Somalia, was completed on 3 March 1995.

Despite not capturing Aideed, SOF had made major contributions to the Somalia 1992-1995 operations. They conducted reconnaissance and surveillance operations;

Below: Special Operations Forces' helicopters, their crews, and other soldiers aboard USS *America* during Operation Support Democracy.

assisted with humanitarian relief; conducted combat operations; protected American forces; and conducted riverine patrols. Additionally, they ensured the safe landing of the Marines and safeguarded the arrival of merchant ships carrying food.

HAITI (1994-1995)

Haiti, occupying the western part of the island of Hispaniola in the Carribbean, had endured unremitting political oppression for hundreds of years. Although the people of this troubled country enjoyed a taste of freedom in 1990 when they elected Jean-Beatrand Aristide as their President, the army took control in a 30 September 1991 coup. Attempting to re-establish the Aristide government, the UN imposed economic sanctions on 23 June 1993; four months later, on October 15, President Clinton ordered US Navy ships to help enforce this embargo. Admiral David Paul Miller, Commander-in-Chief, United States Atlantic Command (CINCACOM), activated Combined Joint Task Force (CJTF) 120 to plan and execute the multinational Operation Support Democracy.

Operation Support Democracy

The U.S. and allied warships in CJTF 120 boarded over 600 ships during the operation's first five months, and the big ships' effectiveness soon drove embargo-busting smugglers to use vessels to carry contraband along shallow coastal routes beyond the larger ships' reach.

CJTF 120 selected the US Special Operations Command Cyclone-class patrol craft (PC) as the best response to the smugglers' new tactic. The PCs were new to USSOCOM's inventory, and needed sea duty certification before assignment to Haiti. After being certified for participating in exercise Agile Provider, the USS *Cyclone* and the USS *Tempest* departed for

Guantanano, Cuba, on 24 May to participate in Support Democracy.

On 30 May, CJTF 120 directed the PCs to begin operations with the warships off the north Haitian coast. The plan to integrate the PCs gradually into the interdiction operation ended when the ships, on their very first voyage, encountered a Bahamian sailing vessel trying to skirt the embargo. As the smugglers' vessel headed for Port-au-Prince, the *Cyclone* ordered it to stand clear of the Haitian coast, but the vessel did not heave to until *Cyclone* fired warning flares and launched a rigid hull inflated boat (RIB) with SEALs aboard. The vessel attempted to play a waiting game that night, but at first light a combined party from the *Cyclone* and the HMCS *Terra Nova* – six Canadians and three SEALs – conducted a boarding and search operation. They found embargoed goods, and the *Cyclone* towed this vessel to Guatanamo.

By 23 June 1994, the CTJF 120 fleet had boarded over 1,100 ships, but embargoed goods flowed steadily into Haiti from neighboring Dominican Republic. General John M. Shalikashvili, Chairman of the Joint Chiefs of Staff, gave approval for the PCs to conduct patrols with Dominican Republic ships. On 11 July 1994, SEALs from the *Cyclone* boarded and cleared the *Vinland Saga*, a Danish vessel carrying a cargo of wheat flour. CJTF 120 directed *Cyclone* and *Tempest* to patrol the inner areas of the coast. These operations provided an opportunity to check sea traffic and collect information. The USS *Hurricane* and USS *Monsoon* patrol craft replaced the *Cyclone* and *Tempest* in September.

Because of the continuing political repres-

Below: The Navy Special Warfare Command USS *Cyclone* with SEALs aboard helped enforce the UN-approved embargo of Haiti in 1994.

Monsoon had the honor of being the first U.S. ship to enter Port-au-Prince Harbor on 19 September. From this point until their departure on 24 October 1994, the PCs maintained harbor patrols.

The Occupation of Haiti

U.S. planners foresaw that Port-au-Prince would be the "center of gravity" for the political and economic struggle that would follow the restoration of the Aristide government. The bulk of the conventional forces from the 10th Mountain Division (and later the 25th Infantry Division) secured and remained in the city. It was also important to maintain stable conditions in the remaining 90 percent of Haiti. For this mission XVIII Airborne Corps Commander Lieutenant General Henry H. Shelton chose to use SOF.

Brigadier General Richard Potter formed Joint Task Force (JTF) Raleigh as the Joint Special Operations Task Force under Lieutenant General Shelton. To implement the plan, the three battalions of 3rd SFG(A) set up three forward operating bases: 1st Battalion at Les Cayes, 2nd at Camp D'Application, and 3rd at Gonaives. Using the "hub and spoke" concept of employment, Operational Detachment-Alpha teams ("A-teams") deployed initially to the forward operating bases (the hubs) and then farther out into the countryside (the spokes). SF teams in these villages became the only source of law and order, and the villagers called on SF captains, sergeants, and warrant officers to act as policeman, judge, and jury for a wide variety of disputes.

A well thought out psychological operations campaign orchestrated by the Joint Psychological Operations Task Force (JPOTF), prepared the way for 3rd SFG(A)'s expansion into the countryside of Haiti. The PSYOP campaign, conducted by elements of the 4th Psychological Operations Group, stressed that cooperating with U.S. forces and avoiding bloody conflicts with the existing illegal regime would lead to the reinstatement of the popular Aristide and the establishment of a working democracy. Using leaflets, radio broadcasts, and airborne loudspeaker platforms, JPOTF soldiers blanketed the countryside with their messages, to great effect. In village after village, the Haitians greeted SOF soldiers with open arms.

While Special Forces soldiers were gaining control over the countryside, Civil Affairs teams from the 96th CA reservists assessed Haiti's creaking infrastructure. The hope was that a

sion in Haiti, the Clinton Administration sought UN Security Council approval for an invasion and occupation of Haiti if the sanctions failed to restore Aristide to the presidency. The Council granted its approval on 31 July 1994. The invasion plan had two phases: first, a 15,000 multinational force would invade, restore public order, and reinstate Aristide; subsequently 6,000 UN forces would train a new Haitian police force to maintain order.

Accordingly, US Army, Air Force, and Navy SOF supported the XVIII Airborne Corps in planning for a full scale invasion of Haiti. The special operations portion of the plan envisioned the takedown of key governmental sites followed by a link-up with conventional forces, similar to what SOF had done for the invasion of Panama in 1989. After the main takedown, Special Forces teams were to secure the countryside. To serve as the SOF mobility and launching platform, an aircraft carrier, USS *America*, was added to the force package in spring 1994.

Operation Uphold Democracy

On 10 September 1994, the administration authorized General Shalikashvili to execute Operation Uphold Democracy within the next ten days. On the night of 16-17 September 1994, SEALs conducted a pre-invasion reconnaissance of the coastline along Cap Haitien, collecting intelligence and hydrographic data on potential landing sites for the Marines. The

SEALs conducted their missions despite the large number of small vessels and Haitians on the beach. The water was thick with traffic, strewn with garbage, and the SEALs heard Haitians beating drums on the shore. The teams met with varying degrees of success, since there were just too many civilians in some areas to permit a full reconnaissance. Nevertheless, the ensuing landings, which proceeded flawlessly (and uncontested) on the morning of 21 September 1994, verified the accuracy of the SEALs' work.

As the deadline for invasion neared, SOF moved their equipment and supplies to their air and sea ports of embarkation. Rangers, SEALs, and Special Operations aviation assets went aboard USS *America*. Other Rangers moved to their waiting aircraft, prepared for an airborne assault. All the elements of a complex plan were in place.

Before the American forces invaded Haiti, however, former President Jimmy Carter, Senator Sam Nunn, and retired General Colin Powell successfully brokered a last-minute deal with the Haitian military. Because of these negotiations, all the American forces moving toward Haiti on 18 September 1994 had their missions aborted, diverted, or reconfigured for a peaceful entry. The invasion thus became a large-scale humanitarian mission, with the U.S. forces landing on 19 September. SEALs provided beach security and terminal guidance to the Marine landing forces. The

Right: Special Operations Forces were trained for a wide range of contingencies in the Balkans; such training would have included fast roping from an MH-60.

new Haitian government, assisted by USAID and various non-governmental organizations, would lift the country up from its endemic chaos and poverty. U.S. soldiers from Company A, 96th CA Battalion, conducted Operation Light Switch in Jeremie, Cap Haitien and other northern cities and towns, restoring electricity to those areas for the first time in years.

SOF operations were notable as a large-scale peacekeeping mission. Even after the UN mission took over on 31 March 1995 (Uphold Democracy became Restore Democracy), SOF still performed this vital mission. The peace and order found in the Haitian countryside were a remarkable tribute to SOF, who fulfilled all of their mission requirements and more. In addition, the PCs demonstrated their versatility during both Support Democracy and Uphold Democracy; they proved their usefulness in coastal operations and showed they could support both SEALs and Special Boat Unit operations.

THE BALKANS
Bosnia-Herzegovina, 1995- to the Present

In the early 1990s rival ethnic states within Yugoslavia declared their independence and used force to align borders to encompass all their ethnic population in neighboring states. The intensity of the fighting and "ethnic cleansing" shocked the UN and NATO into action. From 1992 to 1995, both of these organizations sent forces to the region to force a peace settlement in the former Yugoslavia. But, not until NATO aircraft bombed Bosnian Serb targets (Operation Deliberate Force, August-September 1995) did the warring factions agree to a ceasefire in October. This ceasefire, in turn, led to the Dayton Peace Accords (21 November 1995) and the Paris peace agreement (14 December 1995).

Operation Joint Endeavor

For Operation Joint Endeavor (December 1995-December 1996), the implementation of the peace agreement, NATO's missions included peace enforcement (separating the warring factions, establishing demilitarised zones, and maintaining security) and support for the withdrawal of UN forces from the former Yugoslavia. NATO vested command and control in the Commander-in-Chief, Implementation Force, and his assigned forces, known as Implementation Force (IFOR).

Special Operations Command Europe (SOCEUR) initially became involved in these peace efforts in February 1993 when it established the Joint Special Operations Task Force 2 (JSOTF2). Located at San Vito Air Station, near Brindsi, Italy, JSOTF2 had the following missions: combat search and rescue; fire support; and visit, board, search and seizure. To support the 1995 peace agreement, SOCEUR provided forces to establish the Special Operations Command Implementation Force (SOCIFOR) and superimposed it over JSOTF2 at San Vito. SOCIFOR had several missions, but its most notable one was to provide SOF to the NATO and non-NATO forces in Bosnia. Like Desert Storm and Somalia before, the emphasis was on SOF'S capabilities to interact with foreign military forces. Other missions included personnel recovery and fire support.

All SOF "in the box" (inside of Bosnia-Herzegovina) were assigned to Combined Joint Special Operations Task Force (CJSOTF), the SOF component to the land forces component, Commander, Allied Command Europe Rapid Reaction Corps (COMARRC). A British officer commanded the CJSOTF with an American SOF officer as his deputy. Beneath the CJSOTF, SOCIFOR established a U.S. SOF headquarters (known as FOB 101) using 1st Battalion, 10th SFG(A) assets.

Each of COMARRC's three divisions (called multinational divisions [MNDs]) had a Special Operations Command and Control Element (SOCCE) assigned, which worked for the division commanders, controlled SOF in the divisions' areas, and reported to FOB 101. The SOCCE coordinated SOF activities with the conventional forces; advised the division commander on SOF capabilities and employment options; and provided secure and reliable communications (this last capability was so critical that COMARRC would have delayed the transfer of authority from the UN to NATO if SOF were not deployed).

The SOCCEs sent out Liaison Coordination Elements (LCEs) to the NATO and, most important, non-NATO units within each division's area of operations. The LCEs were assigned to the battalion or brigade commanders. Not unlike the Coalition Warfare Teams of Desert Storm, the fundamental LCE mission was establishing communications between the division and its non-NATO battalions. The LCEs made sure that the information and instructions passed from the division commander to the battalion or brigade commander were understood, which included explaining the intent and movements of allied forces. If needed, the LCEs could also do laser target designation, call for fire, and request medical evacuations. Importantly, the LCEs had their own vehicles so that they could keep up with their parent units.

LCEs performed the following missions: conducting daily patrols with parent battalions; maintaining reliable communications;

assessing the attitudes of local populations and former warring factions; spreading the word on the IFOR mission; providing accurate information on any incidents; and accomplishing route reconnaissance. In addition to their Special Forces members, LCEs were augmented by Special Tactics personnel trained in Special Operations Tactical Air Controller (SOTAC) procedures for close air support. When the battalion or brigade became comfortable with carrying out its mission essential tasks, the LCEs redeployed. No other forces, save SOF, had the requisite capabilities to perform these delicate diplomatic operations.

In the early stages of Joint Endeavor, SOF's flexibility and specialized capabilities were used to ensure the NATO forces arrived in the right place at the right time. SOF's major contributions included: SOF enabling forces were in place on time; SOF aircraft (capable of flying in the most difficult weather) ensured timely SOF deployments into Bosnia-Herzegovina despite weather that grounded all other aircraft; SOF aircraft flew the IFOR commander through adverse weather to reach meetings and ceremonies; SOCIFOR provided a quick reaction force; and SEALs supported the bridging of the Sava River.

Civil Affairs forces likewise had important missions for Joint Endeavor. The CA forces coordinated the reconstruction of the civil infrastructure and organized relief efforts of more than 500 UN, government, and non-government organizations. Civil Affairs personnel, assigned to the Combined Joint Civil Military Operations Center (with CA task forces assigned to each multinational division), assisted in restoring basic services such as public transportation, public works and utilities, public health, and commerce, as well as helping with elections and setting up new national governments. CA specialists worked with organizations like the World Bank and the International Task Force to facilitate the delivery of their services. CA soldiers also helped to develop plans for, and coordinated the repatriation of, refugees.

PSYOP forces had the important task of disseminating factual information to the populace inside the former Yugoslavia. Assigned to the Combined Joint Psychological Task Force, US Army PSYOP forces used print media (the weekly *Herald of Peace* newspaper and posters), "Radio IFOR" broadcasts, and some television broadcasts to accomplish their missions. They also conducted a mine awareness campaign, aimed primarily at children, and distributed literature (such as coloring books) to stress the dangers of land mines and ordnance.

Operation Joint Guard

Operation Joint Endeavor officially ended on 20 December 1996, and the IFOR gave way to Operation Joint Guard's Stabilization Force (SFOR). Planned to last 18 months, Joint Guard built upon the success of Joint Endeavor – NATO-led forces had separated the former warring factions, allowed the transfer of land, moved heavy weapons into storage areas and demobilized troops of the former warring factions. In essence, SFOR was a maintenance force responsible for deterring hostilities and contributing to a secure environment which promoted the restablishment of civil authority.

SOCEUR disbanded SOCIFOR on 20 December and lodged command and control of all SOF inside Bosnia in the revamped CJSOTF. Now commanded by a U.S. SOF officer, the CJSOTF deployed the SOCCEs to each multinational division and LCEs to the Romanian Battalion, Hungarian Battalion, and Russian Brigade. In addition, SOF took on the responsibility of providing Joint Commission Observers (JCOs). These six-man teams roamed the country as "honest brokers" to establish communications between all factions and the SFOR commanders. SOCEUR still had mission responsibility for combat search and rescue; personnel recovery; close air support; and special reconnaissance. Likewise, Civil Affairs and Psychological Operations forces continued accomplishing

under Joint Guard what they had done for Joint Endeavor. Psychological Operations forces worked for the Combined Task Force. All these missions ran until June 1998, when the operation evolved again.

Operation Joint Forge

On 20 June 1998, Operation Joint Forge began as the follow-on operation to Operation Joint Guard. Joint Forge had the same primary goal as Joint Guard – to maintain peace in Bosnia-Herzegovina and sustain the conditions necessary to rebuild that nation. To carry out his mission, NATO continued the Stabilization Force (SFOR), comprised of forces from both NATO and non-NATO nations. SFOR ensured the peace, kept the troops of the former warring factions demobilized, and prevented the revival of hostilities.

The primary changes in Operation Joint Forge were in the SOF's command structure and missions. In Joint Forge, the CJSOTF consolidated operations with Forward Operating Base (FOB) 103. The combined headquarters exercised command and control over all U.S. SOF in MND-North. The combined CJSOTF/FOB reported directly to COMSFOR. U.S. SOF operated in MND-North, except for liaison officers attached to MND-SE and

Below: Special Operations Forces Liaison Coordination Elements (LCEs) attached to the Russian Brigade, working with allied forces in the Balkans.

MND-SW and Civil Affairs and Psychological Operations specialists, who operated throughout Bosnia-Herzegovina.

SOF's missions saw little change in MND-North in Joint Forge. The SOCCE performed as it had in Operation Joint Endeavor, and one LCE was still attached to the Russian Brigade. U.S. SOF in the Bosnia-Herzegovina theater worked in eight-man Joint Commission Observer teams (JCOs) in the MND-North. The JCOs' critical role was to maintain situational awareness and provide "ground truth" to the CJSOTF/SFOR commanders. To do this, they maintained direct contact with leaders of the former warring factions and key members of the local civil and military leadership. They served as contact points between the MND-North commander and local ethnic leaders and as impartial information brokers between different elements of the populace. They also provided the MND-North commander with information about conditions throughout Bosnia-Herzegovina. U.S. SOF provided a Quick Reaction Force that stood ready to defend any JCOs that were threatened.

The majority of SOF personnel for Joint Forge were Civil Affairs and Psychological Operations specialists. They assisted in re-establishing civil institutions and helped pre-

Below: **Members of the MH-60 Pave Hawk aircrew who rescued an F-16 pilot shot down in western Serbia on 2 May 1999 during Operation Allied Force.**

pare for elections that were held in Bosnia-Herzegovina in the autumn of 1998. SOF continued its support to Joint Forge throughout 1999, helping to sustain peace in the area during the Kosovo conflict.

Operation Allied Force

NATO initiated Operation Allied Force on 24 March 1999 to put an end to Serbia's violent repression of ethnic Albanians in Kosovo. The nineteen-nation Allied Force coalition conducted an unrelenting bombing campaign in Serbia and Kosovo for seventy-eight days, eventually forcing Serbian President Slobodan Milosevic to withdraw his forces from the province and stop the "ethnic cleansing" of Kosovar Albanians. The bombing strategy did not prevent Serbia from forcing an estimated 800,000 refugees out of the country, however, which produced an enormous humanitarian crisis in the neighboring states of Albania and Macedonia. Furthermore, the air campaign did not eliminate all of Serbia's surface-to-air missiles, which managed to shoot down two U.S. aircraft.

SOF played a strategic role throughout the Balkans region during Allied Force. In Albania and Macedonia, Civil Affairs units participated in Operation Shining Hope, the humanitarian assistance mission to aid Kosovar refugees. CA elements coordinated large-scale humanitarian relief efforts with U.S. government agencies and international relief organiza-

tions, arranging food, shelter, and medical care for the refugee camps. SOF helicopters airlifted supplies into refugee areas prior to the conventional forces arriving in theater. Within Kosovo itself, SOF aircraft dropped food and supplies to displaced persons.

SOF also carried out an extensive PSYOP campaign. From beyond Serb borders, EC-130E Commando Solo aircraft transmitted daily Serbian-language radio and television programs into the area, informing the Serb people of their government's genocidal practices and televising photographs of Kosovar refugees in Albania and Macedonia. MC-130H aircraft dropped millions of leaflets that decried the Serbs' untenable situation, warning them against committing war crimes, and pointing out how Milosevic's policies were ruining their country.

SOF successfully rescued the only two U.S. pilots downed during Allied Force. In separate missions that took less than a minute on the ground, SOF combat search and rescue teams rescued an F-117A pilot who was shot down near Belgrade on 27 March and an F-16 pilot shot down in western Serbia on 2 May. On each occasion, a mixture of MH-53 Pave Low and MH-60 Pave Hawk helicopters were used to retrieve the downed fliers. These rescues had profound effects on the outcome of the operation.

Operation Joint Guardian

On 9 June 1999, the government of the former republic of Yugoslavia acceded to a "military technical agreement" that ended its army's occupation of Kosovo. Operation Joint Guardian, the mission led by NATO's Kosovo Force (KFOR) to enforce the peace agreement, maintain public security, and provide humanitarian assistance, began immediately thereafter. By 15 June, SOF units had entered the American sector in Kosovo to reconnoiter the area and assess conditions for the conventional forces.

Although everyone involved in the KFOR mission understood that the antipathy between the Serb and Albanian Kosovars would not diminish quickly, the real progress seen in Bosnia-Herzegovina encouraged SOF to apply similar techniques in Kosovo. Accordingly, SOF soon became SFOR's source for "ground truth" in Kosovo's volatile environment. Special Forces teams patrolled the American sector independently and also as the U.S. liaison elements to Polish and Russian units. PSYOP personnel worked to stabilize the situation by distributing native-language leaflets that promoted mine awareness and acceptance of the rule of law. Special Forces soldiers also monitored the Serb military's withdrawal out of the province

and assessed the flow of refugees returning to their homeland.

Civil Affairs soldiers, previously engaged in supporting Operation Shining Hope, moved forward to assist in reconstituting Kosovo's infrastructure. One of their first actions was to establish a civil-military coordination committee, a step towards returning to Kosovo to civilian control. CA soldiers soon improved conditions throughout the province, as they helped organize the importation of heating fuel, repairs to electric grids and water systems, the activation of civilian-run radio station in the capital city of Pristina, and the reopening of schools. They also coordinated the activities of a number of non-governmental organizations and helped a UN-sponsored International Police Task Force begin work in Kosovo.

Special Forces liaison teams, including those attached to a Polish battalion and a Russian brigade, initiated street patrols throughout their areas of operations. To counter ethnic violence, these patrols arranged meetings between local Albanians and Serbs, sought out illegal weapons caches, and assisted war crimes investigators in locating massacre sites. The SOF liaison teams quickly established a rapport with the local citizens and, although not successful in quelling all violent activity, defused some of the area's tensions. Furthermore, the teams' eyewitness reports gave the Joint Guardian leadership a clear understanding of local conditions.

In another application of SOFs unique capabilities, a Special Forces detachment skilled in the Arabic culture and language,

deployed to Kosovo to serve as a liaison coordination element between KFOR and units from the United Arab Emirates and the Kingdom of Jordan. In September 1999, SOF integrated these forces into the Kosovo area of operations, further strengthening the KFOR coalition.

PEACE OPERATIONS AND CRISIS REPONSES

Since the symbolic fall of the Berlin Wall, the United States SOF have had to perform a variety of missions that fall under the category of "Operations Other Than War." At one time, these operations were considered extraordinary, but in the 1990s operations other than war had become the norm. For example, in its first forty years, the UN conducted only thirteen such operations, but in the years from 1988 to 1994 the number of peace operations more than doubled. Although peace operations were not new to the 1990s, what was unprecedented were the numbers, pace, scope, and complexity of recent operations.

Operations other than war included a wide range of missions, such as humanitarian assistance and disaster relief, non-combatant evacuation operations (NEOs) humanitarian demining, peacekeeping operations, crisis response, combating terrorism, enforcement of sanctions or exclusion zones, and show of force. With conventional forces, SOF have participated in these types of operations, often as the lead military organization. Such capabilities as cultural and language familiarity, warrior-diplomat skills, and maturity and professionalism made SOF an ideal force for these operations.

Operation Provide Comfort

SOF's diverse talents made it a natural choice to support humanitarian assistance efforts. Perhaps the best example of SOF's capabilities to deal with a large scale disaster was Operation Provide Comfort. At the end of Desert Storm, in February 1991, Iraqi Kurds revolted against Saddam Hussein, but his forces quickly crushed the rebellion. Hundreds of thousands of Kurds fled to the mountains in northern Iraq and southeastern Turkey.

In April 1991, EUCOM initiated Operation Provide Comfort to stop further Iraqi attacks and to establish a safe haven for the Kurds. On short notice, MC-130Es led in other aircraft to drop emergency supplies to the Kurdish refugees in the mountains of Iraq and Turkey. Next, SOF personnel, supported by MH-53J helicopters, located suitable sites for refugee camps and worked with refugee leaders to organize and distribute supplies to the populace. Civil Affairs units developed plans for medical assistance, food distribution, and daily camp operations, and then managed their implementation. Joint SOF medical teams provided medical assistance and training, such as camp sanitation, and were instrumental in dramatically reducing the death rate. SEALs and Special Boat Unit personnel provided medical support and security in camps. Psychological Operations forces supported efforts to end chaotic conditions by producing millions of leaflets and by loudspeaker presen-

Below: **SOF spearheaded the effort to provide safe havens and aid for Kurdish people being attacked by Iraq forces following Desert Storm.**

tations. Their efforts also helped to convince the Kurds to return to their homes. SOF were credited with saving thousands of lives by providing skilled personnel to rebuild the civil infrastructure, establish supply networks, and furnish medical assistance and training.

Humanitarian Demining Operations

Landmines have proven to be one of the most dangerous and lasting problems created by recent conflicts. USSOCOM and SOF were leaders in the effort to cope with the humanitarian disaster caused by the 100 million mines buried around the world. SOF conducted humanitarian demining operations first in Operation Safe Passage, Afghanistan, in 1988. At that time, over 10 million landmines remained from the Soviet invasion, preventing millions of refugees from returning to Afghanistan. Troops from 5th Special Forces Group (Airborne) deployed to Pakistan to work with the Afghan refugees and the UN Safe Passage became the prototype for subsequent humanitarian demining operations by both the UN and SOF.

The Special Forces soldiers faced enormous challenges. There was no effective Afghan government, and work with the refugees had to be coordinated with the UN, Pakistan, and a vast array of private organizations. In this amorphous situation, the Special Forces troops essentially had to invent humanitarian demining doctrine and sell it to the other agencies on the ground. Even among the Afghans, the mutually suspicious tribes and factions required the Special Forces to use their political skills as well as their technical knowledge.

U.S. SOF established training programs that taught millions of Afghans how to identify, avoid, mark and report mines, and taught thousands of Afghans how to destroy mines safely. More important, they also taught the Afghans how to run the demining program themselves so that they could continue the program without outside assistance. By the time the Special Forces troops left in 1991, they had overcome these obstacles, and Afghans were conducting effective mine clearing operations.

SOF and the UN next conducted demining operations in Cambodia in 1993. Since then, the U.S. humanitarian demining program has expanded dramatically. Each situation was very different because of various types of mines (forty different types of mines were found in Afghanistan alone), the multitude of organizations involved, and the wide ranging terrain and

environmental conditions – from the Sahara Desert to mountainous jungles.

The humanitarian demining program had three critical elements: mine awareness, mine survey and clearance, and national command and control. Mine awareness reduced civilian casualties by teaching people how to spot mines, how to get out of mined area safely, and how to mark and report mined areas. The 4th Psychological Operations Group took the lead in mine awareness training and developed highly effective programs tailored to the specific needs of each country. These programs included the use of every sort of media from radio and television to T-shirts, caps, book bags, and comic books.

The Special Forces Groups developed and taught the mine survey and clearance portions of the program. SOF mine survey teams determined the actual size of the mined area. Mine clearing, the centerpiece of the program, was slow and potentially very dangerous work, so proper training was critical. Special Forces soldiers always emphasized a "train-the-trainer" approach that trained mineclearers as well as indigenous mineclearing instructors, and even-

tually led to the establishment of national demining schools.

Civil Affairs troops worked with the host nation to establish a national demining headquarters. In most nations, civilian agencies ran the mine awareness programs. Coordinating the efforts of several different ministries and determining the sequence of demining operations were politically sensitive tasks that were critical to the success of the demining operations. Civil Affairs troops, therefore, were ideally suited for helping developing nations solve these thorny problems and integrating humanitarian demining into national recovery and development plans.

In 1997, President Clinton committed the U.S. to eliminating the threat of landmines to civilians by 2010. To achieve this ambitious goal USSOCOM's humanitarian demining effort expanded substantially in 1998 and 1999. Whereas in 1997 SOF had deployed to fourteen countries to support humanitarian demining operations, by 1999 that figure had doubled to twenty-eight. One of the more complex operations occurred in Bosnia-Herzegovina, where SOF worked with the UN, the U.S. State

Right: A Croatian student is instructed in demining by U.S. Army 10th Special Forces Group Airborne during Operation Joint Endeavor, 1998.

Department, NATO's Stabilisation Force (SFOR), and the armies representing each of Bosnia's ethnic groups to establish three demining training centers in the country.

In 1998, SOF trained and equipped instructor cadres for the Bosnian Serbs, Croats, and Muslims and guided them through their first demining classes. SOF also helped the local forces transform their ruined buildings into professional training facilities and taught them how to sustain their training operations. By the end of 1999, the three training centers had graduated more than 500 deminers, who helped revitalize the Bosnia-Herzegovina economy by restoring thousands of acres of land to productive use.

By late 1999, humanitarian operations had been conducted by SOCCENT, SOCPAC, SOCSOUTH, and SOCEUR; all five active-duty Special Forces Groups; all six active-duty Psychological Operations Battalions; and the active duty Civil Affairs Battalion. The reserve components fully supported these operations, as well. In Asia, for instance, SOCPAC, the 1st Special Forces Group, the PACOM Psychological Operations Battalion and Civil Affairs troops worked with the national governments of Cambodia and the People's Republic of Laos, the UN, and many non-governmental organizations to make people aware of the landmine danger and to help clear mined areas.

African Crisis Response Initiative

In 1994, Rwanda, in central Africa, experienced human genocide of horrific proportions. As a result of these atrocities, U.S. officials from the Office of the Secretary of Defense visited the Rwandan massacre sites, spoke with refugees, and issued a report that helped to focus attention on the region. The next year, Burundi, Rwanda's neighbor to the south, also experienced political unrest and appeared to be heading down the same road that Rwanda had traveled some months before.

By November 1995, the Defense Department had drafted a proposal to deal with the unrest in Burundi, the centerpiece of which was the training of African peacekeeping troops. The objective was to train African troops to conduct peacekeeping operations within their continent. This initial proposal would become the core for the African Crisis Response Initiative (ACRI), which the U.S. State Department launched in October 1996. However, the U.S. worked only with those African countries that adhered to certain prerequisites, including having democratically elected governments, civilian control of the military, and human rights policies. U.S. SOF, and especially Special Forces soldiers, became an integral part of ACRI.

The African Crisis Response Initiative used military assets from the U.S. and its European allies to train battalion-sized units from various African nations for peacekeeping operations on their continent. Under the command and control of EUCOM, the 3rd Special Forces Group (Airborne) implemented the ACRI plan by developing a program of instruction and sending in teams to conduct training. Drawing from NATO, UN and U.S. doctrine, Special Forces planners developed common peacekeeping tactics, techniques, and procedures. Training African battalions to common doctrine and standards assured that the different forces could effectively work together if deployed on a peacekeeping mission.

As devised by the 3rd Special Forces Group (Airborne), ACRI training consisted of two phases: an initial, intensive sixty-day training period (individual, platoon, company, leader and staff training) followed by sustainment training and exercises. By the end of 1999, Special Forces teams, along with the elements of the 96th Civil Affairs Battalion, and the 4th Battalion Psychological Operations Group, had conducted ACRI training in Senegal, Malawi, Ghana, Mali, Benin, and the Ivory Coast. This multinational peacekeeping effort in Africa held out great promise for the future, and was another example of SOF fulfilling the role of "Global Scouts."

CT-43A Recovery Operation

On several occasions during Joint Endeavor in the Balkans, SOCEUR had to discharge both its normal theater-wide responsibilities and respond to small-scale contingencies. On 3 April 1996, a USAF CT-43A aircraft crashed on a mountainside above Durbrovnik, Croatia, killing all thirty-five people aboard. Included as passengers were Secretary of Commerce Ron

Below: In a tragic accident on 3 April 1996, a USAF CT-43A crashed on a mountainside near Dubrovnik, Croatia. All thirty-five people aboard, including U.S. Secretary of Commerce Ron Brown, died. MH-53 Pave Lows carried Special Operations Forces to the crash site to carry out recovery operations.

Brown and a number of corporate executives, as well as Air Force crew. Special Operations helicopters flew to the crash site through some of the worst flying conditions experienced in the region. SOCEUR completed the recovery operation in four days, despite the extreme cold and wet conditions and rugged mountainside terrain.

Liberian NEO Operations

While these SOF were finishing the CT-43A recovery effort, SOCEUR responded to a crisis in Liberia, West Africa, where a civil war endangered Americans and other foreign nationals. The U.S. had to deploy forces quickly to save lives, protect the American embassy, and initiate a non-combatant evacuation operation (NEO). The only integrated force with its own airlift and strike force ready and available was SOCEUR. In fact, within hours of deploying from Dubrovnik to Stuttgart on 7 April, SOF aboard an MC-130H had launched for Sierra Leone, the intermediate staging base for Operation Assured Response. Using its Air Force MH-53J helicopters (augmented later by Army MH-47D helicopters), SOCEUR sent first SEALs, on 9 April, and then other SOF personnel to provide security for the U.S. embassy and implement an orderly evacuation of Americans and third country nationals. On 13 April the Psychological Operations Task Force arrived and was ready to conduct force protection loud speaker operations for Assured

Below: During Operation Assured Response, April 1996, SOF evacuated over 2,100 non-combatants from the U.S. Embassy in Liberia, West Africa.

Response. SOF had the situation well in hand and had evacuated 136 Americans and 1,677 foreign nationals when the US Marines relieved SOCEUR on 20 April 1996.

Operation Shadow Express

SOF returned to Liberia in the fall of 1998 after violent civic unrest in Monrovia again threatened the U.S. embassy. On 18 September, government forces fired on Krahn leader Roosevelt Johnson and his entourage as they were talking to U.S. officials at the embassy entrance. The attack wounded two U.S. personnel and killed four Krahn. The Americans returned fire, killing two policemen. The Americans and the Johnson party retreated into the embassy compound, setting the stage for an extended siege.

The next day, Liberian President Charles Taylor demanded Johnson's surrender, and an attack on the embassy appeared imminent. EUCOM responded by directing SOCEUR to dispatch a twelve-man survey and assessment team (ESAT), which was led by Major Joe Becker, an Air Force SOF helicopter pilot, and Senior Chief Petty Officer Pat Ellis, a SEAL, and included several SOF intelligence specialists. The ESAT team arrived at the embassy on 21 September and, within a few hours, ascertained that an armed force was massing to attack the compound. SCPO Ellis and Major Becker alerted ECOMOG, a Nigerian-led African peacekeeping force then in Monrovia. The ESAT team and the Marine embassy guards devised a defense plan, with the ESAT on the chancery roof and the Marines defending from within the building. Shortly thereafter,

an ECOMOG checkpoint stopped two truckloads of men armed with rocket-propelled grenade launchers who were approaching the embassy. The U.S. State Department subsequently arranged for the Johnson entourage to relocate to a third country. The ESAT team planned the move, coordinated logistical support, and provided security for the Johnson group's departure.

On 26 September, the Defense Department ordered additional U.S. forces into the region. In anticipation of this mission, SOCEUR dispatched USS *Chinook*, a SOF patrol coastal ship from Naval Special Warfare Unit 10 (NSWU-10), toward Liberia from Rota, Spain, with a 36-foot rigid hull inflatable boat (RIB) and four special boat operators aboard. Within 12 hours of notification on the 26th, SOCEUR deployed a SOF command and control element from Naval Special Warfare Unit 2 (NSWU-2), accompanied by approximately twenty SEALs, two Air Force combat controllers, and an Air Force flight surgeon, on an MC-130 to a forward operating location in Freetown, Sierra Leone. The force landed in Freetown on the 27th. *Chinook* came in to Freetown's port 30 minutes after the aircraft landed, took seventeen SEALs on board, and embarked for Liberia, with the remaining SOF staying in Freetown to maintain a tactical operations center. By the 28th, *Chinook* was positioned 2,000 yards offshore from the embassy, ready to provide an in-extremis response force.

Below: SCPO Pat Ellis (center), part of a survey and assessment team which reported on an impending attack on the U.S. Embassy in Monrovia, Liberia.

From 29 September to 7 October, SOF maintained a highly visible maritime presence off the embassy's coastline. First *Chinook*, and later a second patrol coastal vessel, USS *Fireboat*, surveyed the Monrovia harbor and repeatedly conducted launch and recovery rehearsals of the RIB. The two patrol coastals also stood ready to evacuate the embassy, if necessary. The 10-day "presence operation" provided a calming influence on the situation and reaffirmed SOF's ability to deploy forces rapidly into an uncertain environment.

Operation Silver Wake
In September 1996, a Special Forces sergeant first class was one of a four-person Military Liaison Team that went into Albania, in southeast Europe. As part of the Joint Contact Team Program, this team coordinated Albania's requests for military visits that fostered civilian control of the military in a democratic society. This mission, however, was cut short by an incipient revolt in southern Albania. In January, the Special Forces sergeant assisted the American embassy in revising its emergency evacuation plan; this assistance included surveying helicopter landing zones.

After releasing him to the Military Liaison Team in late January, the American Ambassador recalled the Special Forces sergeant to the American embassy in late February, as the Albanian people's displeasure with their government had erupted again in open revolt. This lone non-commissioned officer became the focal point for non-combatant evacuation operations preparations. His activities ranged from coordinating a visit

from the EUCOM Survey and Assessment Team to prompting the embassy staff to define what should be done and when to do it as the revolt approached Tirana, and conducting area assessments that provided the embassy with accurate military judgements.

JTF Silver Wake notified the embassy that 26th Marine Expeditionary Unit helicopters would start the evacuation on 13 March. The Special Forces sergeant then went to the evacuation site in the embassy housing area, where he helped to write the passenger manifests and set up "sticks" of approximately twenty persons per helicopter. The helicopters approached the compound after dark. The Special Forces sergeant guided the first helicopter in by flashing "SOS" with his flashlight, despite the risk from random gunfire. For the remainder of the NEO, he provided invaluable service to the embassy staff and Marine evacuation force. The NEO ended on 26 March 1997, and the JTF evacuated nearly 900 civilians safely without incident.

During the first days of the NEO, an AC-130U from JSOPTF2 at Brindsi flew over Tirana and the surrounding area, providing close air support, armed reconnaissance, and intelligence. On at least one occasion, the AC-130U's mere presence halted an AAA battery's fire. Its crew also directed evacuation helicopters away from SA-2 surface-to-air missile batteries. The crew ensured that the NEO proceeded safely.

Operation Noble Obelisk
In April 1997, an Operation Detachment Alpha or "A" Team (thirteen Special Forces soldiers) from the 3rd Special Forces Group (A) deployed to Freetown, Sierra Leone, for

Joint Combined Exchange Training. Their mission was to train and promote a professional, apolitical military that was supportive of the elected government. However, on 25 May 1997, rebel forces and military members toppled the government. Once shooting erupted at their training site, U.S. Special Forces soldiers manned security positions inside their compound, communicated with SOCEUR and EUCOM, and established intermittent contact with the embassy.

The next day, the detachment moved to Freetown 20 miles away. The Special Forces soldiers had to pass through two rebel roadblocks and near an army post, but the rapport with their former trainees enabled the Americans to proceed safely to the embassy. In Freetown, the detachment commander divided his team to secure the two embassy compounds, and team members performed advance force operations, including reconnoitering the helicopter landing zone on the coast. They also defused a tense situation during a meeting of the senior ambassadors and rebel forces at the British High Commission residence. All of these activities required movement through a town riven by looting and indiscriminate fire.

On 29 May, team members conducted an early morning patrol through the rebel-held areas to secure the landing zone for the Marines from the 22nd MEU. They established sniper positions, security, and coordinated with the Nigerians before the Marine helicopters arrived. The next day, the NEO began. After escorting official U.S. personnel to the landing zone, Special Forces soldiers served as a buffer by establishing two blocking positions between the Marines and the marauding rebels. They succeeded in turning back rebel forces trying to reach the landing zone. The NEO evacuations ran from 30 May through 3 June, and a total of 2,509 people (including 454 American personnel) were evacuated.

ECUADOR, MAY 1999
A test of SOF's force protection skills occurred on the evening of 2 May 1999 in northern Equador, South America. A convoy transporting thirty-seven U.S. SOF personnel and Ecuadorian soldiers to a joint counter-drug training exercise was attacked by local bandits. The six-vehicle convoy was negotiating a hairpin turn on a muddy jungle road when it came upon a roadblock set up by a dozen masked and armed robbers.

The bandits had already stopped two

Left: Constant readiness is a feature of SOF training, displayed by members of the 10th Special Forces Group (Airborne) following a static line jump.

passenger buses and several cars, and were holding about fifty civilians along the side of the road. Two bandits opened fire on the convoy, hitting the lead vehicle. The four Special Forces soldiers in that vehicle and a Civil Affairs soldier in the second vehicle engaged the bandits with their sidearms. Ecuadorian soldiers opened fire as well. After a firefight that lasted several minutes, eight of the bandits fled, leaving behind two dead and two prisoners, one of whom was wounded. One U.S. personnel and one Ecuadorian soldier suffered minor wounds, but there were no civilian casualties.

When the Ecuadorian soldiers interrogated the prisoners, the watching crowd turned ugly, shouting for the prisoners' execution. The SOF soldiers took control and protected the prisoners from the angry crowd while a Special Forces medic treated the wounded. The dead and captured attackers were then taken to the training site and turned over to local police. The government of Ecuador subsequently praised the action as professional and appropriate.

COLOMBIA, JULY 1999

SOF's ability to support far-flung contingencies was again demonstrated in July 1999, during the recovery of a U.S. Army reconnaissance aircraft that had crashed in the Colombian Andes. The crash killed five U.S. Army and two Colombian soldiers who had been engaged in an airborne counterdrug reconnaissance mission.

A search plane found the wrecked aircraft the day after the crash, but poor weather and the rugged terrain inhibited recovery efforts. At the direction of Gen. Charles

Willhelm, USCINCSOUTH, Special Operations Command South (SOCSOUTH) deployed two MH-60L helicopters and support from D Company, 160th SOAR(A), and a liaison element. USSOCOM provided refueling assets, combat controllers, weather forecasters, and the requisite operational support. Two 16th SOW MC-130E Combat Talon and one MC-130H Combat Talon II moved the AFSOC elements from Hurlburt Field, FL, to Bogota, Colombia. An eight-man Special Forces element from the 7th SFG(A) – already supporting the counterdrug operational planning mission in Bogota with the U.S. country team – was incorporated into the operation to provide communications, coordination with host nation units, and their unique operational skills. Brig. Gen. James Parker, Commander SOCSOUTH, was assigned to lead the effort.

The MH-60L crews had trained in high-altitude operations and were familiar with the region and the host nation forces. The helicopters transported and inserted the Special Forces soldiers and a USAF combat controller into the crash site. These SOF helped Colombian and other U.S. personnel search the wreckage. The MH-60Ls evacuated remains from the crash site to the forward operating location, whereupon an MC-130E and host nation aircraft carried them forward to Bogota. The Combat Talons also provided refueling capabilities at remote airfields that lacked adequate fuel stores.

The crash site proved to be an exceptionally dangerous environment. The wreck-

Below: **During Operation Noble Obelisk, May 1997, Special Forces soldiers were having their morning PT when rebel forces began shooting in their compound.**

age was situated on a steep mountainside, with much of it suspended from trees and brush. The ground teams made an exhaustive search of the wreckage and surrounding area but were unable to enter the aircraft fuselage or move large pieces of the aircraft. To meet that challenge, a Special Forces team with mountaineering experience and unique demolitions capabilities was brought in from C Company, 3rd Battalion, 7th SFG(A), based in Puerto Rico. The team employed their specialized skills to good effect and completed the recovery of remains and equipment from the crash site. Upon completion of their mission, the Special Forces soldiers destroyed the remaining wreckage with explosives.

Approximately 120 SOF participated in the mission. At the conclusion of the recovery operation, Gen. Willhelm commended all of the participants, declaring that the "unknown tactical situation, adverse weather, and rugged terrain made this the most difficult and challenging operation of its type that I have seen in my 36 years of service."

FUTURE CHALLENGES

The optimism engendered by the Cold War coming to a close in the early 1990s quickly gave way to the stark reality of a new world order. Few would have predicted that the ancient problems of ethnic hatred, religious intolerance, and nationalism would undermine international stability as they did. U.S. Special Operations Forces, however, were prepared for the changed world order because of significant improvements made under the auspices of USSOCOM since 1987. Command and control problems were solved, and SOF commanders controlled force modernization and readiness through MFP-11. Interoperability within the joint SOF community was never better. Acceptance of SOF by the conventional military increased considerably during these years. The Nunn-Cohen Amendment to the Goldwater-Nichols Department of Defense Reorganization Act provided the mechanism that empowered the special operations revitalization. Because of their unique skills, regional expertise, cultural sensitivity, and operation experiences, SOF became the "force of choice" for the uncertain times of the 1990s.

But, SOF did not rest on its laurels, and USSOCOM aggressively looked at future challenges to develop enhanced capabilities that would keep its forces at the "tip of the spear." Former C-in-C General Schoomaker recognized the constancy of a chaotic world order for the foreseeable future. For the SOF community to retain its place in the national security structure, it had to institutionalise the process of change.

PART TWO

TODAY'S U.S. SPECIAL OPERATIONS FORCES

TODAY'S U.S. SPECIAL OPERATIONS FORCES

Recent history has caused the United States to maintain specialized forces capable of performing extremely difficult, complex, and politically sensitive missions on short notice, in peace and war, anywhere in the world. In 1987, Congress mandated the creation of the U.S. Special Operations Command (USSOCOM) with the responsibility to prepare and maintain combat-ready Special Operations Forces (SOF) to successfully conduct special operations, including civil affairs (CA) and psychological operations (PSYOP).

U.S. SOF provide unique capabilities not found in other elements of the U.S. armed forces or those of other nations. While other U.S. military units can conduct special operations, and some other nations have special operations capabilities, no other force in the world has USSOCOM's range of capabilities, which include land, air, and maritime forces that can be employed either as joint- or single-service units.

Today's U.S. SOF are the product of an evolutionary process. The lessons learned from past operations and events, as well as the requirements of current missions and operations, have brought about a unique force with distinctive characteristics, capabilities, and limitations.

The characteristics of SOF personnel are shaped by the requirements of their missions and include foreign language capabilities; regional orientation; specialized equipment, training, and tactics; flexible force structure; and an understanding of the political context of their mission. These characteristics make SOF unique in the U.S. military and enable SOF personnel to work as effectively with civilian populations as they do with other military forces to influence situations favorably toward U.S. national interests. Because of these characteristics, SOF can be formed into small, versatile, self-contained units with a number of important capabilities. They can:

- organize quickly and deploy rapidly to provide tailored responses to many different situations;
- gain entry to and operate in hostile or denied areas;
- provide limited security and medical support for themselves and those they support;
- communicate worldwide with unit equipment;
- live in austere, harsh environments without extensive support;
- survey and assess local situations and report these assessments rapidly;
- work closely with host nation military and civilian authorities and populations;
- organize indigenous people into working teams to help solve local problems;
- deploy at relatively low cost, with a low profile and less intrusive presence than larger conventional forces.

Across the Spectrum of Conflict

Based on these capabilities, SOF provide the the United States with rapidly deployable and flexible joint task forces for both war and peacetime activities. In peacetime, SOF can assist a nation in creating the conditions for stable development – thereby reducing the risk of or precluding armed conflict. By training indigenous forces to provide their own security, and using integrated CA and PSYOP programs to strengthen government infrastructures, small teams can help prevent local problems from developing into threats to internal and international stability. SOF work closely with the host nation government, military forces, and population to assist them in resolving their own problems. Their efforts to resolve or contain regional conflicts or respond to natural disasters may preclude,

Below: **U.S. Army 5th Special Forces Group soldiers on parachute insertion exercise with British and Kuwaiti commandos in 1998.**

in some cases, the need to deploy large conventional forces.

These same SOF teams often forge strong links with the military establishment and civilian groups with whom they come in contact. This can be of inestimable value to U.S. forces if they have to work later with these same organizations, either as coalition partners, or in localized combat operations. SOF contact with foreign military hierarchies is also an effective, low-cost means of cultivating respect for human rights and democratic values.

In war, SOF conduct operational and strategic missions that directly or indirectly support the joint force commander's (JFC's) campaign plan. SOF missions originate with the JFC — often with the advice of the joint force special operations component commander (JFSOCC) — and are directed toward exactly the same ends as the operations of conventional forces. It is as an integrated part of a joint or combined force that SOF prove of greatest assistance to the conventional commander.

SOF can help the JFC seize the initiative, reduce risk, facilitate maneuver, and achieve decisive results by attacking operational and strategic targets. SOF also can carry out PSYOP to deceive and demoralize the enemy. As force multipliers, SOF work with indigenous forces to increase their contribution to the campaign plan, and conduct coalition support to help integrate multinational forces into a cohesive, combined task force to carry out coalition goals. CA and PSYOP can also contribute directly to the commander's maneuverability by reducing the number of civilians on or near battlefield areas.

Additionally, SOF play a vital role in post-conflict operations. Many of the talents used in pre-conflict situations are applicable after fighting has ceased, and are directed toward establishing (or re-establishing) the infrastructure required for a peaceful, prosperous society. SOF training skills, coupled with CA and PSYOP expertise, help speed the return to normal conditions, thereby allowing conventional forces to quickly re-deploy.

SOF also can conduct stand-alone operations in situations where a small, discreet force provides the nation's leaders with options that fall somewhere between diplomatic efforts and the use of high-profile conventional forces. Moreover, the relatively small size and the capabilities of highly trained, joint SOF units enable them to react rapidly and provide the United States with options that limit the risk of escalation, which otherwise might accompany the commitment of larger conventional forces. Unconventional warfare, direct action, and special reconnaissance missions, such as insurgency, counterterrorism, counterdrug

Above: On the firing line, Kuwaiti soldiers receive live ammunition weapons instruction from U.S. Special Operations Forces in 1998.

Below: U.S. Army SOF on a "direct action" training exercise in urban warfare tactics, an increasing activity for today's Special Operations Forces.

Above: Army Special Forces soldiers clear a room (of hostages or terrorists) during training for Military Operations in Urban Terrain (MOUT).

Below: Air Force Special Tactics Squadron members perform a breathtaking "high altitude low opening" (HALO) jump on exercise.

activities, surgical counterproliferation, and counterinsurgency, may be handled best by such a force.

Counterproliferation of weapons of mass destruction (WMD) is USSOCOM's highest operational priority. SOF can enhance the effectiveness of U.S. military, other government agencies, and international organizations in deterring proliferation of WMD and reacting appropriately should deterrence measures fail.

Against a growing security challenge, SOF also offer a wide variety of skills to combat terrorism. One area of focus includes defensive antiterrorism measures, such as training and advising of security techniques, procedures, and systems that reduce vulnerability. The other major element of SOF operational capabilities centers on offensive counterterrorism measures directed at preventing, deterring, and vigorously responding to terrorist acts against U.S. interests, wherever they occur.

Limitations

As with any highly specialized capability, it is equally important to understand the limitations of SOF. Some points to bear in mind are:

- SOF operators require extensive training, often years in duration. They cannot be replaced quickly and their capabilities cannot be expanded rapidly. Squandering scarce SOF resources on inappropriate missions or inordinately dangerous tasks runs the risk of depleting the SOF inventory early in a conflict.

- SOF are not a substitute for conventional forces; they provide different capabilities that expand the options of the employing commander. SOF should not be used for operations whenever conventional forces can accomplish the mission.
- SOF are not the solution to peacetime operations. SOF have a role to play in peacetime operations, just as they have a role to play in war. Peacetime operations almost always require an integrated, interagency approach to solve the problems encountered. SOF alone cannot do this.
- SOF logistics support is austere. A large number of SOF units generally cannot maintain themselves for extended periods of time without significant support from the conventional support structure.

Missions and Activities

Special operations are characterized by the use of small units in direct and indirect military actions focused on strategic and operational objectives. These actions require units with combinations of specialized personnel, equipment, training, and tactics that go beyond the routine capabilities of conventional military forces. The enduring, overarching purposes of SOF are derived from historical experience, Congressional legislation, and the evolving security environment. In support of the national military strategy, SOF are currently organized and trained in nine principal mission areas. Based on their unique capabilities, SOF are also frequently tasked to participate in other activities that are not principal SOF missions. These collateral activities tend to shift in response to the changing international environment.. The principal missions and collateral activities of SOF are listed below.

SOF Principal Missions

SOF are organized, trained, and equipped specifically to accomplish their assigned roles, as described below, in nine mission areas:

- *Counterproliferation (CP)* – to combat proliferation of nuclear, biological, and chemical weapons across the full range of U.S. efforts, including the application of military power to protect U.S. forces and interests; intelligence collection and analysis; and support of diplomacy, arms control, and export controls. Accomplishment of these activities may require coordination with other U.S. government agencies.
- *Combating terrorism (CBT)* – to preclude, preempt, and resolve terrorist actions throughout the entire threat spectrum, including antiterrorism (defensive measures taken to reduce vulnerability to ter-

rorist acts) and counterterrorism (offensive measures taken to prevent, deter, and respond to terrorism), and resolve terrorist incidents when directed by the National Command Authorities or the appropriate unified commander or requested by the Services or other government agencies.

- *Foreign internal defense (FID)* – to organize, train, advise, and assist host-nation military and paramilitary forces to enable these forces to free and protect their society from subversion, lawlessness, and insurgency.
- *Special reconnaissance (SR)* – to conduct reconnaissance and surveillance actions to obtain or verify information concerning the capabilities, intentions, and activities of an actual or potential enemy or to secure data concerning characteristics of a particular area.
- *Direct action (DA)* – to conduct short-duration strikes and other small-scale offensive actions to seize, destroy, capture, recover, or inflict damage on designated personnel or materiel.
- *Psychological operations (PSYOP)* – to induce or reinforce foreign attitudes and behaviors favorable to the originator's

Below: A Naval Special Warfare Command Mark V Special Operations Craft (SOC) performs a high-speed turn, with a SEAL manning one of the guns.

objectives by conducting planned operations to convey selected information to foreign audiences to influence their emotions, motives, objective reasoning, and, ultimately, the behavior of foreign governments, organizations, groups, and individuals

- *Civil affairs (CA)* – to facilitate military operations and consolidate operational activities by assisting commanders in establishing, maintaining, influencing, or exploiting relations between military forces and civil authorities, both governmental and non-governmental, and the civilian population in a friendly, neutral, or hostile area of operation.
- *Unconventional warfare (UW)* – to organize, train, equip, advise, and assist indigenous and surrogate forces in military and paramilitary operations normally of long duration.
- *Information operations (IO)* – to undertake actions to achieve information superiority by affecting adversary information and information systems while defending one's own information and information systems.

SOF Collateral Activities

Based on their unique capabilities, SOF are frequently tasked to participate in the following activities:

- *Coalition support* – to integrate coalition units into multinational military operations by training coalition partners on tactics and techniques and providing communications.
- *Combat search and rescue (CSAR)* – to penetrate air defense systems and conduct joint air, ground, or sea operations deep within hostile or denied territory, at night or in adverse weather, to recover distressed personnel during wartime or contingency operations. SOF are equipped and manned to perform CSAR in support of SOF missions only. SOF perform CSAR in support of conventional forces on a case-by-case basis without interference with the readiness or operations of core SOF missions.
- *Counterdrug (CD) activities* – to train host-nation CD forces and domestic law enforcement agencies on critical skills required to conduct individual and small-unit operations in order to detect, monitor, and interdict the cultivation, production, and trafficking of illicit drugs targeted for use in the United States.
- *Humanitarian demining (HD) activities* – to reduce or eliminate the threat to noncombatants and friendly military forces posed by mines and other explosive devices by training host-

nation personnel in their recognition, identification, marking, and safe destruction; to provide instruction in program management, medical, and mine-awareness activities.

- *Humanitarian assistance (HA)* – to provide assistance of limited scope and duration to supplement or complement the efforts of host-nation civil authorities or agencies to relieve or reduce the results of natural or manmade disasters or other endemic conditions such as human pain, disease, hunger, or privation that might present a serious threat to life or that can result in great damage to, or loss of, property.
- *Security assistance (SA)* – to provide training assistance in support of legislated programs which provide U.S. defense articles, military training, and other defense-related services by grant, loan, credit, or cash sales in furtherance of national policies or objectives.
- *Special activities* – subject to limitations imposed by Executive Order and in conjunction with a Presidential finding and Congressional oversight, to plan and conduct actions abroad in support of national foreign policy objectives so that the role of the U.S. government is not apparent or acknowledged publicly.

Below left: SEALs load into a US Air Force MH-53 Pave Low on the flight deck of the USNS *Leroy Grumman* during a search and seizure exercise.

Above: An explosive charge is detonated on a booby-trapped mine that was found during Army 10th Special Forces Group demining training in Croatia, 1998.

Below: Civil Affairs (CA) operations are among Special Operations Forces' principal missions. Here SOF soldiers distribute leaflets to civilians in Bosnia.

Above: Members of the U.S. Army's 13th Psychological Operations Battalion undergo riot control training at a mock prisoner of war camp.

Below: USAF Special Operations personnel receive jungle survival training with a live snake held by a Royal Thai Army Special Forces instructor.

The Role of SOF in National Defense

In the largest sense, this is a period of strategic opportunity for the United States. The threat of global war has receded and the core U.S. values of representative democracy and market economics are embraced in many parts of the world, creating new opportunities to promote peace, prosperity, and enhanced cooperation among nations.

While the United States is taking full advantage of this period of strategic opportunity and positive change, the world remains a complex, dynamic, and dangerous place. The United States will likely continue to face several significant security challenges including regional coercion or aggression, proliferation of potentially dangerous weapons and technologies, terrorism and international crime, threats to the homeland, failed states and humanitarian disasters, asymmetric challenges, and "wild card" or unpredictable scenarios.

A Posture of Global Engagement

Globalization – the process of accelerating economic, technological, cultural, and political integration – means that, more and more, the United States is affected by events beyond its borders. Its strategic approach to the increasing interdependence brought about by globalization recognizes that the nation must be involved in a leading role abroad in order to influence security at home.

The President's *National Security Strategy for a New Century* stresses the "imperative of engagement" and enhancing the nation's security through integrated approaches that allow the nation to shape the international environment; respond to the full spectrum of crises; and prepare now for an uncertain future. The nation's strategic approach uses all appropriate instruments of national power to influence the actions of other states and non-state actors, exert global leadership, and remain the preferred security partner for the community of states that share the interests of the United States.

The Military Challenge

The United States' military strategy is based on the concept that it will continue to deploy its armed forces globally and will remain engaged to influence the shaping of the global

Above: Members of the USAF 353rd Special Operations Group take cover in a hangar during a simulated chemical warfare attack.

Below: Operations in Panama, Haiti, and Somalia in the 1990s led to increased emphasis in Military Operations in Urban Terrain training for today's SOF.

Above: USAF Special Operations MH-53 Pave Low in Sarajevo, capital of Bosnia-Herzegovina in the late 1990s during peace-keeping operations.

environment, creating favorable conditions for U.S. interests and global security. It emphasizes that the U.S. armed forces must respond to the full spectrum of crises in order to protect the national interests. It further states that, as they pursue shaping and responding activities, the armed forces must also take steps to prepare now for an uncertain future.

Today the U.S. armed forces prepare for and conduct operations in environments ranging from peacetime to global war. Moreover, both peacetime operations and war could take place either in high-technology industrial states or in lesser-developed parts of the world. The military challenge is to field forces that can fight and win against threats ranging from the modern high-technology nation-state, with its complex infrastructure, to such non-state entities as terrorists, ethnic factions, religious radicals, and criminal cartels.

These diverse and contradictory environments require flexible and versatile forces that can function effectively, with speed and precision, across the full range of military operations anywhere in the world. These forces must have a keen sense of the political implications of their actions, and must be able to adapt quickly to changing rules of engagement, with decisive and appropriate action.

Relevance of SOF

SOF have an important and growing role in addressing challenges to U.S. interests and global security. First, SOF provide significant capabilities in support of the core national objectives through a combination of each of their nine principal missions. Second, SOF have the unique capability to provide addi-

tional support through application of their collateral activities.

But to remain effective, SOF must also be prepared to adapt to changing missions, technology, and security environments. To these ends, and in support of the national "shape, respond, and prepare now" strategy, USSO-COM provides an array of unique SOF flagship capabilities. Chief among these are:

- *Ubiquitous Presence.* Combat-ready SOF units are routinely deployed around the world to support peacetime engagement and to prevent conflict. Should conflict arise, these "global scouts" can quickly transition to combat operations and spearhead a decisive victory.

- *Strategic Agility.* SOF will provide greater

Above: U.S. Army Rangers fast-rope into a target from a 160th Special Operations Aviation Regiment MH-47 during an insertion exercise.

strategic and operational agility through the development of a more flexible and responsive force structure. The key elements to this structure are maintaining an unparalleled national mission capability and developing more robust theater special operations commands (SOCs).

- *Global Access.* Although theater engagement provides SOF access to most parts of the world, SOF must retain the capabil-

Below: A SEAL emerges from a dry deck shelter aboard the submerged nuclear-powered attack submarine USS *Silversides* off the coast of Florida.

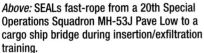

Above: SEALs fast-rope from a 20th Special Operations Squadron MH-53J Pave Low to a cargo ship bridge during insertion/exfiltration training.

Above: Army 3rd Special Forces Group soldier uses a Tactical Satellite Communication Radio while providing security for U.S. aircraft in Liberia.

ity to go where U.S. forces are unwelcome. The capability to conduct clandestine operations anywhere in the world in support of the National Command Authorities (NCA) or theater C-in-Cs is one of the defining attributes of SOF.

- *Information Dominance.* The information age has opened up a wide range of new opportunities, seemingly endless possibilities, and significant vulnerabilities for all

Below: Members of the U.S. Army 10th Special Forces Group Airborne practice hand-to-hand combat, just one of the skills the SOF candidate must master.

military forces, SOF included. Accordingly, USSOCOM is examining new ways to enhance SOF capabilities to ensure uninterrupted information exchange, reduce an adversary's ability to use information, and influence situations to support mission accomplishment.

Personnel and Readiness

By the end of FY 2001, U.S. Special Operations Forces personnel totaled 45,690. The active force (29,164) made up 64 percent; reserve force (10,043), 22 percent; National Guard (3,695), 8 percent; and civilians (2,788) 6 percent.

USSOCOM's FY 2001 President's budget request is predicated on maintaining and sustaining readiness as the top priority, which is

crucial to mission success. The Special Operations Forces aim to maintain a consistently high state of readiness, and people and training are key factors in achieving that goal. SOF are made up of some of America's most dedicated men and women from the Army, Navy, and Air Force – from active, National Guard, and reserve units.

The selection and retention of high-quality, motivated, and dedicated personnel are most important because SOF operate in circumstances where the reputation of the United States may rest on the successful completion of the mission. Given the unique nature of special operations and the often isolated environments, it takes a discriminating selection and assessment process and hard work to find the right person. After selection, personnel are trained extensively in the individual combat skills, foreign languages, and technical specialties required for their profession. Next, they join a SOF aircrew, team, or squad and participate in extensive unit training. Finally, they are cross trained in essential, special skills, and advanced techniques.

SOF training places great emphasis on individual and team professional development. An essential part of all training and education is the building of teams who work well together; who know the strengths, capabilities, and weaknesses of each member of the team; and who share a common doctrine that allows precise communication.

Special operations are often extremely physically demanding. The body and mind are the fundamental operating system, and their capability to withstand stress is enhanced by high levels of physical fitness. Special operators require a high level of physical fitness

Above: A group of Basic Underwater Demolition/SEAL (BUD/S) students man-handle logs to build both teamwork and body conditioning.

because missions often take place in harsh climates, over extended periods of time, far from conventional support, and frequently with little time to adjust to climatic changes. A unit that stresses top physical condition for its members – all of the time – can count on them being ready for any contingency.

Regional orientation has grown in importance over the past few years and requires SOF to maintain proficiency in a number of languages. Regional orientation, however, is much more than language training. It is not enough to speak the language. To communicate effectively, one must know the culture and customs, to include the subtleties of non-verbal communications. For example,

Below: SOF trainees cross a rope bridge during 1723rd Combat Control Squadron course on water and land navigation, equipment operation, and survival skills.

foreign internal defense and unconventional warfare operations have as their focus preparing foreign forces, either military or paramilitary, to conduct operations on a wide range of tasks from combat to internal development, in peace as well as in war. Successful conduct of these operations relies on the ability of SOF teams to establish rapport with and positively influence those they train. As such, these operations place a high premium on not only knowing the language of the people being taught, but in having a thorough understanding of the culture and the area where these operations take place. Units that conduct these operations invest a great deal of time and energy in language proficiency, cultural awareness, regional orientation, cross-cultural communications, and negotiation within the context of culture.

Training

SOF require a combination of basic military training and specialized skills training to

Above: Army 55th Special Operations Squadron soldiers are hoisted by an MH-60G while training in special patrol insertion-extraction (SPIE).

achieve operational proficiency. Training is designed to produce individuals and units that have mastered the tactics, techniques, and procedures through which units accomplish their missions. The SOF training system encompasses three processes: institutional training, component training, and joint training.

There are two types of institutional training: joint and common institutional training and service special operations training. USSOCOM has oversight of joint and common institutional training; ensuring programs of instruction adhere to joint doctrine and reflect current tactics, techniques, and procedures. Institutional spe-

Below: A member of the Army 12th Special Forces Group aims his M-16 while securing the perimeter of a drop zone during an air drop exercise.

Above: SEALs prepare to push their inflatable boat from a 1550th Combat Crew Training Wing helicopter during a joint Navy/Air Force exercise.

cial operations training, conducted by USSOCOM's service component schools, develops SOF-unique abilities through intensive training at the John F. Kennedy Special Warfare Center and School at Fort Bragg, North Carolina; the Naval Special Warfare Center at Coronado, California; and the Air Force Special Operations School at Hurlburt Field, Florida. Courses cover a broad range of topics and scenarios from doctrine and foreign policy to mission-specific skills to cross-cultural communications skills and language training.

The focus of component training is to ensure units are capable of performing assigned wartime missions through the

Below: Air Force 20th Special Operations Squadron MH-53J Pave Low refuels during joint Army-Air Force exercise organized by USSOCOM.

accomplishment of individual and collective tasks. Component training, managed by the USSOCOM service component commands, is governed by the doctrine of the military departments and primarily driven by mission requirements identified in the various geographic regions by the theater Special Operations Commands.

Although each of these processes is important, SOF places great emphasis on joint training with conventional forces. SOF joint training is primarily accomplished through participation in exercises sponsored by the Chairman, Joint Chiefs of Staff (CJCS)/C-in-C and USSOCOM's joint/combined exchange training (JCET) events. SOF participate in over sixty CJCS exercises annually, to meet geographic C-in-C needs.

Additionally, SOF are able to train to meet the regional, cultural, and language demands of each theater. Furthermore, SOF participation in JCETs has averaged 200 events annually. These events are

Above: Air Force Special Operations Squadron soldiers participate in field movements during a joint Special Operations Command Europe exercise.

conducted overseas with host nation forces. JCETs focus on SOF tasks that are essential for mission accomplishment and also provide valuable forward presence in support of the geographic C-in-C's strategic objectives. JCETs provide SOF access to areas that may not typically be open to larger conventional forces. In this respect, JCETs open doors – politically, diplomatically, and militarily – for U.S. forces to train with foreign military forces. Joint training provides Army, Navy, and Air Force special operators the opportunity to train as a joint team, performing tasks and activities that span the entire range of military operations.

Below: A search and rescue swimmer is hoisted aboard a Helicopter Combat Support Squadron 16 (HC-16) UH-1N Iroquois during training.

U.S. SPECIAL OPERATIONS FORCES AROUND THE WORLD

United States Special Operations Forces are conducting more missions, in more places, and under a broader range of conditions than ever before. In FY 1999, SOF units deployed to 152 countries and territories – a figure that does not include classified missions or special access programs. In any given week, 5,000 SOF operators are deployed in approximately 60 countries worldwide.

Operations conducted during FY 1999, and numerous joint/combined exercises in the United States and overseas, continue to reinforce two key principles. First, SOF provide complementary capabilities that, when used in conjunction with conventional forces, expand the military options of a Joint Force Commander (JFC). Second, SOF are most effective when they are fully integrated into a JFC's campaign plan. The theater Special Operations Commands (SOCs) ensure that SOF capabilities are considered throughout the entire planning process and that SOF are fully integrated into both peace and wartime plans.

Below: **The overall areas of responsibility (AORs) of the individual commanders-in-chief of U.S. forces throughout the world.**

UNITED STATES JOINT FORCES COMMAND AND SOCJFCOM

On 1 October 1999, the Unified Command Plan (UCP 99) redesignated the U.S. Atlantic Command (USACOM) as the U.S. Joint Force Command (USJFCOM), fully asserting its mission as the joint force provider, trainer, and integrator. UCP 99 depicts the evolution from USACOM, a geographic C-in-C with some functional roles, toward a functional unified command performing joint force training, integrating, and force-providing functions while retaining some geographic unified command responsibilities.

In concert with UCP 99, CINCUSJFCOM's strategic vision is to lead the transformation of U.S. armed forces to the capabilities envisioned in *Joint Vision 2010.* CINCUSJFCOM maximizes America's present and future military capabilities through joint training, total force integration, and the provision of ready CONUS-based conventional forces to support other C-in-Cs, the Atlantic theater, and domestic requirements. Toward this end, USJFCOM has been established as the center of excellence for training, training support, and integration of U.S. forces and America's

allies in preparing to conduct the full spectrum of joint, multinational, and interagency operations in order to protect and defend national interests.

The change to USJFCOM has significantly amended the focus of SOCJFCOM. This, a sub-unified command of USJFCOM, located in Norfolk, Virginia, further enhances USJFCOM's center of excellence by providing the capability to fully integrate SOF operations in its joint, multinational, and interagency training and integration program. SOCJFCOM also assists in CINCSOC's joint SOF training responsibilities through its Joint Special Operations Task Force (JSOTF), Joint Psychological Operations Task Force (JPOTF), and Joint Civil-Military Operations Task Force (JCMOTF) training charter.

In September 1999, CINCUSJFCOM approved a new SOCJFCOM mission statement to under-score this changing role, as follows:

SOCJFCOM conducts worldwide joint SOF training and facilitates joint integration to enhance the effectiveness and interoperability of Special Operations Forces in joint, multi-

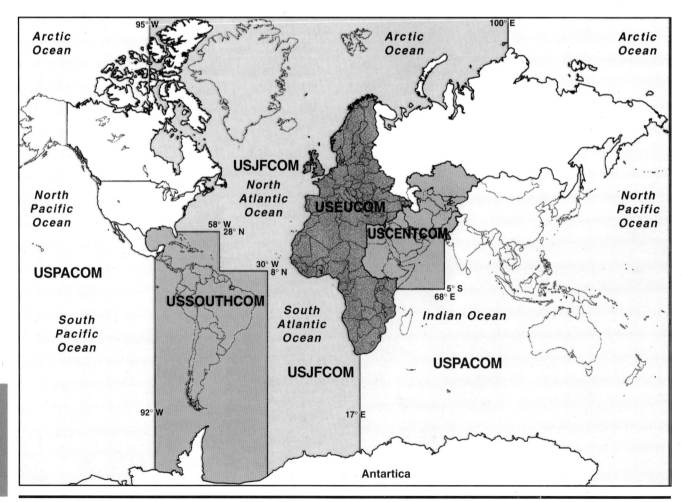

national, and interagency environments.

Additionally, as a theater SOC, SOCJF-COM will conduct special operations as directed by CINCUSJFCOM.

From this mission statement, SOCJFCOM has derived four essential tasks:

- Conduct worldwide joint SOF training to enhance SOF effectiveness within the joint, multinational, and interagency environment in support of USJFCOM's training program; focus training on C-in-C staffs and JTF commanders and staffs (the mission employers of SOF), and the identified training needs of the JSOTF, JPOTF, JCMOTF commanders and staffs (the doers).
- Improve JTF to JSOTF and JSOTF to JTF component interoperability through participation in the USJFCOM Joint Exercise Program.
- Facilitate joint integration, to include concept development and experimentation, to enhance SOF effectiveness within the joint, multinational, and interagency environment.
- Conduct special operations in support of USJFCOM, which encompasses: being prepared to form a JSOTF to conduct special operations in support of USJFCOM; conducting regional surveys; and being prepared to deploy a Humanitarian Assistance Survey Team within 24 hours of notification.

As USJFCOM continues to spearhead the improvement of the joint combat capability of U.S. military forces worldwide, SOCJFCOM will facilitate this evolution by its focus on joint SOF training and integration that enhances the effectiveness and interoperability of SOF in joint, multinational, and interagency operations.

UNITED STATES SOUTHERN COMMAND AND SOCSOUTH

The area of responsibility (AOR) of the U.S. Southern Command (USSOUTHCOM) encompasses the land mass and surrounding waters of Latin America south of Mexico, the Caribbean Sea, and the Gulf of Mexico. This area contains thirty-two independent countries and fifteen dependencies, including French, British, Dutch, and U.S. territories – 12.5 million square miles or approximately one-sixth of the world's land area. Every country, except Cuba, conducts national elections and employs a representative form of government. Economically, the region is considered vital to the United States' continued prosperity. Nearly 40 percent of the crude oil

Above: U.S. Joint Forces Command (USJF-COM) training helps Special Operations Forces to be fully integrated in both peace and wartime plans.

Below: In support of Operation Uphold Democracy, U.S. Special Operations Forces were in Haiti in 1994 to help insure security for demonstrators.

NUEVA REPÚBLICA

SINTONIZA A A.M. 1160

Ed. V

9 de Enero, 1990

NORIEGA EN MIAMI PARA SER PROCESADO

MIAMI (AP) El depuesto dictador panameño M.A.N. arribó a los EE.UU. donde enfrentará cargos por narcotráfico luego de entregarse a las tropas estadounidenses que rodeaban la Embajada del Vaticano, donde buscó santuario la pasada nochebuena.

Noriega, quien antagonizó a dos presidentes de los EE.UU. hasta que fue depuesto el 20 de diciembre, fue llevado a la base de la Fuerza Aerea Homestead, 25 millas al sur de Miami.

Noriega, que dominó como lider militar desde 1983, se declaró inocente de los cargos que lo acusan de haber utilizado su posición oficial para lucrarse brindándole protección al notorio Cartel de Medellín.

En Washington, el Presidente Bush expresó que Noriega se entregó voluntariamente a las autoridades estadounidenses y con el "pleno consentimiento" del gobierno panameño, y añadió en su pronunciamiento a la nación que estaba comprometido a brindarle a Noriega un juicio justo.

Los EE.UU. acordaron tres condiciones exigidas por Noriega: que le sería permitido realizar llamadas telefónicas, que su decisión sería mantenida en secreto hasta el momento del arresto, y que le seria permitido usar su uniforme. Oficiales de la administración acotaron que los EE.UU. también le garantizó a Noriega que no sería juzgado bajo la nueva ley federal que permite la aplicación de la pena de muerte para un "zar de droga". Las fuentes mencionaron que los EE.UU. no trataron diréctamente con Noriega. Las garantias le fueron notificadas por los oficiales del Vaticano.

NUMERO PRONTUARIO 41586

Left: During Operation Just Cause in Panama (1989-1990) U.S. PSYOP forces disseminated newspapers and leaflets, and sent out radio/TV broadcasts.

consumed in the United States comes from the Caribbean Basin. Brazil is the world's eighth largest economy, equal to China and larger than Canada. Argentina's gross domestic product (GDP) is approximately the same as the GDP of Australia, Russia or India. Over 400 million people of the area speak seven official languages: English, Spanish, Dutch, Portuguese, French, Quechua, and Aymara. Extreme differences in geography, topography, prosperity, stability, and ethnicity characterize the theater.

Special Operations Command, South (SOCSOUTH), is the Southern Command's subordinate unified command for special operations. It is responsible for all Special Operations Forces in the theater, except CA and PSYOP forces. Forward based at Naval Station Roosevelt Roads, Puerto Rico, SOCSOUTH is comprised of a joint headquarters with three forward-based operational units: C Company, 3rd Battalion, 7th Special Forces Group (Airborne); Naval Special Warfare Unit FOUR; and D Company, 160th Special Operations Aviation Regiment (Airborne). CONUS-based SOF from USSOCOM, in support of the USSOUTHCOM Theater Engagement Plan, continuously augment the

command. This assisance can be expanded to the full range of SOF capabilities required for contingency response. SOCSOUTH supports the USSOUTHCOM Strategy of Cooperative Regional Peacetime Engagement by providing SOF capabilities that assist in shaping the theater's security environment, while ensuring appropriate forces are postured to respond when U.S. interests are perceived to be threatened. Toward this end, SOCSOUTH manages over 200 SOF deployments annually, averaging 42 missions in 16 countries at any given time.

SOCSOUTH contributes to the accomplishment of USCINCSOUTH theater objectives by:

- Assisting U.S. agencies in training host-nation forces to target drug production and trafficking, and supporting interagency efforts to interdict the flow of drugs in the transit zone.
- Enhancing regional stability by assisting friendly nations in dealing with internal and external threats to their security, while fostering professionalism and respect for human rights.

Below: In Panama, Spanish-speaking U.S. Special Forces went from village to village insuring peaceful capitulation of PDF forces and offering CA assistance.

- Building military-to-military contacts that generate mutual trust, improve collective military capabilities, and promote democratic ideals.
- Staying ready to conduct special operations in conflict and peace in support of U.S. interests.

Many of the region's democracies remain fragile, their basis undermined by widespread economic, sociological, and political problems. They face security problems that are multidimensional and localized. Latin America has the most uneven distribution of income and wealth of any region, where the poorest 40 percent of the population receives only 10 percent of the income. Poverty is widespread. Rapid population growth, proliferating transnational threats, international drug trafficking, organized crime, terrorism, environmental degradation, illegal migration, the proliferation of land mines, and extra-legal paramilitary forces challenge the well-being and moral fiber of every country in the Western Hemisphere, including the United States. Domestic crime threatens U.S. economic interests and the security of the nation's citizens abroad – one-half of the world's abductions occur in Colombia alone. The region's porous borders, the expanding influence of insurgent organizations, and the symbiotic relationship between the illicit drug industry and insurgent forces vastly increase the complexity of the challenge facing the United States and its Special Operations Forces.

The emphasis of the region's military forces is moving away from traditional roles. The concepts of balance of power, deterrence, and collective defense against extra-hemispheric threats are fading. Regional security considerations now include threats to the domestic order that challenge a state's ability to hold the country together and to govern. Today, many regional militaries focus on issues that garner the support of the people for the government, including response to natural disasters and their aftermath; domestic threats; and dealing with non-state organizations including terrorists, organized crime, and paramilitary groups.

To assist in the U.S. effort to meet these challenges, SOCSOUTH provides a flexible means of accomplishing a wide range of missions. As the theater's only rapid response force, SOCSOUTH is commonly called upon to handle emergencies requiring immediate military assistance. When Hurricane Georges struck the Dominican Republic, SOF helicopters and soldiers were the first U.S. forces in the country. As Hurricane Mitch was devastating Honduras,

Above: Army and Air Force Special Forces recovery teams are taken to the Andes Mountains, Colombia, where an Army recce plane has crashed.

SOCSOUTH deployed forces that rescued over 900 people on the day of their arrival.

After the lifesaving efforts were complete, SOF language and communications skills were employed to coordinate the initial multinational relief efforts in Honduras, El Salvador, Guatemala, and Nicaragua. In one case, SEALs and SOF helicopters recovered a fisherman with a life-threatening disorder from a ship off the coast of Costa Rica when other U.S. assets were forced to turn back due to bad weather. In another instance, SOF helicopters, SF soldiers, and Special Tactics Team airmen employed their unique skills to recover human remains and sensitive equipment from exceptionally rugged terrain when a U.S. Army reconnaissance low-level aircraft crashed in the Andes Mountains of Colombia.

In December 1999, severe flooding in Venezuela resulted in the deaths of an estimated 30,000 people. Within hours of notification, a task force from SOCSOUTH deployed to the disaster area to assist in rescue efforts. The nature of operations rapidly shifted and SOCSOUTH was tasked to provide the command and control element for a humanitarian assistance operation that remained in place for an extended period.

Counterdrug support is a major area of focus in the Southern Command. Deployed on a continuous basis throughout the source and transit zones, SOF supports interagency and host-nation land-, riverine-, sea-, and air-interdiction efforts to disrupt the production, cultivation, and movement of illegal drugs. The presence of Naval Special

Warfare Patrol Coastal ships plays a vital role in detection and monitoring efforts. SEALs and Special Boat Unit personnel are constantly engaged in training missions to assist participating nations in controlling their coastlines and waterways. Air Force SOF provide critical training that helps host nations develop counterdrug aviation operational and logistical support infrastructures. Army SF teams are continuously training host-nation counter-narcotics forces in a wide range of relevant skills.

The Colombian Government is making substantial efforts to neutralize those organizations responsible for illicit drug activities in its country and requested U.S. assistance in training and equipping an Army Counterdrug Brigade capable of day or night operations in all weather and terrain. Currently, SOCSOUTH is the USSOUTHCOM executive agent for the training. The initial Colombian Army Counterdrug Battalion attained operational capability in December 1999.

C Company, 3rd Battalion, 7th Special Forces Group (Airborne) hosts the annual SOF Counterterrorism Tactics and Techniques Symposium (CTTTS). This USSOUTHCOM activity brings security forces from throughout the region together to exchange ideas and foster dialog on the common issue of combating terrorism. Additionally, SOCSOUTH deployed forces on numerous occasions to improve force protection for U.S. units and enhance the safety of U.S. citizens and interests during periods of internal strife in several nations of the region.

SOCSOUTH provides SOF expertise to the USSOUTHCOM exercise program. It serves as executive agent for two JCS exercises, and as co-executive agent for a third. Cabanas is a joint and combined field training exercise with South American countries that focuses on peacekeeping operations skills. Tradewinds, for which SOCSOUTH is executive agent for the ground phase, is an annual opportunity for the defense and police forces of the Caribbean Regional Security System and the Caribbean Community to conduct interoperability and skills training from the individual to battalion staff level. These exercises serve to promote regional stability. Ellipse Echo is an annual contingency response event that provides superb training in warfighting and planning skills to U.S. SOF. Additionally, SOCSOUTH participates in a variety of other exercises designed to enhance U.S. joint interoperability, such as Blue Advance, Unified Endeavor, and Fuertes Defensas.

UNITED STATES EUROPEAN COMMAND AND SOCEUR

The U.S. European Command (USEUCOM) is the second largest geographic area of responsibility in the unified combatant command structure. Spanning three continents and encompassing eighty-nine countries, its geographical area encompasses 13 million square miles and is home for more than one billion people. Within this vast AOR, USEUCOM is tasked to be ready to promote peace and stability and to defeat adversaries. To accomplish these theater objectives, the Commander-in-Chief, USEUCOM, relies heavily on Special Operatins Command, Europe (SOCEUR) to provide him with timely unconventional military options.

As a sub-unified command for special operations, COMSOCEUR provides operational direction and control of special operations, CA, and PSYOP forces in the USEUCOM AOR. Comprising Army, Air Force, and Navy SOF stationed in Europe, the SOC routinely receives augmentation from continental U.S.-based forces to accomplish its assigned tasks. From these varied assets, COMSOCEUR forms task forces capable of executing special operations as well as conducting assessments and response to crises throughout the USEUCOM AOR. COMSOCEUR also functions as Director, Special Operations Directorate, of the EUCOM staff to provide theater strategic input and advice

to the theater commander concerning special operations.

SOCEUR's operations and activities reflect the USEUCOM strategic objectives to promote peace and stability, and defeat adversaries. SOCEUR plays an important role in promoting peace and shaping the international environment in the EUCOM area of responsibility by reducing the conditions that lead to conflict. Key SOCEUR engagement activities include joint and combined exercises and training (JCET) events, the Joint Contact Team Program (JCTP), the African Crisis Response Initiative (ACRI), and humanitarian demining operations.

JCETs are training activities that fulfill SOF unit training and CINCEUR engagement needs in countries throughout the theater. This combination of training and engagement allows SOF units to perform mission-

Above: U.S./Peruvian special warfare teams parachute amidst surfers as other team members pass in an inflatable boat during joint nation exercises.

essential tasks and regionally focused training while simultaneously establishing U.S. presence and influence in priority engagement countries.

The JCTP is a USCINCEUR initiative to provide greater U.S. military interaction with former Warsaw Pact countries and Soviet client states; SOF units provide excellent models for these nations to emulate in their evolving militaries.

ACRI is a U.S. Department of State initiative to develop the capabilities of selected

Below: 3rd Special Forces Group (Airborne) under EUCOM trained Senegalese soldiers during the African Crisis Response Initiative in the 1990s.

Above: SEALs supported bridging of the Sava River as part of Special Operations Command Implementation Force during Operation Joint Endeavor (1995-1996).

African countries to respond to regional crises with capable, professional, indigenous military forces. Humanitarian demining is a joint venture between the Departments of State and Defense. This program continues to save hundreds of lives each year throughout the EUCOM AOR by training host-nation personnel in demining and in educating the public on the dangers of landmines and unexploded ordnance.

SOCEUR's AOR exhibits the full range of human conditions, and the strategic environ-

Below: Special Operations Forces are prepared for operations in all climates and terrains; this AFSOC soldier is clearing snow from a vehicle in Norway.

ment is correspondingly diverse. In many cases, U.S presence is welcomed on a bilateral, or more often multilateral, basis. U.S. presence is minimal in many cases – particularly in Sub-Saharan Africa – due to the size of the theater. SOCEUR manages its engagement programs on a country-by-country basis and follows the EUCOM lead by dividing its AOR into several regions for easier manageability, as follows.

Western Europe/NATO

Western Europe will continue to be the stable anchor within the AOR. The template for stability and cooperation in the region is NATO. U.S. Special Operations Forces train with NATO air, land, and sea special operations forces in all climates and terrain, from the frozen fjords of Norway to the sweltering deserts of Africa. Interoperability, combined command and control, and the exchange of methods and tactics ensure the United States and its allies are ready to conduct combined or coordinated special operations anywhere in the theater. SOCEUR has been in the forefront of integrating new member nations into the NATO alliance – assessing, training, and exercising with host-nation special forces.

Central Europe

Central Europe is experiencing a new wave of nationalism and, to a lesser degree, ultra-nationalism. The end of communism has revealed long-suppressed internal and external security issues involving intractable ethnic/religious hatreds and old boundary disputes rooted in modern history. Political opportunists are seen to be seizing on these issues to acquire national leadership positions. The risk of political instability within the developing central European democracies – particularly the Balkan states – is expected to remain high through the next several years.

To counter these threats, SOCEUR has joined former Warsaw Pact forces to develop Special Operations Forces that meet NATO standards for interoperability. JCETs conducted in Central Europe provide unique training opportunities for each of SOCEUR's component forces. They also serve to demonstrate the strengths and capabilities of the U.S. military, as well as the benefits of a responsible and well-trained, professional NCO corps – a capability normally lacking in Soviet-modeled forces. In the recent Balkans conflict, joint Special Operations Forces, under the direction of COMSOCEUR, were employed to expand the range of military options available to USCINCEUR. Most notable were two successful combat recoveries of American pilots downed by enemy fire over Serbia. Additionally, CA and PSYOP forces provided immeasurable assistance in the ever-evolving process of modern day warfare. The Balkans have historically demanded world attention and SOF will continue to play a central role in this volatile region.

New Independent States

With their emergence as sovereign nations, the New Independent States (NIS) simultaneously began the process of changing their institutions from authoritarian to democratic and from provincial to national. While some have successfully taken their place on the world stage as democracies, others have tended to revert to authoritarianism, and a few are split by severe ethnic divisions. This is an emerging region for USEUCOM and SOCEUR.

Above: Members of AFSOC 352nd Special Operations Group and 16th Special Operations Wing plot a Bosnian flight with French pilot (seated).

Below: An AFSOC translator in discussion with an Italian officer about monitoring of no-fly zone operations in Bosnia-Herzegovina.

Initial efforts in this area have focused on regional assessments and teaching these nations the role of the military in a democracy.

SOF play a key role in the NIS by providing the C-in-C with U.S. eyes and ears in a region still plagued by uncertainty and instability. In 1998, SOCEUR sponsored the first NIS SOF conference held offsite in Stuttgart, Germany. This benchmark event brought military personnel from Moldova, Georgia, and the Ukraine together to view U.S. SOF demonstrations and discuss opportunities for future JCET and JCTP events. International interest and tensions in the region are expected to dramatically increase as resident deposits of oil and minerals are developed. Accordingly, development of SOF familiarity and experience in the region is becoming a high priority.

Africa

Africa is a complex and diverse region with many countries evolving into clusters of stability and instability. While some are prosperous and semi- or fully democratic, others are stagnating under non-democratic military or civilian leaders, and a few are consistently chaotic due to coups, civil wars, or lack of a strong, central government. Special Operations Forces represent the greatest percentage of American "boots on the ground" in this vast continent. Conduct of ACRI and humanitarian demining training under the auspices of SOCEUR has had a demonstrable stabilizing influence in this unstable part of the world. Likewise, port visits and coastal maritime engagement programs maintain a critical presence in areas where other U.S. forces either cannot or will not go. A very active JCET program permits each of the three SOF components to routinely train in an environment that has recently precipitated four responses to crises by SOCEUR forces.

UNITED STATES CENTRAL COMMAND AND SOCCENT

The Central Region is one of the most dynamic and diverse areas of the world. It is an area that has been, and will continue to be, vitally important to the United States. The Central Region is the birth place of three of the world's major religions; has a population of over 428 million people; and consists of seventeen different ethnic groups, six major languages, hundreds of dialects, varied forms of government, and a wide range of per capita incomes.

CENTCOM's strategy of "Shaping the Central Region for the 21st Century" seeks to integrate the efforts of U.S. Central Command with those of other U.S. government agencies, non-governmental/private volunteer organizations, and the nation's friends in the region to

Above: Members of the Army 5th Special Forces group perform a HALO jump from a USAF C-141B during joint U.S. and Egyptian exercises, 1998.

Below: After fast-roping from an AFSOC MH-53 Pave Low, SEALs provide cover for each other during a search and seizure exercise.

obtain the shared goal of a peaceful, stable, and prosperous Central Region. Implementing this strategy involves the full spectrum of engagement, including warfighting and contingency planning, combined and bilateral exercises, United Nations sanctions enforcement and monitoring, and security assistance and demining operations. SOCCENT plays an integral part in all these activities.

Special Operations Command, Central (SOCCENT) implements the Command's theater strategy through numerous initiatives and programs. SOCCENT's culturally sensitive forces provide a direct link to host-nation counterparts and work to formalize coalition operations procedures, agreements, and doctrine for coalition warfare. SOCCENT has several forward-positioned command and control (C2) elements. SOCCENT Forward exercises C2 for all SOF forces within the AOR. SOCCENT For-ward is located in Bahrain. Naval Special Warfare Unit Three (NSWU-3), also located in Bahrain, provides C2 and support for all Naval Special Warfare forces in theater. The SOC Coordination Element (SOCCE) Kuwait is primarily dedicated to providing SOF C2 for Operation Desert Spring. SOCCE Qatar provides logistic and administrative assistance in preparation for the SOCCENT headquarter's relocation into the AOR.

SOCCENT headquarters is currently located at MacDill Air Force Base, Florida. The command is organized in a similar way to other joint commands with responsibilities divided among six directorates: personnel, operations, plans, intelligence, logistics, and communications. Command manning is heavily reliant upon individual mobilization augmenties (IMAs).

SOCCENT is committed to support the CENTCOM's regional strategy through a variety of initiatives that reflect the National Security Strategy elements of shaping the international environment, responding to the full spectrum of crises, and preparing now for an uncertain future. Some recent operations and initiatives conducted by SOCCENT forces are described below.

Desert Fox

In December 1998, Operation Desert Fox was executed in response to reported Iraqi non-compliance with the United Nations Special Commission (UNSCOM). SOCCENT deployed special operations liaison elements and a SOCCE augmentation force in anticipation of extended hostilities.

Maritime Interception Operations (MIO)

SOCCENT supported UN sanctions enforcement through MIO conducted in support of UN

Security Council Resolution 687 that imposed international trade and economic sanctions against Iraq. NSWU-3 in Bahrain provided both assets and personnel for this effort.

Desert Spring

In August 1999, all Iris Gold exercises were incorporated under Operation Desert Spring. The original purpose of the exercise remains the same: to provide combat support units to the Kuwaiti Brigades for terminal guidance of close air support liaison to Combined Task Force (CTF) Kuwait. Operation Desert Spring has expanded to include up to nine SF teams and a special operations C2 element.

Demining

SOCCENT forces plan, establish, and conduct humanitarian demining operations to provide a self-sustaining, indigenous humanitarian capability. Training is performed to locate, identify, and create databases for mine locations; eliminate the threat of land mines and unexploded ordnance (UXO); reduce the risk to life, livestock, and property; return land to productive use; and train and maintain the indigenous force in demining techniques. Demining operations have been conducted in Yemen and Jordan and are planned for Ethiopia and Eritrea. The partnership established through the demining program has become the prototype for all other demining programs throughout the world.

Counterdrug

SOCCENT conducts counterdrug operations in support of Presidential Decision Directive 44. During 1999, SOF forces provided light infantry and mountaineering training for Turkmenistan's state border service. In addition, SOF forces conducted a Warrant Officer Leadership and Development Course with thirty Turkmen participants. Additional counterdrug training operations are planned in Egypt and Kenya.

Integrated Survey Program (ISP)

SOCCENT forces conduct surveys of U.S. facilities, including embassies and consulates, within the AOR on a recurring basis. These surveys support State Department emergency action plans (EAP) for each post. In addition, surveys provide planning information for Non-Combatant Evacuation Operations (NEO).

In August 1998, while conducting a survey in Nairobi, Kenya, ISP personnel were inside the U.S. embassy when a terrorist bomb exploded. The team quickly formed a defensive perimeter around the embassy to prevent pedestrian interference and potential follow-on attack. In addition, several members of the team established a first aid triage cen-

ter treating injured embassy personnel. Their quick decisive actions were critical in saving additional lives. Nine SF personnel and one member of the Air Force special tactics squadron were awarded the Soldier's Medal for their actions.

Central Asian States

USCENTCOM recently assumed responsibility for all military activities for the five countries in the Central Asian Region: Turkmenistan, Uzbekistan, Kazakhstan, Kyrgyzstan, and Tajikistan. SOCCENT's inherently small foot-

Below: Air Force MH-53J CSAR helicopter from 20th Special Operations Squadron lifts off from USS *George Washington* during joint exercises.

Above: Army 5th Special Forces Group soldiers and British and Kuwaiti commandos parachuted simultaneously from four C-130s in 1998 exercises.

print and culturally sensitive forces play a critical role in nurturing CENTCOM's relationships in this region.

JCS and JCET Exercises

SOCCENT's joint and combined exercise and training programs are vital peacetime engagement tools that support the C-in-C's theater strategy. Two primary goals of these programs are to enhance SOF's warfighting capability through maintaining combat readiness and to maintain access and presence in the AOR. The exercises also provide the prin-

Above: A 38th Air Rescue Squadron HH-60G Pave Hawk refuels from a 17th Special Operations Squadron HC-130 Combat Talon.

cipal means by which to improve coalition warfighting capabilities while simultaneously building strong military-to-military relationships. During 1999, SOCCENT forces conducted over fifteen JCET and eight JCS exercises with fifteen countries.

UNITED STATES PACIFIC COMMAND AND SOCPAC

Special Operations Command, Pacific (SOCPAC), located at Camp H. M. Smith, Oahu, Hawaii, is a sub-unified command and serves as the SOF component command for

Below: A member of Naval Special Warfare Unit One-SEAL Team Five rappels down a wall during refresher training on Guam.

the U.S. Pacific Command (USPACOM). The AOR of the Commander-in-Chief, U.S. Pacific Command (USCINCPAC), represents the largest geographic area of the unified commands. It covers over half of the earth's surface with over 105 million square miles and nearly 60 percent of the world's population. Distance, diversity, and change characterize the PACOM AOR.

Although the Asian-Pacific Rim has recently experienced an economic slowdown, over the last decade Asia's economic growth rate was twice that of the world as a whole. This growth has increased competition for both natural resources and markets. Thirty-six percent of U.S. merchandise trade is within the region and over three million American jobs are linked to Asian export markets. Sovereignty claims to areas such as the Spratly Islands have become important due to the resource potential of the surrounding seas.

Economic growth has fueled an expansion of military technologies and capabilities. The six largest armed forces in the world operate in the Pacific AOR. Military capabilities in the region are increasingly modern due to technical development and economic growth. This enhanced military capability has resulted in several nations possessing the capability to build and deliver weapons of mass destruction (WMD). Other regional nations also have the economic and technical sophistication to develop WMD capabilities on short notice, should they believe a threat exists.

The political challenges are also changing. Asian-Pacific nations are proud of their cultures and sensitive about issues of independence and sovereignty. These nations are strikingly diverse in size, population, culture, and history. The 43 nations, 20 territories, and 10 U.S. territories represent 75 official languages and over 20 distinct religions. The potential threats posed in parts of the region, such as the Korean peninsula, Indo-Pakistani border, and Indonesia, remain USCINCPAC concerns. Local insurrection, territorial disputes, religious and ethnic conflicts, and illegal drug trafficking have economic, political, and military implications for USCINCPAC and all theater service components.

USCINCPAC's strategy harmonizes employment of military resources with the other elements of national power. This strategy recognizes contributions made, both directly and indirectly, by military forces in shaping the international environment through activities that promote peace and stability. The strategy focuses on continued military presence in the region – demonstrating U.S. commitment, developing trust, and deterring aggressors.

SOCPAC supports USCINCPAC's shaping strategy through operations such as demining activities, counterdrug operations, bilateral/multilateral exercises, JCET program activities, Pacific Situation Awareness Teams (PSATs), and the annual Pacific Area Special Operations Conference (PASOC). Such engagement seeks to demonstrate continued American intent and capability; reassure allies and friends; promote regional stability, cooperation and trust; deter potential regional aggressors; build force interoperability; and maintain access to host-nation support and facilities.

Above: A combined U.S./Thai Special Forces parachute jump team exits a U.S. Marine KC-130 during joint and combined exercise training (JCET).

Landmines continue to inflict hundreds of civilian casualties every month. Additionally, the mine threat removes arable land from production and reduces the flow of commerce. Various factions laid these mines over the last forty years. SOF, in cooperation with the host nation and U.S. government agencies, have designed and managed a training program to improve mine awareness, detection and recovery, and the treatment of casualties. SOCPAC conducted four demining operations in Laos in 1998 and again in 1999. Additionally, two initial demining assessments were conducted in Thailand in 1999, with further demining operations scheduled. Other countries plagued by landmines are looking at ways to participate in the program.

Southeast Asia remains one of the world's largest drug-producing areas. U.S. Special Operations Forces assist host nations in improving their capability to deal with this significant problem. Specifically, SOF conduct training to improve planning, expertise, and small-unit tactics of host-nation military and law enforcement agencies to increase their ability to battle narco-criminals. Thailand, Malaysia, Laos and Cambodia have all participated in this training, which benefits both host nation and U.S. forces as they share techniques, sharpen skills, and improve operational effectiveness.

One of the cornerstones of the shaping element is the SOCPAC-managed JCET program. This program fulfills SOF training requirements and allows the sharing of skills between SOF elements and their host-nation counterparts. These activities include airborne and air mobile patrolling, lifesaving, reconnaissance, and small-unit tactics. JCET activities improve SOF and host nation capabilities, and also demonstrate USCINCPAC's commitment to constructive engagement.

In addition, humanitarian and civic action projects, carried out in conjunction with JCET events, provide tangible benefits for the host-nation civilian population. During 1999, SOCPAC conducted thirty-seven JCET events in twelve countries. Participants include in-theater and CONUS units from both active and reserve components. USCINCPAC uses this cornerstone program for initial military-to-military contact, annually demonstrated through presence in some of the smaller countries, and as part of an ongoing military program in many of the larger nations.

USCINCPAC deployed its Pacific Situation Assessment Team (PSAT), consisting of SOCPAC personnel, during 1998 and 1999. PSAT enhances coordination between USCINCPAC and the U.S. Chief of Mission's country team by providing on-site advice regarding the suitability and feasibility of the application of military forces and resources in support of U.S. government responses to crisis situations.

The annual PASOC is another forum that supports USCINCPAC's theater engagement program. This week-long conference, comprising over 200 delegates – including twenty-six flag officers – from twenty-two countries, provides USCINCPAC and COMSOCPAC with an "azimuth check" for U.S. peacetime engagement. In addition, PASOC provides a unique opportunity to develop, in a multilateral setting, senior foreign military contacts that will facilitate the conduct of future exercises, crisis response, and other operations within the AOR.

SOCPAC provides USCINCPAC with a highly capable crisis response force. Crisis response is USCINCPAC's top SOF priority and is provided by USCINCPAC's rapidly deployable Joint Task Force-510 (JTF-510). With SOCPAC as the nucleus, JTF-510 is specifically structured for, and capable of, timely response to special contingencies, humanitarian assistance, disaster relief, noncombatant evacuation operations, and other crises. JTF-510 is usually the first to deploy in real-world crises and in each major exercise.

SPECIAL FORCES, KOREA

Special Operations Command, Korea, (SOCKOR), located at Camp Kim in Yongsan, Korea, is the theater SOC responsible for special operations on the Korean peninsula and, when established, the Korean Theater of Operations (KTO). The KTO and SOCKOR exist because there has never been a peace treaty officially ending the Korean War. Military forces on the Korean Peninsula maintain a heightened state of readiness to respond to the resumption of hostilities with little or no warning. The KTO achieves unity of effort through a complex web of command relationships comprised of three military elements with different but complementary missions, all commanded by a single C-in-C.

The KTO is unique because the C-in-C in Korea is not a U.S. unified commander. As the Commander-in-Chief, United Nations

Command (CINCUNC), he is the international commander responsible for maintaining the armistice that has existed in Korea since 1953. As the Commander-in-Chief, Republic of Korea (ROK)/U.S. Combined Forces Command (CINCCFC), he is a bi-national commander who supports CINCUNC by deterring North Korean aggression and, if necessary, defeating a North Korean attack. As the commander of U.S. Forces, Korea (COMUSKOREA), he is the subordinate unified commander of USPACOM responsible for providing U.S. forces to CINCUNC/CFC.

Because of the unique command relationships in Korea, SOCKOR is the only theater SOC that is not a subordinate unified command. Established in 1988 as a functional component command of U.S. Forces, Korea (USFK), SOCKOR is the principal organization responsible for the integration of U.S. Special Operations Forces in Korea. Its primary mission focus is simple: be ready to employ U.S. SOF and win, should war resume in Korea.

During armistice, SOCKOR is responsible to CINCUNC/CFC and COMUSKOREA for SOF war planning, targeting, training, and participation in exercises and contingency operations on the Korean peninsula. SOCPAC supports SOCKOR in these responsibilities and routinely demonstrates its capability to reinforce SOCKOR rapidly during a crisis. During armistice, contingencies, and hostilities, SOCKOR exercises operational control of the U.S. Army Special Forces Detachment, Korea (SFD-K), which is the longest continuously serving SF unit in Asia. This organization is key to ensuring interoperability between ROK and U.S. SOF. The SF liaison NCOs of SFD-K live, train, and work with the ROK Special Forces Brigades on a daily basis, and thus play a critical role in the shaping of ROK and U.S. SOF operations to support CINCUNC/CFC.

Should war resume in Korea, SOCKOR will combine with the Republic of Korea Army Special Warfare Command to establish the Combined Unconventional Warfare Task Force (CUWTF). As the special operations component of CFC, the CUWTF will plan and conduct joint and combined special operations throughout the KTO in support of CINCUNC/CFC, exercising operational control of all assigned and attached U.S. and ROK SOF. Additionally, SOCKOR will function as the Special Operations Command, UNC, integrating all third-country SOF committed to CINCUNC. When fully reinforced with U.S. forces, SOCKOR comprises the largest JSOTF in the world.

SOF helps to shape the strategic environment by contributing directly to CINCUNC/CFC's deterrence efforts through long-term deployments of SOF, such as AC-130 gun-

ships, during critical periods. Through the integration of ROK and U.S. SOF in combined exercises, SOCKOR assists in expanding allied SOF capabilities to respond to the spectrum of threats as well as to ensure that there is post-reunification relevance for ROK SOF. Although not under the operational control of SOCKOR, U.S. CA and PSYOP forces have also assumed significantly greater roles in support of CINCUNC/CFC through the newly established Combined Civil Affairs Task Force (CCATF) and Combined Psychological Operations Task Force (CPOTF). The U.S. SOF elements apportioned to the CCATF and CPOTF are helping to shape the combined capabilities of CFC to execute CA and PSYOP missions across the full range of military operations.

To add to the challenge posed by a return

Above: Army Special Forces based in Seoul, Korea, plan their moves in the escape and evasion portion of combat search and rescue exercises.

to hostilities, there are a number of "wild card scenarios" that may occur, including North Korean terrorist actions, direct military confrontations, threats of the use of WMD, missile launches, and other forms of provocation to gain political and economic concessions. Other potential crises include massive refugee flow, natural or manmade disasters, transfer of or loss of control of WMD, the outbreak of civil war within North Korea, and collapse of the North Korean state. Therefore, as U.S. SOF train for war, they must also prepare for the uncertainty and complexity of post-hostilities and a wide range of potential crises requiring swift and skilled military intervention.

HOW USSOCOM IS ORGANIZED

The United States Special Operations Command (USSOCOM) is one of nine unified commands in the U.S. military's combatant command structure. It is composed of Army, Navy, and Air Force Special Operations Forces. The Commander-in-Chief of USSOCOM (USCINCSOC) has two roles. In his capacity as a supporting C-in-C, he provides trained and ready SOF. In his role as a supported C-in-C, the USCINCSOC must be prepared to exercise command of selected special operations missions when directed by the National Command Authorities.

The U.S. Congress mandated the creation of USSOCOM in 1987 to correct serious deficiencies in the ability of the United States to conduct special operations and engage in low-intensity conflict activities. The command was assigned many service-like responsibilities, including training, ensuring combat readiness, monitoring personnel promotions and assignments, and developing and acquiring SOF-peculiar equipment. USSOCOM was also given responsibility for managing a separate major force program (MFP), MFP-11, which ensures that the SOF program has visibility at the Department of Defense and Congressional levels.

These last two tasks give USSOCOM great flexibility in training, equipping, and employing its forces. USCINCSOC is the sole unified commander with responsibility for planning, programming, and budgeting of military forces. In addition, he has the

Right: In the hot seat, General Charles R. Holland, U.S. Air Force, assumed command of U.S. Special Operations Command on 27 October 2000.

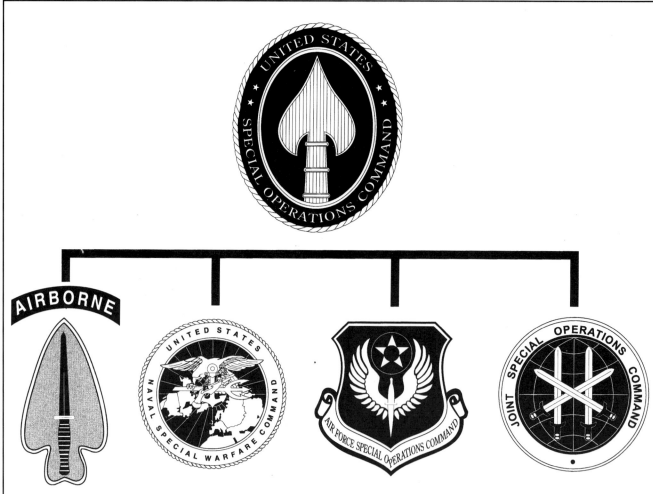

USSOCOM, formally established as a unified combatant command at MacDill Air Force Base, Florida, on 16 April 1987, is commanded by a four-star flag or general officer with the title of Commander-in-Chief, U.S. Special Operations Command (USCINCSOC). All SOF of the Army, Navy, and Air Force, based in the United States, were eventually placed under USCINCSOC's combatant command. USSOCOM's three service component commands are the Army Special Operations Command, the Naval Special Warfare Command, and the Air Force Special Operations Command. The Joint Special Operations Command is a sub-unified command of USCINCSOC.

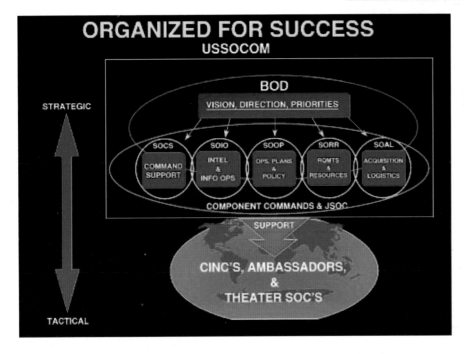

ORGANIZED FOR SUCCESS
USSOCOM

STRATEGIC

TACTICAL

BOD
VISION, DIRECTION, PRIORITIES

SOCS
COMMAND SUPPORT

SOIO
INTEL & INFO OPS

SOOP
OPS, PLANS & POLICY

SORR
RQMTS & RESOURCES

SOAL
ACQUISITION & LOGISTICS

COMPONENT COMMANDS & JSOC

SUPPORT

CINC'S, AMBASSADORS, & THEATER SOC'S

Left: Headquarters, U.S. Special Operations Command (HQ USSOCOM). In November 1998, USCINCSOC reorganized the USSOCOM headquarters staff from a standard J-staff configuration to five functional centers. This action strengthens USSOCOM's ability to support its customers by ensuring a flexible command structure adaptable to future challenges. An overview of the new organization is shown here.

authority similar to that of a service chief for the development and acquisition of special operations-peculiar equipment, materials, supplies, and services. In short, he is the only C-in-C with a checkbook.

Under the same legislation that created USSOCOM, Congress also established the Office of the Assistant Secretary of Defense for Special Operations and Low-Intensity Conflict (ASD(SO/LIC)) as the policy and resource focal point for all special operations and low-intensity conflict activities of the Department of Defense. Aided by these reforms, enormous improvements in the readiness and capabilities of the U.S. Special Operations Forces were made.

Special Operations Acquisition and Logistics (SOAL) Center

The SOAL combines the acquisition function of the command and the logistics functions of the J-4 staff to provide research, development, acquisition, and logistics support to USCINCSOC. The SOAL plans, directs, reviews, and evaluates materiel development, procurement, and sustainment for USSOCOM; conducts liaison with USSOCOM components to ensure operational requirements are met by developmental programs; develops and promulgates USSOCOM acquisition and logistics policies and procedures; and manages a select group of special operations-peculiar programs.

Benefits derived from this include:
- "Cradle-to-grave" management of SOF-related systems.
- Improved life-cycle cost management.
- Portfolio and materiel management.
- Elimination of organizational stove pipes or barriers to collaboration.
- Worldwide logistic support of SOF.

Special Operations Requirements and Resources (SORR) Center

The SORR combines the planning (J-5 and J-7) and resourcing (J-8) functions, to include the USSOCOM Strategic Planning Process. The mission of the SORR is to support SOF through the development of resourcing, operational mission and force structure analysis, strategic assessments, and requirements reviews.

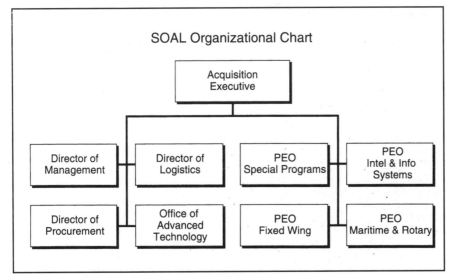

SOAL Organizational Chart

Acquisition Executive

- Director of Management
- Director of Logistics
- PEO Special Programs
- PEO Intel & Info Systems
- Director of Procurement
- Office of Advanced Technology
- PEO Fixed Wing
- PEO Maritime & Rotary

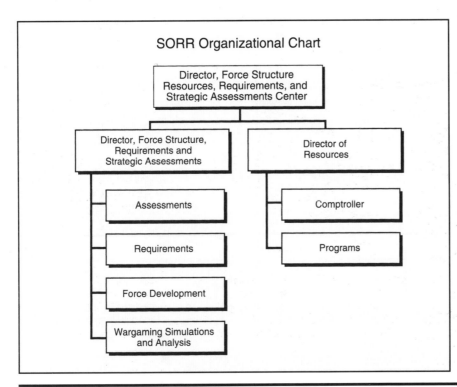

SORR Organizational Chart

Director, Force Structure Resources, Requirements, and Strategic Assessments Center

- Director, Force Structure, Requirements and Strategic Assessments
  - Assessments
  - Requirements
  - Force Development
  - Wargaming Simulations and Analysis
- Director of Resources
  - Comptroller
  - Programs

Above: Training of Special Operations Forces incorporates familiarity with weapons systems of all nations – allies and real or potential enemies.

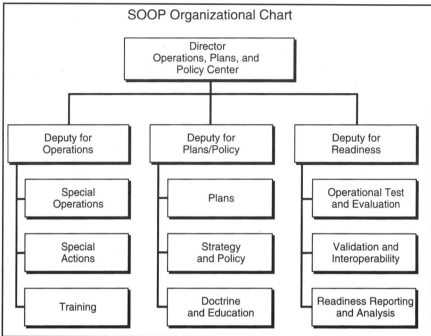

SOOP Organizational Chart

Director
Operations, Plans, and
Policy Center

Deputy for Operations
- Special Operations
- Special Actions
- Training

Deputy for Plans/Policy
- Plans
- Strategy and Policy
- Doctrine and Education

Deputy for Readiness
- Operational Test and Evaluation
- Validation and Interoperability
- Readiness Reporting and Analysis

Special Operations Operations, Plans, and Policy (SOOP) Center

The SOOP combines the J-3 and the J-5 staffs to provide focused operational support in the areas of doctrine, plans, policy, operations, training, and special actions. Its mission is to ensure all special operations deployments and plans supporting the NCA, regional C-in-Cs, and ambassadors are tailored to mission requirements, reflect current force capabilities, and are consistent with USCINC-SOC Title 10 responsibilities and core missions. In support of these objectives, the SOOP oversees SOF doctrine, education, tempo, and remediation, as well as the training and exercise programs, in order to optimize force readiness and SOF relevance.

The SOOP also develops joint plans, policy, strategic assessments, and force structure, and directs deployment, employment, and readiness of approximately 46,000 Army, Navy, and Air Force SOF worldwide, including sensitive special mission units; validates operational requirements; and manages training resources, humanitarian programs, joint training exercises, and operational testing.

Special Operations Intelligence and Information Operations (SOIO) Center

The SOIO combines the J-2 and J-6 staff functions to provide for integrated information management in intelligence, communications, information protection, network management, and audio/visual support. SOIO integrates command and control, communications, computer, intelligence, surveillance, and reconnaissance (C4ISR), and information operations (IO) to gain information superiority throughout the spectrum of engagement and conflict. The SOIO validates requirements and develops special operations C4ISR and IO training, doctrine, and procedures.

Special Operations Command Support (SOCS) Center

Created from the remaining command functions, the SOCS is a process-oriented support center that provides personnel and special staff support to the headquarters and its components. The SOCS includes public affairs, executive services, medical, chaplain, historian, equal opportunity, security, quality integration, engineering, protocol, headquarters command, and joint secretariat support services. The USSOCOM chief of staff directs the center.

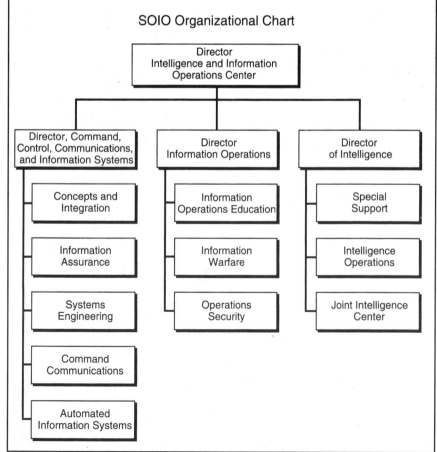

SOIO Organizational Chart

Director
Intelligence and Information
Operations Center

Director, Command, Control, Communications, and Information Systems
- Concepts and Integration
- Information Assurance
- Systems Engineering
- Command Communications
- Automated Information Systems

Director Information Operations
- Information Operations Education
- Information Warfare
- Operations Security

Director of Intelligence
- Special Support
- Intelligence Operations
- Joint Intelligence Center

Above: Instruction at the Air Force Special Operations School, Hurlburt Field, Florida, covers a wide range of strategic and tactical considerations.

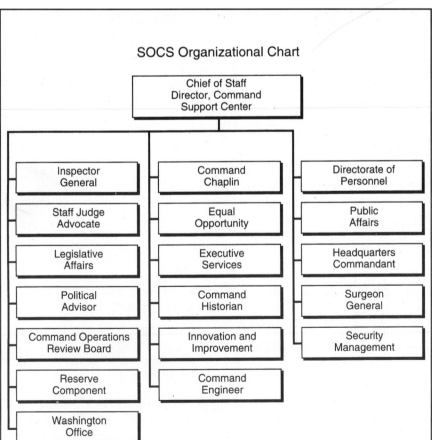

SOCS Organizational Chart

Chief of Staff Director, Command Support Center

Inspector General	Command Chaplin	Directorate of Personnel
Staff Judge Advocate	Equal Opportunity	Public Affairs
Legislative Affairs	Executive Services	Headquarters Commandant
Political Advisor	Command Historian	Surgeon General
Command Operations Review Board	Innovation and Improvement	Security Management
Reserve Component	Command Engineer	
Washington Office		

Above: Armed with German MP5 9mm submachine guns, members of Navy Sea-Air-Land (SEAL) team during a public demonstration of their skills.

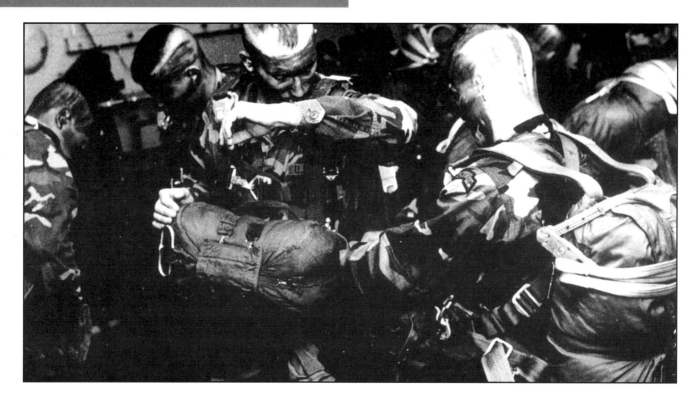

Above: Men from Army Special Operations Command 75th Ranger Regiment prepare for an airborne assault aboard a transport aircraft.

Service Component Commands

USSOCOM's mission can be effectively accomplished only with the support of the Army, Navy, and Air Force and elements of the Marine Corps who provide quality personnel, common equipment, base operations support, logistical sustainment, and core skills training. This support allows USCINCSOC to focus on SOF-specific training and equipment, as well as the integration of SOF into the entire range of military operations.

All active and reserve Army, Navy, and Air Force Special Operations Forces based in the United States are assigned to USSOCOM. The USSOCOM's service component commands of USSOCOM are the U.S. Army Special Operations Command, the Naval Special Warfare Command, and the Air Force Special Operations Command. The Joint Special Operations Command is assigned as a sub-unified command of USSOCOM. Component command organization and force structure are presented in detail in the accompanying charts.

Joint Special Operations Command (JSOC)

The Joint Special Operations Command was established in 1980 and is located at Fort Bragg, North Carolina. JSOC is a joint headquarters designed to study special operations requirements and techniques; ensure interoperability and equipment standardization;

plan and conduct joint special operations exercises and training; and develop joint special operations tactics.

Theater Assets: Theater Special Operations Commands (SOCs)

The theater Special Operations Command, established as a sub-unified command of the combatant unified commands, is the geographic C-in-C's source of expertise in all areas of special operations, providing the C-in-C with a separate element to plan and control the employment of joint SOF in military operations. Theater SOCs normally exercise operational control of SOF (except civil affairs and psychological operations) within each geographic C-in-C's area of responsibility. Additionally, the SOCs can provide the nucleus for the establishment of a Joint Special Operations Task Force (JSOTF) or Joint Task Force when formed.

The theater SOC commander is responsible to the geographic C-in-C for planning and conducting joint special operations in the theater, ensuring that SOF capabilities are matched to mission requirements, exercising operational control of SOF for joint special operations, and advising the C-in-C and component commanders in theater on the proper employment of SOF. While the USCINCSOC provides funding and personnel for the SOCs, each SOC reports directly to the geographic C-in-C.

Operational experience, both in peace and war, indicates that SOF are most effective when closely integrated into campaign plans. The SOCs' efforts have paid great dividends

in this regard. The result is the full integration of SOF into theater and country peacetime plans, as well as the geographic C-in-Cs' war plans. The key role of the theater SOCs and the recent accomplishments of SOF in the theaters are highlighted in following pages.

CA and PSYOP Support to Geographic C-in-Cs

CA and PSYOP are Special Operations Forces' principal missions, but their functional command and control relationships are structured to support both special operations and conventional forces. USSOCOM provides forward-deployed CA and PSYOP support to the geographic C-in-Cs to accomplish planning and coordination for forward presence, peacetime support, contingency, and wartime operations.

CA support provided to combatant commanders comes from both the active and reserve components. Although the reserve component comprises approximately 90 percent of the total CA force, the support offered by all CA forces is integrated into theater engagement and contingency and operational planning.

PSYOP support to geographic C-in-Cs is vital to attaining theater objectives. Normally located on the geographic C-in-C's staff, PSYOP forward liaison detachments (FLDs) are an important resource in planning politically sensitive, yet invaluable, PSYOP. Currently, the only PSYOP group in the active component force structure, the 4th PSYOP Group (Airborne), provides FLDs to USEUCOM, USPACOM, USSOUTHCOM, and United Nations Command (Korea).

U.S. ARMY SPECIAL OPERATIONS COMMAND (USASOC)

The U.S. Army Special Operations Command, headquartered at Fort Bragg, North Carolina, commands, and is responsible to USSOCOM for the readiness of, Army Special Operations Forces (ARSOF), including active, Army National Guard, and U.S. Army Reserve forces consisting of Special Forces, Rangers, special operations aviation, civil affairs (CA), psychological operations (PSYOP), and combat- and service-support units which may be deployed to unified combatant commands around the world.

These units include:

- Five active and two Army National Guard (ARNG) Special Forces groups totaling fifteen active and six ARNG battalions.
- One active Ranger regiment with three battalions.
- An active special operations aviation regiment with one detachment in Puerto Rico.
- Four reserve CA commands, seven reserve CA brigades, and one active and twenty-four reserve CA battalions.

- One active and two reserve PSYOP groups totaling five active and eight reserve PSYOP battalions.
- One active special operations support command composed of one special operations signal battalion, one special operations support battalion, and six special operations theater support elements.
- Two active and two reserve chemical reconnaissance detachments (CRD).
- The John F. Kennedy Special Warfare Center and School

Rangers

Providing a responsive strike force and fighting primarily at night, Army Rangers rely on elements of surprise, teamwork, and basic soldiering skills to plan and conduct special missions in support of U.S. policy and objectives. Having taken part in every major combat operation in which the U.S. has been involved since the end of the Vietnam War, they are capable of deploying rapidly by land, sea, or air to conduct direct-action operations.

Above: Members of Army 10th Special Forces group (Airborne) suspended beneath a UH-60 Blackhawk helicopter during insertion/extraction practice.

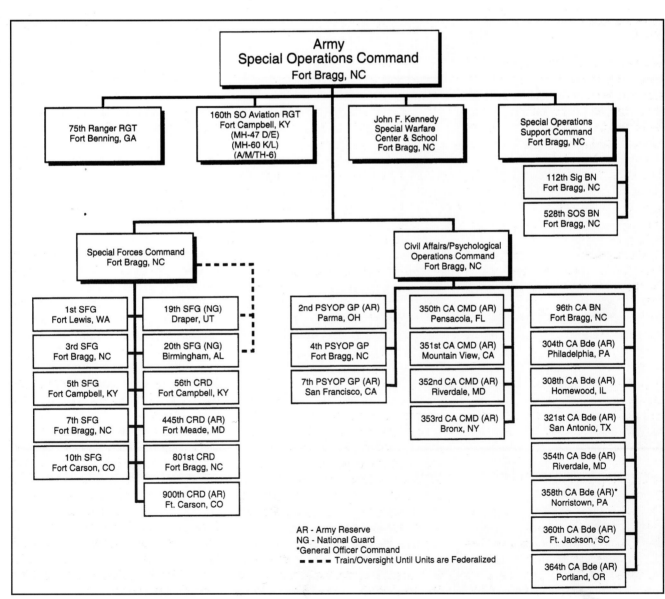

85

Above: 160th Special Operations Aviation Regiment soldiers aboard an MH-47 Chinook after a fast-rope insertion/extraction operation.

Below: Constant training hones Army Special Forces' skills. Here, men "maintain security" at a mock-up site at Army SOC headquarters, Fort Bragg.

Aviation

The 160th Special Operations Aviation Regiment employs state-of-the-art equipment to provide extremely accurate heliborne lift and attack capabilities in a wide range of mission profiles, including force insertion and extraction, aerial security, armed attack, electronic warfare, and command and control support.

Special Forces (SF)

Special Forces soldiers receive training in a variety of individual and special skills. These skills include operations, intelligence, communications, medical aid, engineering, and weapons. SF soldiers train, advise, and assist host-nation military or paramilitary forces in a variety of conventional and unconventional warfare techniques. SF soldiers are highly skilled operators, trainers, and teachers. Regionally oriented, they are specially trained in their respective area's native language and culture.

Civil Affairs (CA)

Civil affairs units support the commander's relationship with civil authorities, and the civilian populace, by promoting mission legitimacy and thereby enhancing military effectiveness. U.S. Army Reservists, comprising 97 percent of the force, bring civilian job skills to support civil military operations and civil administration. Some of these specialized skills include: public safety, agriculture, finance, economy, and support of dislocated civilian operations.

Psychological Operations (PSYOP)

PSYOP units support operations across the operational continuum to induce or reinforce attitudes and behaviors favorable to U.S. national goals in selected foreign-target audiences. Intense cross-cultural and language training provide PSYOP personnel with an invaluable regional orientation.

Special Operations Chemical Reconnaissance Detachment (CRD)

CRDs conduct chemical reconnaissance in permissive, semi-permissive, and denied areas for special operations force commanders and theater C-in-Cs. These special detachments are the only CRDs with this mission within the U.S. Army.

Special Operations Support Command (SOSCOM)

SOSCOM provides combat service support, combat health support, and signal support to Army Special Operations Forces. To support this complex and demanding mission, the command's subordinate units (the 528th Support Battalion and the 112th Special Operations Signal Battalion) provide the necessary connectivity to sustain and support ARSOF around the world.

The John F. Kennedy Special Warfare Center and School

The John F. Kennedy Special Warfare Center and School – the Army's special operations university – is responsible for special operations training, leader development, doctrine, and personnel advocacy. The center and school's Training Group conducts the complete spectrum of special operations training.

KEY COMBAT UNITS

The 75th Ranger Regiment

Rangers are the premier airfield seizure and raid unit in the Army. A typical Ranger battalion or regiment mission would involve seizing an airfield for use by follow-on general purpose forces and conducting raids on key targets of operational or strategic importance. Once secured, follow-on airland or airborne forces are introduced into theater and relieve the Ranger force so that it may conduct planning for future SOF operations.

The 75th Ranger Regiment, headquartered at Fort Benning, Georgia, is composed of three Ranger battalions:

- 1st Battalion, Hunter Army Airfield, Georgia;
- 2nd Battalion, Fort Lewis, Washington;
- 3 rd Battalion, Fort Benning, Georgia.

Each of the three Ranger Battalions is identical in organization. Each consists of three rifle companies and a headquarters and headquarters company. Each battalion is authorized 580 Rangers. However, the battalions may be up to 15 percent over-manned to make allowances for schools and TDYs.

Each battalion can deploy anywhere in the world with 18 hours' notice. Because of the importance the Army places on the 75th Ranger Regiment, it must possess a number of capabilities, including: infiltrating and exfiltrating by land, sea, and air; conducting direct action operations; conducting raids; recovery of personnel and special equipment; conducting conventional or special light-infantry operations.

Ranger units have a limited anti-armor capability (84mm Carl Gustav and Javelin) and lack organic indirect fire support (60mm mortars only). The only air defense artillery (ADA) system is the Stinger. Ranger units have no organic combat support or combat service support and deploy with only five days of supplies. There are no organic transportation assets. Ranger units require logistical and

Above: U.S. Army Rangers prepare to fire a Carl Gustav 84mm recoilless rifle, part of the 75th Ranger Regiment's limited anti-armor capability.

Below: 75th Rangers Regiment soldiers with a variety of weapons undergoing training in Military Operations in Urban Terrain (MOUT).

mission support from other services and/or agencies. Ranger battalions are light infantry and have only a few vehicles and crew-served weapons systems.

Standard weapon systems per battalion are:

- 84mm Ranger Antitank Weapons System (RAWS): 16
- 60mm mortars: 6
- M240G machine guns: 27
- M249 Squad Automatic Weapons (SAW): 54
- MK 19 grenade launcher: 12
- .50 cal machine gun: 12
- Javelin: 9

Each Ranger Battalion possesses twelve Ranger Special Operations Vehicles (RSOVs) for its airfield seizure mission. The vehicle is a modified Land Rover. Each vehicle carriers a six or seven-man crew. Normally, each vehicle mounts an M240G MG and either a MK-19 grenade launcher or a M2, .50 cal MG. One of the passengers mans an anti-armor weapon (RAWS, AT-4, LAW, and Javelin). The main purpose of the vehicle is to provide the operation force with a mobile, lethal defensive capability. They are not assault vehicles, but useful in establishing battle positions that provide the force some standoff capability for a short duration. Each battalion also possesses ten 250cc motorcycles that assist in providing security and mobility during airfield seizures. Most commonly used as listening

Above: Today's Rangers rely on elements of surprise, teamwork, and basic soldiering skills while deploying on direct-action operations.

Below: Relying on well-practiced teamwork, U.S. Army Special Forces soldiers secure a building's exit after a room-clearing exercise.

posts/observation posts (LP/OPs), or as an economy of force screen for early warning, the motorcycles offer the commander tactical mobility.

Special Forces Group (Airborne)

The Special Forces Group (Airborne) is comprised of one Headquarters and Headquarters Company (HHC), one Support Company (SPT CO), and three Special Forces Battalions (SF BN). The HHC consists of 28 officers, 3 warrant officers, and 58 enlisted soldiers. The SPT CO consists of 13 officers, 12 warrant officers, and 151 enlisted soldiers. Each SF BN consists of 39 officers, 24 warrant officers, and 320 enlisted soldiers.

Special Forces Groups are tasked to:

- Conduct operations in remote and denied areas for extended periods of time with little external direction and support.
- Develop, organize, equip, train, and advise or direct indigenous military and paramilitary forces.
- Plan and conduct unilateral SF operations.
- Train, advise, and assist US and allied forces or agencies.
- Perform other special operations as directed by the NCA or a unified commander.

Special Forces Groups are trained to infiltrate by air (parachute, conventional landing in fixed-/rotary-wing aircraft, rappel, and fast-rope); infiltrate/exfiltrate by sea (from surface or sub-surface mother craft, dropped by para-

Above: Army Special Forces are capable of deploying rapidly by land, sea, or air to conduct special missions in support of U.S. policy and objectives.

Below: Army 1st Special Forces Group soldiers prepare to conduct a training jump with their Thai special forces' counterparts during 1990s exercises.

Above: Alert U.S. Army Special Forces soldiers make a quiet insertion in a Zodiac rubber boat, part of the wide range of equipment available to them.

Below: A soldier disarms and disables the "enemy" during hand-to-hand combat practice carried out by members of the 10th Special Forces Group (Airborne).

chute from fixed wing aircraft, or delivered by rotary wing aircraft); and infiltrate/exfiltrate by land in all weathers and conditions.

1st Special Forces Operational Detachment – Delta

One Army SOF unit about which very little is published, and whose existence is not acknowledged by USSOCOM, is 1st Special Forces Operational Detachment - Delta (1SFOD-Delta), more familiarly known as "Delta." It was the brainchild of Colonel Charles (Charlie) A. Beckwith, US Army, who, as a major, served on an exchange posting with the British S.A.S. in 1962-63. On his return to the United States he sought to form a new unit with the same organization, ideals, and functions as the S.A.S., and eventually overcame the resistance of a very conservative chain-of-command, with Delta being officially formed on 19 November 1977. Its credo, as laid down by Charlie Beckwith, was "surprise, speed, success."

The title of this unit sometimes causes misunderstandings. 1SFOD-D was a totally new unit and had nothing to do with the "Delta Project (Detachment B-52)" set up by Army Special Forces in Vietnam in the mid-1960s (and which was, at one time, commanded by Beckwith), which was a totally different organization and concept. The reason for the name of the new unit was, in fact, quite simple. At that time, according to Beckwith, there were already three Special Forces Detachments, designated Alpha, (commanded by a captain); Bravo (by a major); and Charlie (by a lieutenant-colonel). It was, suggested Beckwith, a natural progression in titles and ranks to call the new detachment "Delta" and for it to be commanded by a colonel.

Delta was always intended for use overseas, although even then it could be deployed only at the invitation of the host government, which has not always been forthcoming. The main mission is counter-terrorism, and its priority tasks are hostage rescue, wanted-man "snatches," covert reconnaissance, and explosive ordnance disposal.

Delta is based at Fort Bragg, in a large and well-protected area known as "The Stockade." Not surprisingly, the organization of Delta reflects the ideas brought back to the United States by Colonel Beckwith. Thus, the unit is composed of a headquarters and three operational squadrons, each of which is composed of two or more troops, each of four four-man squads. There are also a support squadron, a communications squadron, and a covert troop using special equipment and techniques. The main aviation support for Delta comes from 160th Special Operations Aviation Regiment (160 SOAR) but Delta also has its own aviation troop which uses helicopters with civilian color schemes and registration in a similar manner to the British 22 S.A.S. with its two Agusta A 109s.

Delta is manned by volunteers who can come from anywhere within the Army, although, in practice, the majority come from the Green Berets and Rangers. Under Colonel Beckwith's command, Delta's selection and training processes were essentially similar to those used by the British S.A.S., although it is reasonable to assume that these have been refined and adapted over the intervening years to meet the demands of a larger Army and changed conditions.

Delta has undertaken a host of operational deployments, some of which have appeared in the Press and some of which have been learnt about through other means; there have also doubtless been deployments which remain totally classified to this day. Some of the operations have been unsuccessful, but in most the aim has been achieved. Among the known deployments have been:

- Operation Eagle Claw (24-25 April 1980). The attempted rescue of the US hostages in the embassy compound in Teheran.
- Air Garuda Boeing 737 (March 1981). A single four-man team killed four hijackers at Bangkok airport, successfully releasing hostages.
- Brigadier-General Dozier rescue (January 1982). Dozier was taken hostage by Red Brigade terrorists. A Delta team deployed to Italy, but the Italians carried out the rescue, which was successful.

Above and below: U.S. Army 1st Special Forces Operational Detachment – Delta, while not officially acknowledged, has been involved in a number of direct-action operations, including the aborted attempt to rescue U.S. hostages in Iran ("Desert One"). Helicopters used in the operation are shown aboard USS *Nimitz*.

- Operation Urgent Fury (25 October 1983). Delta and SEAL Team Six took part in the U.S. invasion of Grenada.
- Olympic Games, Los Angeles (1984). Delta played a major role in the security arrangements for the Los Angeles Games, for which Colonel Beckwith, by then retired, was the security consultant.
- TWA Flight 847 hijack (June 1985). Having been hijacked, the aircraft was flown to Algiers, where two US passengers were murdered. Delta was deployed to Europe but the Algerian government refused permission for them to take action.
- Achille Lauro Incident (October 1985), in which an American, Leon Klinghoffer, was murdered aboard the liner *Achille Lauro*, which had been hijacked by four Palestine terrorists.
- Atlanta City prison riots (1987). Delta

Right: Americans who were held hostage aboard the Italian cruise ship *Achille Lauro* on their way home aboard an Air Force C-141B Starlifter.

Below: The U.S. Army's Delta detachment carried out behind-the-lines missions in Iraq, working with Allied special operations services.

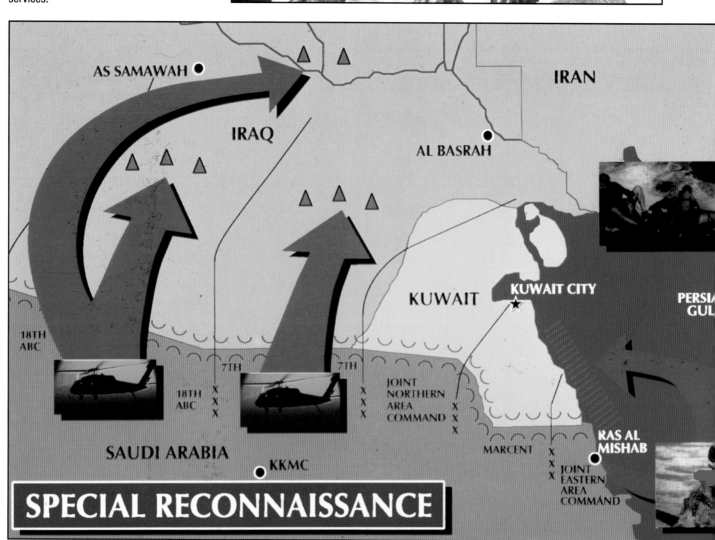

SPECIAL RECONNAISSANCE

Above: General Schwarzkopf thanks SCUD-hunters, including Delta members, who had undertaken hazardous missions during the Gulf War.

Below: U.S. Army 1st Special Forces Operational Detachment – Delta helped direct helicopters and fixed-wing aircraft to special targets in Iraq.

deployed to help quell the riot, but prisoners surrendered before they arrived.

- Operation Just Cause (1989). Delta and SEAL Team Six took part in the invasion of Panama, where their prime task was to apprehend General Noriega.
- Operation Desert Storm (1990-1). Delta deployed to Iraq, where they worked along-side British, Australian, and New Zealand S.A.S. units in seeking out and destroying and calling down fire on SCUD missile launchers.
- "Branch Davidian" siege (1993). Delta teams were sent to Waco, Texas, to join the FBI and other agencies in breaking the siege of the religious sect's headquarters. Delta was not used, possibly due to disagreements with the FBI.
- Operation Restore Hope (1993). Delta was deployed to Somalia where it became embroiled in the attempts to arrest "General" Aidid.
- Operation Uphold Democracy (1994). Delta took part in the peacekeeping operation in Haiti.
- Atlanta Olympic Games (1996). Delta was again on stand-by to deal with terrorist incidents at the Games.
- Bosnia (1996-). It is believed that Delta teams (possibly accompanied by SEAL Team Six) have deployed to Bosnia on several occasions. One possible mission was to arrest the war criminal Radovan Karadzic, although, in the event, this has never happened.

NAVAL SPECIAL WARFARE COMMAND (NAVSPECWARCOM)

The Naval Special Warfare Command, located in Coronado, California, is responsible to USSOCOM for the readiness of active and reserve Naval Special Warfare (NSW) forces. NSW Group One and Special Boat Squadron One in Coronado, California and NSW Group Two and Special Boat Squadron Two in Little Creek, Virginia, are the major operational components.

Naval Special Warfare forces are organized to support Naval and joint special operations within the theater unified command. These forces are organized, equipped, and trained to be highly mobile and quickly deployable. They comprise:

- Two active NSW groups.
- Five active NSW units stationed overseas.
- Two active special boat squadrons.
- Thirteen active patrol coastal ships.
- Three active special boat units.
- Two active Sea, Air, Land (SEAL) delivery vehicle (SDV) teams.
- Six active SEAL teams.
- The Naval Special Warfare Development Group.
- The Naval Special Warfare Center.

SEAL Teams

The single, most important trait that distinguishes SEALs from all other military forces is that SEALs are, by doctrine, maritime special forces. SEALs strike from and return to the sea, and take their name from the elements in and from which they operate (Sea, Air, Land).

Operating mainly in sixteen-man platoons from sea-based platforms, SEALs primarily conduct clandestine ground and waterborne reconnaissance and direct action missions in a maritime, littoral, or riverine environment in support of joint and fleet operations. Their stealth and clandestine methods of operation allow them to conduct multiple missions against targets that larger forces cannot approach undetected. Using state-of-the-art equipment and employing the elements of surprise, firepower and mobility, SEALs can launch attacks against unsuspecting enemies many times their size. Their training is extremely demanding, both mentally and physically, and produces combat swimmers that are considered to be the best in any service.

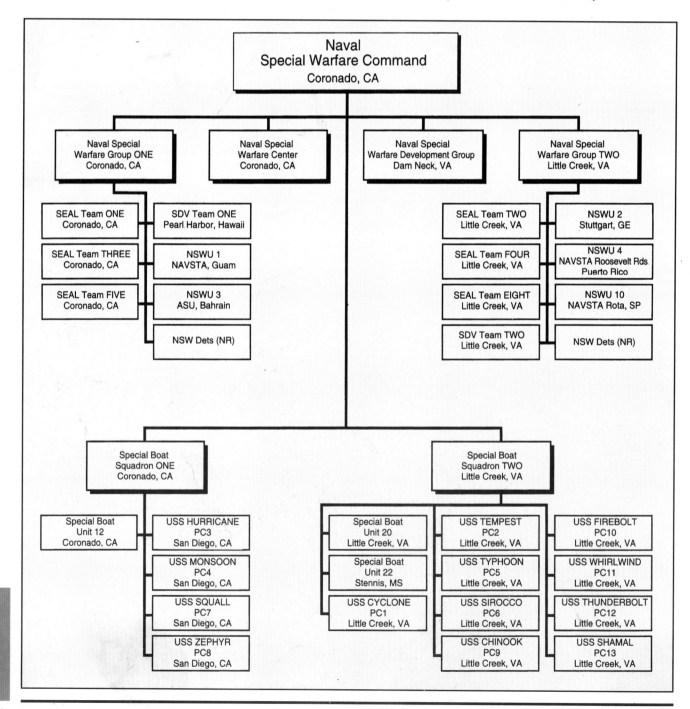

SEALs can operate independently or integrate within carrier battle groups, amphibious ready groups, and joint special operations forces. Forward-based and forward-deployed, SEALs, Special Boat Units, and SEAL Delivery Vehicle Teams can be operational anywhere in the world in 72 hours or less. With half of the world's industry and population located within one mile of an ocean or navigable river, Naval Special Warfare forces can readily execute operations across the spectrum of conflict in more than 70 percent of the sovereign nations of the world.

Below: NSW Rigid inflatable boats and equipment can be deployed on USN amphibious ships or transported in standard C-130 or larger aircraft.

Above: SEALs are, by doctrine, maritime special forces, but they can be inserted by land, sea or air to carry out direct-action missions anywhere in the world.

SEAL Delivery Vehicle (SDV) Teams

SDV teams are specially trained SEALs and support personnel who operate and maintain SDVs and dry deck shelters (DDS). SDVs are wet submersibles designed to conduct clandestine reconnaissance, direct action, and passenger delivery missions in maritime environments. DDSs deliver SDVs and specially trained forces from modified submarines. When teamed with their host submarines, SDV and DDS platoons provide the most clandestine maritime delivery capability in the world.

Above: SEALs' primary mission areas include special reconnaissance and unconventional warfare, launching attacks on unsuspecting enemies.

Special Boat (SB) Squadrons and Units

SB squadrons and units are composed of specially trained naval personnel. They are responsible for operating and maintaining a variety of special operations ships and craft, such as rigid inflatable boats and patrol coastal ships, to conduct coastal and riverine interdiction and support naval and joint special operations. These specialized units have great strategic mobility and can respond to crises worldwide. They provide the Navy's only riverine operations capability and small-craft support for SOF.

Above: Special Boat Unit 26 (SBU-26) member in a PBR Mark 2 riverine patrol boat watches USS *Seahorse* his unit is escorting into the Panama Canal.

Below: A line is rigged to the sail of USS *Woodrow Wilson* (SSBN-624) as SEALs practice entering and exiting the submerged nuclear-powered submarine.

SEAL Team Six

Following the disaster at Desert One (Operation Eagle Claw, April 1980, the aborted attempt to rescue fifty-three hostages in the US embassy, Teheran), the U.S. Navy, along with all other services, reviewed its counterterrorist organizations, capabilities, and training. This led to the creation of SEAL Team Six in October 1980 as a specialist maritime counterterrorist unit, and it became operational in April 1981. At this point an earlier counterterrorist unit, designated Mobility Team 6 (known as "Mob 6"), was disbanded. Mob 6 was an offshoot of SEAL Team Two and had been developing counterterrorist techniques before Eagle Claw, but for a variety of reasons it proved more practicable to disband it rather than to develop it into the

Below: Students on a Basic Underwater Demolition/SEAL (BUD/S) course learn to breathe only through their mouths with their masks filled with water.

Above: Armed with 9mm MP5 sub-machine guns, members of a SEAL team entertain a crowd as they secure a "prisoner" during a public demonstration.

new unit. SEAL Team Six's title was subsequently changed to the cover name Naval Special Warfare Development Group (NAVSPECWARDEVGRU), although it is quite clear that, while it may have a developmental role, it is basically an operational unit.

NAVSPECWARDEVGRU is located on the east coast, at Dam Neck, Virginia. The strength of the unit has not been published, but a reasonable guess would be about 200-300, organized into troops which specialize in the unit's different roles. The unit will also need its own support (headquarters, logistics, medical, supplies, etc) which probably accounts for another 200-300.

It seems reasonable to assume that SEAL Team Six/NAVSPECWARDEVGRU has been involved in covert operations, particularly

Above: Primarily, SEALs strike from and return to the sea. Here, a SEAL team member wears diving gear during a special forces exercise.

involving submarines, which have not been publicly acknowledged. However, it is known that it has been involved in operations targeted at extracting specific individuals, some of which have been successful, including two rescues of deposed, legal rulers (Scoones of Grenada in 1985 and Aristide of Haiti in 1991) and the capture of Panamanian ruler, General Noriega (1989). The unit is also reported to have been involved in attempts to capture alleged war criminals in the former Yugoslavia, although, as far as is known, none of these has, as yet, been successful. NAVSPECWARDEVGRU is known to cooperate closely with units of other nations with a similar role, including the British Special Boat Service (S.B.S.) and Italy's navy frogman group, COMSUBIN.

U.S. AIR FORCE SPECIAL OPERATIONS COMMAND (AFSOC)

The Air Force Special Operations Command, located at Hurlburt Field, Florida, is responsible to USSOCOM for the readiness of active, Air Force Reserve, and Air National Guard SOF for worldwide deployment. Three special operations wings, two special operations groups, and one special tactics group are assigned. AFSOC's Air Force Special Operations Forces (AFSOF) are comprised of highly trained, rapidly deployable airmen who are equipped with specialized, fixed- and rotary-wing aircraft to provide SOF mobility, forward presence and engagement, precision employment/strike, and information operations.

The Command has the following active, Air National Guard (ANG), and Air Force Reserve units assigned:

- One active special operations wing with eight special operations squadrons; squadrons include five fixed-wing, one rotary-wing, an aviation foreign internal defense (FID) unit, and a fixed-wing training squadron.
- Two active overseas-based special operations groups; each theater-oriented group com-prises two fixed-wing and one rotary-

wing special operations squadron, and a special tactics squadron.
- One AF Reserve special operations wing with two fixed-wing special operations squadrons.
- One ANG special operations wing with one fixed-wing special operations squadron.
- One active special tactics group with four special tactics squadrons and a combat weather squadron.
- One active flight test squadron.
- The Air Force Special Operations School.

Air Force Special Operations Forces' unique active, ANG, and AF Reserve units provide a global ability to conduct special operations missions ranging from precision application of firepower, to clandestine infiltration, exfiltration, resupply, and refueling of SOF operational elements. Capabilities include airborne radio and television broadcast for psychological operations (PSYOPs), as well as aviation FID to provide other governments military expertise for their internal development. Special tactics squadrons combine combat control, weather, and pararescue personnel to ensure air power is integrated and operable with special operations and conventional ground forces.

USAF Special Operations School

The USAF Special Operations School's (USAF-SOS) mission is to educate U.S. military and other personnel in the missions and functions of special operations. Since special operations forces routinely interact with foreign militaries and America's allies, cross-cultural issues and communications are taught in regional orientation courses. Operational courses include aviation FID, crisis response management, joint PSYOP, joint planning and staff officer courses, and revolutionary warfare.

KEY COMBAT UNITS

16th Special Operations Wing

The 16th SOW is located at Hurlburt Field, Florida and is the oldest and most seasoned unit in AFSOC. The wing's mission is to organize, train, and equip Air Force Special Operations Forces for global employment. The 16th SOW focuses on unconventional warfare, including counterinsurgency and psychological operations during operations other than war.

The 16th SOW is the largest Air Force unit within AFSOC. It operates a fleet of more than 90 aircraft with a military and civilian work

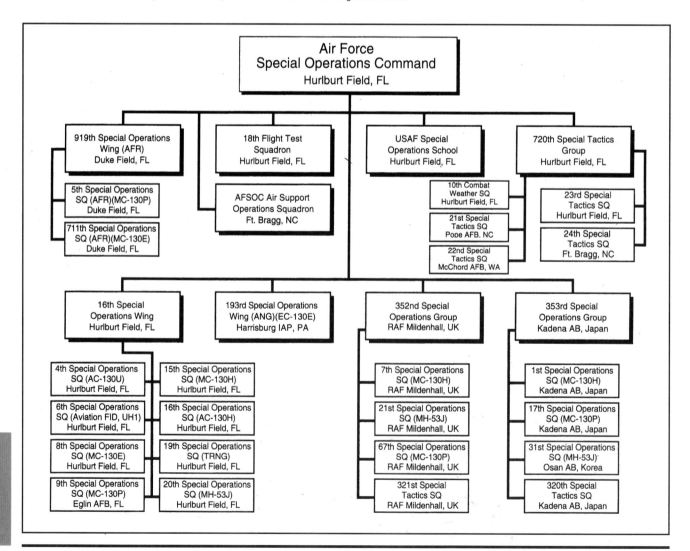

force of nearly 7,000 people. It includes the 6th Special Operations Squadron (SOS), the 4th SOS, the 8th SOS, the 9th SOS, the 15th SOS, the 16th SOS, the 20th SOS and the 55th SOS.

- The 6th Special Operations Squadron is the wing's aviation foreign internal defense (FID) unit. Its members provide US military expertise to other governments in support of their internal defense and development efforts (IDAD).

- The 8th SOS and 15th SOS employ the MC-130E Combat Talon I and MC-130H Combat Talon II aircraft, respectively, supporting unconventional warfare missions and Special Operations Forces. The MC-130 aircrews work closely with Army and Navy Special Operations Forces. Modifications to the MC-130 allow aircrews to perform clandestine missions minimizing the chances of being detected by hostile radar systems. Both units' primary missions are day and night, adverse weather, infiltration, exfiltration, and resupply of Special Operations Forces in hostile or denied territory. In addition, the MC-130E Combat Talon I is capable of clandestine penetration of hostile or denied territory to provide aerial refueling of special operations helicopters.

- The 9th SOS, at nearby Eglin AFB, flies the MC-130P Combat Shadow tanker for worldwide clandestine aerial refueling of special operations helicopters. It has the additional capability of infiltration, exfiltration, and resupply of Special Operations Forces by airdrop or airland tactics.

- The 4th SOS and 16th SOS fly the AC-130U and AC-130H Spectre gunships,

Above: AFSOC combat controllers establish drop zones, landing zones, air traffic control, medevac, and combat search and rescue services.

Below: 16th Special Operations Squadron AC-130H, headquartered at Hurlburt Field, Florida, aircraft deploy countermeasures during a training attack.

Above: Spectre Gunships operated by 16th SOW are Vietnam-era aircraft upgraded with improved sensors, fire control, and navigation suites.

respectively. Unique equipment on these modified C-130s enables crews to provide highly accurate firepower in support of both conventional and unconventional forces, day or night. Primary missions include close air support, armed reconnaissance, and air interdiction. Other missions include perimeter defense, forward air control, night search and rescue, surveillance, and airborne command and control.

- The 20th SOS employs the MH-53J Pave Low III helicopter. Its specialized mission consists of day or night, all-weather, low-level penetration of denied territory to provide infiltration, exfiltration, resupply, or fire support for elite air, ground, and naval forces.
- The 55th SOS flies the MH-60G Pave Hawk helicopter. Its mission is to provide a rapidly deployable, worldwide, multimission and combat rescue capability for

Below: AFSOC Special Tactics Teams are preferably deployed by static line or military freefall parachute for time-sensitive operations.

wartime special operations and peacetime contingency tasking. It is used to infiltrate, resupply, and exfiltrate U.S. and allied Special Operations Forces during long-range, low-level penetrations of hostile or denied territory at night.

352nd Special Operations Group

The 352nd SOG at RAF Mildenhall, United Kingdom, is the designated Air Force component for Special Operations Command Europe. Its squadrons are the 7th SOS, which flies the MC-130H Combat Talon II; the 21st SOS, equipped with the MH-53J Pave Low III; the 67th SOS, with the MC-130P Combat Shadow; and the 321st Special Tactics Squadron.

The mission of the 352nd SOG is to act as the focal point for all Air Force special operations activities throughout the European and Central Commands theaters of operation. The group is prepared to conduct a variety of high priority, low-visibility missions supporting U.S. and allied special operations forces throughout the European theater during peacetime, joint operations exercises and combat operations. It develops and implements peacetime and wartime contingency plans to effectively use fixed wing, helicopter and personnel assets to conduct infiltration, exfiltration and resupply of United States and allied Special Operations Forces.

Special Operations Command Europe is a sub-unified command of the US European Command. The 352nd SOG has three flying

Above: An MC-130 of the 352nd Special Operations Group taxis at RAF Mildenhall, UK, in support of Special Operation Command, Europe.

Below: Members of the 18th Flight Test Squadron are highly qualified technicians supporting the advanced technology elements of Air Force SOC.

squadrons, a maintenance and tactical communications squadron and a special tactics squadron. The organizations are:

- The 7th SOS – MC-130H Combat Talon II. Mission is identical to that of the 15th SOS.
- The 21st SOS – MH-53J Pave Low III helicopter. Mission is identical to that of the 20th SOS.
- The 67th SOS – MC-130P. Mission is identical to that of the 9th SOS.
- The 352nd Maintenance Squadron is responsible for maintenance of assigned fixed wing aircraft and helicopters.
- The 321st Special Tactics Squadron pararescuemen and combat controllers provide for the establishment of drop zones, landing zones, air traffic control, combat medical care and evacuation, and combat search and rescue for fixed and rotary wing assets. In addition, combat controllers trained in SOTAC conduct terminal guidance of fires delivered by fixed and rotary wing aircraft. Also, the 321st has combat weathermen assigned to provide weather support for Air Force and Army special operations.

353rd Special Operations Group

The 353rd SOG, with headquarters at Kadena Air Base, Japan, is the Air Force component for Special Operations Command Pacific. The 353rd SOG is composed of three flying

squadrons and the 320th STS. The 320th and two of the flying squadrons are located at Kadena Air Base: the 1st SOS which flies the MC-130H Combat Talon II, and the 17th SOS, which flies the MC-130P Combat Shadow. The third flying squadron is located at Osan Air Base, Korea; the 31st SOS which flies the MH-53J Pave Low III helicopter.

The group's mission is to act as the focal point for all Air Force special operations activities throughout the Pacific. The group is prepared to conduct a variety of high-priority, low-visibility air support missions for joint and allied Special Operations Forces in the region. It maintains a worldwide mobility commitment, participates in theater exercises, and supports humanitarian assistance and disaster relief operations. The group develops wartime and contingency plans to effectively use the full range of helicopter and fixed wing capabilities, to include infiltration, exfiltration and resupply of US and allied Special Operations Forces. The primary peacetime responsibility of the 353rd SOG is to oversee the training and maintenance of its assigned units. The group ensures the combat readiness of these units through comprehensive involvement in numerous theater and joint chiefs of staff-directed military exercises and training activities throughout the Pacific.

The 353rd SOG comprises the US Air Force's special operations air arm in the US Pacific Command. The commander is desig-

Above: An AFSOC MH-53 is guarded during Operation Sustain Hope which brought relief to thousands of Kosovar refugees in Albania and Macedonia.

Below: An 8th Special Operations Squadron, 353rd SOG, MC-130H Combat Talon II displays the bulbous housing for its AN/APQ-170 radar.

nated Commander, Air Force Special Operations Command, Pacific, a sub-unified command to the Special Operations Command, Pacific. The 353 rd SOG has three flying squadrons, a maintenance and tactical communications squadron and special tactics squadrons:

- The 1st SOS – MC-130H Combat Talon II, Kadena AB, Japan. Mission is identical to that of the 15th SOS.
- The 17th SOS – MC-130P Combat Shadow, Kadena AB, Japan. Mission is identical to that of the 9th SOS.
- The 31st SOS –MH-53J Pave Low III, Osan Air Base, Korea. Mission is identical to that of the 20th SOS.
- The 320th Special Tactics Squadron pararescuemen and combat controllers provide for the establishment of drop zones, landing zones, air traffic control, combat medical care and evacuation, and combat search and rescue for fixed and rotary wing assets. In addition combat controllers trained in SOTAC conduct terminal guidance of fires delivered by fixed and rotary wing aircraft. Also, the 320th has combat weathermen assigned to provide weather support for Air Force and Army special operations.

720th Special Tactics Group

The 720th STG, with headquarters at Hurlburt Field, FL, has special operations combat controllers, pararescuemen, and combat weathermen who work jointly in Special Tactics Teams (STT). There are six Special Tactics Squadrons (STS) and one Combat Weather Squadron. The 320th STS at Kadena AB, Japan and the 320th STS at RAF Mildenhall, England, are assigned to and under the operational control of the 353rd and the 352nd Special Operations Groups, respectively. The 720th also includes the 10th Combat Weather Squadron with headquarters at Hurlburt Fld, Florida, and detachments co-located with US Army Special Operations Command units.

Air Reserve and Air National Guard Components

AFSOC gains three Air Reserve Component units when the organizations are mobilized. One is the 919th Special Operations Wing (AFRES) at Duke Field, Florida, training Air Force reservists in MC-130E Combat Talon I and MC-130P Combat Shadow aircraft operations. The second is the 193rd Special Operations Group (ANG) at Harrisburg International Airport, PA., which flies the

Above: A member of the 20th Special Operations Squadron mans an M-2 .50-cal machine gun at the door of an MH-53J Pave Low helicopter.

EC-130E Commando Solo. The third component unit is the 123rd Special Tactics Flight (ANG) at Standiford Field, KY.

Special Tactics Team (STT)

The STTs are comprised of combat controllers, pararescue, and support personnel operating operate in a ground role with joint or combined Special Operations Task Forces. They can be deployed by airlift, sea-lift or overland means, airlift being the preferred method of deployment and critical for time sensitive operations. ST teams may be employed using a variety of tactical methods including: static line or military freefall parachute; Scuba, small boat or amphibious means; overland using mounted or dismounted techniques; airland via fixed or rotary wing aircraft; airmobile procedures including, rope, ladder or STABO. ST teams deploy with the minimum equipment and supplies needed to complete a mission. One C-130 can deploy a single ST team and its associated equipment.

U.S. MARINE CORPS

While the U.S. Marine Corps is not part of the U.S. Special Operations Command, no review of America's special forces would be complete without reference to the Corps in general and to some of its units in particular, since some USMC personnel have been seconded to USSOCOM, although the number is small (currently fewer than sixty). During the organization of the USSOCOM in the late 1980s, the USMC elected to remain separate from the new Command. Instead, it instituted an aggressive Special Operations Capable (SOC) training program to optimize the inherent capability of Marine Expeditionary Units (MEUs). These are 2,200-strong expeditionary intervention forces with the ability to rapidly organize for combat operations in virtually any environment.

Thus were formed forward-deployed MEU(SOC)s to conduct selected maritime special operations. MEU(SOC)s are designed to be the Marine Corps' first-on-the-scene force. Normally embarked aboard three to four ships of an Amphibious Ready Group (ARG), a MEU(SOC) unit is task-organized and comprised of a command element (CE); a reinforced infantry battalion as the ground combat element (GCE); a reinforced helicopter squadron as the aviation combat element (ACE); and a combat service support element (CSSE) designated the MEU Service Support Group (MSSG).

MEU(SOC) Operational Employment, Mission and Capabilities

The MEU(SOC)'s maritime special operations capabilities are based upon its expeditionary and amphibious nature, and are primarily an enhancement of the traditional capabilities of Marine forces afloat. These capabilities do not transform MEU(SOC)s into dedicated Special Operations Forces or national-level counter-terrorist forces rather, they make them far more useful as forward-deployed forces in a wider range of contingency and crisis-response situations.

The primary objective of the MEU(SOC) program is to provide the National Command Authorities and geographic combatant commanders with an effective means of dealing with the uncertainties of future threats, by providing forward-deployed units which offer

Below: Ever ready to hit the beaches, Special Operations Capable (SOC) Marines are valued for their distant reconnaissance and surveillance skills.

a variety of quick reaction, sea-based, crisis-response options, in either a conventional amphibious role, or in the execution of select-ed maritime special operations.

Task organized from MEU(SOC) assets is a Maritime Special Purpose Force (MSPF) that provides a special operations capable force that can be quickly tailored to accomplish a specific mission, and employed either as a complement to conventional naval operations or in the execution of a selected maritime special operations mission. Particular empha-sis is placed on operations requiring precision skills that normally are not resident in tradi-tional amphibious raid companies. Command and control of the MSPF remains with the MEU(SOC) commander. The MSPF is not designed to duplicate existing capabilities of SOF, but is intended to focus on operations in a maritime environment. The MSPF is not capable of operating independently of its par-ent MEU; operating in conjunction with the MEU, however, it is capable of conducting operations with, or in support of, SOF. The MSPF task organization can be enhanced with the addition of ARG elements such as the Assault Craft Unit Detachment (LCACs) or the Naval Special Warfare Task Unit (NSWTU) detachment assigned to the ARG.

Below: **A Special Marine Air Ground Task Force member shoots the M40A1 sniper rifle from a helicopter during an exercise in urban warfare tactics.**

The MSPF is specifically trained and equipped to conduct direct action missions using close quarters battle (CQB) skills. The capabilities of the MSPF include:
- Reconnaissance and surveillance.
- Specialized demolitions.
- In-extremis hostage recovery.
- Seizure/recovery of offshore energy facilities.
- Seizure/recovery of selected personnel or material.

Above: **A 1st Recon Battalion detachment, headquartered at Camp Pendleton, California, free-rappels from a CH-46 near Camp Reasoner.**

- Visit, board, search and seizure operations.
- Tactical recovery of aircraft and personnel.

The MEU(SOC) is task trained to operate with SOF as mission requirements dictate. This interoperability may be in the role of a supporting force or as the supported force if directed by the Chairman, Joint Chiefs of

Staff. The NSWTU (SEALs/Special Boat Unit) embarked aboard amphibious shipping may be employed in a supporting/supported role with the MSPF or other elements of the MEU(SOC). Effective operational and tactical interoperability between the MEU(SOC) and the embarked NSWTU, across the spectrum of MEU(SOC) operations, is essential. Prior to deployment, the MEU(SOC) will be required to demonstrate interoperability with the NSWTU.

As a global force-in-readiness, the MEU(SOC) is organized, trained, and equipped as a self-sustaining, general-purpose expeditionary force that possesses the capability to conduct a wide spectrum of conventional and selected maritime special operations, rather than a force which is tailored for a specific operation or area of responsibility. The immediate response utility of the MEU(SOC) requires that it be capable of commencing mission execution within six hours of receipt of a warning, or alert order. Commencement of mission execution is signified by the launch of forces by air and/or surface means. This may range from the insertion of reconnaissance and surveillance assets to the launch of an assault force.

MEU(SOC)'s mission is to provide the geographic combatant commanders with a forward-deployed, rapid crisis-response capability by conducting conventional amphibious and selected maritime special operations under the following conditions: at night; under adverse weather conditions; from over the horizon; under emissions control (EMCON); from the sea, by surface and/or by air.

The inherent capabilities of a forward-deployed MEU(SOC) are divided into four broad categories:

- **AMPHIBIOUS OPERATIONS:**
  Amphibious assault, the capability to establish a force on a hostile shore.
  Amphibious raid, the capability to conduct a swift incursion into, or temporary occupation of, an objective followed by a planned withdrawal.
  Amphibious demonstration, the capability to deceive the enemy by a show of force with the expectation of deluding the enemy into a course of action unfavorable to him.
  Amphibious withdrawal, the capability to conduct the extraction of forces by sea in naval ships or craft from a hostile or potentially hostile shore.
- **DIRECT ACTION OPERATIONS:**
  In-extremis hostage recovery, the capability to conduct recovery operations in-extremis, by means of an emergency extraction of hostages.
  Seizure/recovery of offshore energy facilities, the capability to conduct seizure, recovery, and/or destruction of offshore

Above: Recon Marines jump the surf in a Zodiak rubber boat. Their prime mission is reconnaissance ten miles past the forward edge of the battle area.

gas and oil platforms.
Visit, board, search and seizure operations, the capability to conduct vessel boarding/seizure in support of Maritime Interception Operations (MIO) on an uncooperative, underway ship.
Specialized demolition operations, the capability to conduct specialized breaching; to employ specialized demolitions in support of other special operations. This includes an explosive entry capability to facilitate close quarters battle/combat, and dynamic assault tactics/techniques.
Seizure/recovery of selected personnel or material, the capability to conduct clandestine seizure/recovery of personnel and/or sensitive items in a benign or hostile environment.
Counterproliferation of weapons of mass destruction (WMD).
- **MILITARY OPERATIONS OTHER THAN WAR (MOOTW):**
  Peacekeeping, peace enforcement, security, non-combatant evacuation, reinforcement, joint/combined training/instruction, humanitarian assistance/disaster relief operations.

Above: Marines from Task Force Mogadishu provide covering fire during a raid on a weapons cache during Operation Restore Hope, Somalia, 1993.

Below: During Urban Warrior experiments by USMC Warfighting Laboratory, Marines use a lifting device to enter a building in 1998.

ment of the overall mission.

Fire support planning, coordination, and control in a Joint/Combined Environment.

Signal intelligence (SIGINT)/Electronic Warfare (EW), the capability to conduct tactical SIGINT, limited ground based EW, and communications security (COMSEC) monitoring and analysis.

Military operations in urban terrain (MOUT), the capability to conduct operations in densely populated and built-up urban areas employing appropriate tactics, equipment, and supporting arms.

Reconnaissance and surveillance, the capability to clandestinely obtain specific, well-defined, and time-sensitive information of strategic, operational, or tactical significance.

Initial terminal guidance, the capability to clandestinely establish and operate navigational, signal, and/or electronic devices for guiding helicopter and surface waves from a designated point to a specific landing zone or beach.

Counterintelligence operations, the capability to conduct CI and human intelligence operations that protect the MEU(SOC) against espionage, sabotage, terrorism, and subversion by developing and providing information the commander can use to

• **SUPPORTING OPERATIONS:**
Tactical deception operations, the capability to design and implement operations to mislead/deceive opposing forces through electronic means, feints, ruses, demonstrations or portrayals which cause the enemy to react or fail to react in a manner that assists in the accomplish-

Above: Marines at the Military Operations in Urban Terrain (MOUT) facility experiment with a 1,400-pound Grizzly small urban mover.

Below: Force Recon companies are attached to MEU(SOC)s as the first into operations, scout swimmers, and the unit's eyes behind the lines.

undertake countermeasures to protect resources.

Airfield/port seizure.

Limited expeditionary airfield operations, the capability to conduct tactical air operations at austere locations, including short-field, unimproved runways.

Show of force operations.

Joint Task Force (JTF) enabling operations, the capability to temporarily provide organic resources, coordination, and command and control functions to any Command JTF in order to expedite the smooth transition of the JTFHQ into the area of operations.

Sniping operations, during daylight or at night, in urban and rural environments, including helicopter-borne sniper operations.

U.S.M.C. Reconnaissance

Reconnaissance groups are elite reconnaissance teams within the U.S.M.C. There are two varieties, Recon, and Force Recon. Recon operates in strictly a reconnaissance role. Force Recon's missions are analogous to the U.S. Navy SEALs (albeit that they are not under USSOCOM's command). Within the 1998 reorganization of Marine reconnaissance elements, there are Recon battalions and Force Recon companies. The Recon battalions work in support of the division gathering intelligence to something like 10 miles

Above: First and foremost, Force Recon Marines are the "shooters," carrying out sniping, quick raids, enemy captures – similar operations to those of SEALs.

past the forward edge of the battle area. The Force Recon companies gather all intelligence past this 10 mile limit. The Force Recon company having this mission is trained in more elaborate insertion/extraction methods such as jump/Scuba/SPIE rig, etc.

U.S.M.C. Fleet Anti-Terrorist Team (FAST)

Another elite Marine Corps unit, and one about which very little is published, is the Fleet Anti-Terrorist Security Team, formed in 1987 in response to the world-wide increase in threats to U.S. armed forces and government facilities. Their prime mission is to provide additional, highly trained protection over short periods, when the threat is beyond the capabilities of the usual security forces. Following the principle that "prevention is better than cure," however, FAST companies are also responsible for carrying out threat assessments, for helping security officers to prepare proper security plans, and for improving individual standards in a security force (for example, of surveillance and marksmanship).

FAST companies are some 300-strong

and can be deployed very rapidly when the need arises. Following the bombing of U.S. troops in Saudi Arabia on 25 June 1996, in which nineteen people were killed and 500 injured, FAST Marines from Norfolk, Virginia, were actually on-site within ten hours of the explosions. They then not only provided additional security by deploying their own Marines, but also carried out security assessments, which, in many cases, found the existing arrangements wanting.

FAST units have deployed with U.S. forces on numerous operations including: the Gulf War; Liberia (Operation Sharp Edge); Panama (Operations Just Cause and Promote Liberty); Haiti (Operation Safe Return); Cuban refugee evacuation (Operation Safe Passage); and the United Nations withdrawal from Somalia.

Below: Fleet Anti-Terrorist Team (FAST) soldiers question a local inhabitant during Operation Just Cause, in Panama, in December 1989.

MAJOR WEAPONS AND EQUIPMENT

Tasked to be the repository of knowledge on the world's small arms, U.S. Special Operations Forces are therefore trained on virtually every weapon likely to be found on operations anywhere in the world. Their own personal weapons are versions of the famed M16A2 rifle (the "Armalite") and Heckler & Koch .45 ACP caliber, 10-round Mk 23 SOCOM pistol, but they have a wide variety of other equipment available to them. This brief review covers major weapons systems and equipment that are subject of upgrades, excluding a wide range of intelligence, communications, and information systems. It presents weapons and equipment divided into prime SOF users, but some systems are used by more than one SOF service.

AIR FORCE SPECIAL OPERATIONS COMMAND

AC-130H/U Spectre Gunship

Dimensions: Length: 97ft 9in. Wingspan: 132ft 7in. Height: 38ft 6in.
Maximum gross weight: 155,000lb.
Powerplant: Four Allison T56-A-15 turboprops, 4,300hp per engine.
Performance: Speed, 374mph at 20,000ft. Ceiling 33,000ft, with 100,000lb payload. Range, 2,356 miles with max payload, 2,500 miles with 25,000lb cargo, 5,200 miles with no cargo. Unrefueled combat radius (1 hour loiter), 500nm.
Crew: Max 21; min tactical crew, AC-130U – 13, AC-130H – 14.

The AC-130 Gunship is a basic C-130 modified with side mounted guns and various sensors that make it highly adaptable to a variety of special missions. The Gunship can provide sustained and surgically precise firepower in a variety of scenarios. Within permissive environments, the AC-I30 is effective in the following roles: close air spport (CAS); interdiction; armed reconnaissance; point defense; escort (convoy, naval, train, rotary wing); surveillance; combat search and rescue (CSAR); landing/drop zone (LZ/DZ) support; limited airborne

Below: Thirteen AC-130U Spectres have been delivered to AFSOC. Ongoing avionics modifications include enhanced situational awareness.

command and control.

These heavily armed aircraft incorporate side-firing weapons integrated with sophisticated sensor, navigation and fire control systems to provide surgical firepower during extended loiter periods, at night and in adverse weather. The side-firing gunship delivers ordnance while in a pylon turn around the target. Targets are visible and can be attacked throughout the entire orbit and attack run-in headings are usually not desired. The Gunship is particularly effective at troops in contact (TIC) fire support.

Firing altitude depends on terrain, threat environment, and weather. Gun selection depends on target type and damage desired. To limit collateral damage, a live-fire area may be required to bore-sight weapons prior to employment. The Gunship weapons do not have a hard-kill capability against heavy armor or bunkers. However, the 105mm has Superquick fuses with both point detonation and 0.05 sec delay, concrete penetrators, and proximity fuses for airburst. All 20mm, 25mm, and 40mm have point detonate fuses. Although the AC-130H and AC-130U use very dissimilar avionics and other systems, fire support to the ground party is generally comparable.

Mission success is largely determined by the threat. The AC-I30 operates best during cover of darkness. It is extremely vulnerable during daylight operation and is most suited for operations in a low threat environment. By operating over an overcast, the AC-130U can degrade daylight threats, but must rely on the radar as its only sensor. Mission execution and desired objectives are seriously degraded by radar guided antiaircraft artillery, surface-to-air missiles, and some IR MANPAD systems. If radar threats are known or suspected, preemptive jamming or SEAD (suppression of enemy air defenses) is required. SEAD is preferable. Certain threats may dictate higher employment altitudes. However, sensor resolution decreases with altitude: as range increases fire control accuracy degrades slightly, reducing the Gunship's ability to hit point targets. The threat environment limits the use of laser illuminators (the "BURN"), as it illuminates both the aircraft and the ground party to anyone properly equipped.

Thirteen AC-130Us have been delivered for full operational capability in FY 2001. Extensive modernization is being carried out to AC-130H/U flight decks, and development is under way to equip the aircraft with more effective ammunition that will enable the aircraft to fire from beyond the range of antiaircraft weapons.

Spectre has an impressive combat history. During Vietnam, Gunships destroyed more than 10,000 trucks and were credited with many life-saving close air support missions. AC-130s suppressed enemy air defense systems and attacked ground forces during Operation Urgent Fury in Grenada. This enabled the successful assault of Point Salines airfield via airdrop and airland of friendly forces. Gunships had a starring role during

Above: **AFSOC has 14 MC-130E Combat Talons, each capable of carrying 52 SOF troops. Flight-deck avionics upgrades are planned.**

Operation Just Cause in Panama by destroying Panamanian Defense Force Headquarters and numerous command and control facilities by surgical employment of ordnance in an urban environment. As the only close air support platform in the theater, Spectre was credited with saving many friendly lives.

MC-130E/H Combat Talon I and II
Data: Essentially as AC-130; weapons and equipment fit differ.

These aircraft are equipped with inflight refueling equipment, terrain-following, terrain-avoidance radar, an inertial and GPS navigation system, and a high-speed aerial delivery system. Some MC-130Es are also equipped with the surface-to-air Fulton recovery and helicopter air refueling systems.

The mission of the MC-130E Combat Talon I and MC-130H Combat Talon II is to provide global, day, night, and adverse weather capability to airdrop and airland personnel and equipment in support of US and allied Special Operations Forces. The MC-130 conducts infiltration, exfiltration, resupply, psychological operations, and aerial reconnaissance into hostile or denied territory using airland and/or airdrop. Both Combat Talons are capable of inflight refueling, giving them an extended range limited only by crew endurance and availability of tanker support. The MC-130E Combat Talon I is capable of air refueling helicopters in support of extended helicopter operations. MC-130 missions may be accomplished either single-ship or in concert with other special

operations assets in varying multi-aircraft scenarios. Combat Talons are able to airland/airdrop personnel/equipment on austere, marked and unmarked LZ/DZs, day or night.

MC-130 missions, which may require overt, clandestine or low visibility operations, are normally flown at night using a high-low-high altitude profile. The high altitude portion is generally flown prior to penetrating and after exiting the target area. This portion of the flight will be flown at an average ground speed of 260 knots and at an altitude which minimizes fuel consumption and enemy detection. The aircraft will descend to low-level, terrain-following altitudes to penetrate hostile territory. Mission success may require the flight to be conducted at the lowest possible altitude consistent with flying safety, and at a ground speed between 220 and 260 knots. Night vision goggles (NVGs) may be used for night operations.

MC-130E/H aircraft are equipped with inflight refueling equipment, terrain-following, terrain-avoidance radar, an inertial and GPS navigation system, and a high-speed aerial delivery system. Some MC-130Es are also equipped with the surface-to-air Fulton recovery and helicopter air refueling systems.

The special navigation and aerial delivery systems are used to locate small drop zones and deliver people or equipment with greater accuracy and at higher airspeeds than possible with a standard C-130E/H aircraft.

Fourteen MC-130Es and twenty-four MC-130Hs have been delivered. Special-to-role equipment includes: APQ-170 radar in an enlarged nose radome, with a FLIR turret underneath; low-level extraction system; defensive systems. Modernization plans include improved terrain following capability and enhanced situational awareness on MC-130H.

MC-130P Combat Shadow
Data: Essentially as AC-130; weapons and equipment fit differ.

The mission of the MC-130P is clandestine formation/single-ship intrusion of hostile territory to provide aerial refueling of special operations helicopters and the infiltration, exfiltration, and resupply of special operations forces by airdrop or airland operations. To perform these missions, the primary emphasis is on night vision goggle (NVG) operations, but they can be accomplished during the day.

The MC-130P primarily flies missions at night to reduce probability of visual acquisition and intercept by airborne threats. Secondary mission capabilities may include airdrop of small special operations teams, small bundles, and combat rubber raiding craft; as well as NVG takeoff and landing procedures, tactical airborne radar approaches, and inflight refueling as a receiver.

Some aircraft have been modified with the Universal Air Refueling Receptacle Slipway Installation (UARRSI) system for inflight refueling as a receiver and all aircraft are modified with the self-contained navigation systems (SCNS) and Global Positioning System (GPS). The Special Operations Forces Improvement (SOFI) modification gives the aircraft an NVG HUD, a new modified radar, and an Infrared Detection System (IDS), greatly increasing the range and navigational accuracy.

The aircraft normally carries eight crewmembers. Depending on mission profile and duration, additional crewmembers are carried. All crewmembers are NVG/formation and helicopter air refueling qualified. Special qualifications include high altitude low opening (HALO) airdrop, NVG airland, formation lead, inflight refueling (IFR), and Rigging Alternate Method Zodiac (RAMZ).

The MC-130P employs night terrain contour (NTC) procedures using NVGs. The profile is flown at 500 feet above ground level using terrain masking. If necessary, the mission can be flown with visual and electronic-controlled emissions. The range of the mission depends on several factors: length of time on the low-level route, enroute weather, winds, and the air refueling offload requirements. Portions of the profile may be flown at high altitude to minimize fuel consumption. NTC procedures will be used to avoid enemy detection in a non-permissive environment to get the aircraft to the objective area.

Air refueling is the primary mission of the MC-130P. The MC-130P normally flies in a formation of aircraft to provide the capability of multiple simultaneous refueling of large helicopter formations. An airborne spare tanker is also a part of the formation.

AFSOC MC-130P (referred to as the HC-130 prior to 1996) were deployed to Saudi Arabia and Turkey in support of Desert Storm. They operated from main bases and remote locations. Their missions included air refueling of Special Operations Forces helicopters over friendly and hostile territory, psychological operations, and leaflet drops.

EC-130 Commando Solo
Data: Essentially similar to AC-130.

Commando Solo is an airborne electronic broadcasting system utilizing four EC-130E RivetRider (RR) aircraft operated by the 193rd Special Operations Group, Pennsylvania Air National Guard. Commando Solo conducts psychological operations and civil affairs broadcast missions in the standard AM, FM, HF, TV and military communications bands. Missions are flown at maximum altitudes possible to ensure optimum propagation patterns. This system may also be used to: support disaster assistance efforts by broadcasting public

information and instruction for evacuation operations; provide temporary replacement for existing transmitters or expanding their areas of coverage; other requirements, which involve radio and television broadcasting in its frequency, range.

The EC-130 flies during either day or night scenarios and is air-refuelable. A typical mission consists of a single-ship orbit, which is offset from the desired target audience. The targets may be either military or civilian personnel. Secondary missions include command and control communications countermeasures (C3CM) and limited intelligence gathering. Six aircraft have been modified to EC-130E specifications.

The EC-130 was deployed to both Saudi Arabia and Turkey in support of Desert Shield and Desert Storm. Their missions included broadcasts of "Voice of the Gulf," and other programs intended to convince Iraqi soldiers to surrender. More recently, in 1994, Commando Solo was utilized to broadcast radio and television messages to the citizens and leaders of Haiti during Operation Uphold

Above: An MC-130P Combat Shadow about to refuel an MH-53M Pave Low IV during a humanitarian aid mission over flooded Mozambique in March 2000.

Below: Six C-130Es have been modified to EC-130E Commando Solo status. Besides PSYOP broadcasts, they can be used to jam enemy communications.

Democracy. The EC-130s deployed early in the operation, highlighting the importance of PSYOP in avoiding military and civilian casualties. President Aristide was featured on the broadcasts which contributed significantly to the orderly transition from military rule to democracy.

MH-53J/M Pave Low III/IV
Dimensions: Length, 88ft. Height, 25ft. Rotary diameter, 72ft.
Maximum takeoff weight: 50,000lb.

Below: In support of suppressive fire support tactics, the tail gunner in an MH-53J Pave Low helicopter blasts rapid rounds from his 7.62mm minigun.

Powerplant: Two General Electric T64-GE/-100 engines, 4,330shp per engine.
Performance: Speed: 130 knots; range, 600nm (unlimited with aerial refueling); ceiling, 16,000ft.
Armament: Combination of three 7.62mm miniguns or .50 caliber machine guns.
Crew: Two officers (pilots) and four enlisted (two flight engineers and two aerial gunners).

The Pave Low heavy-lift helicopter is the largest and most powerful helicopter in the Air Force inventory, and the most technologically advanced helicopter in the world. The terrain-following and terrain-avoidance radar, forward-looking infrared sensor, inertial navigation system with GPS, along

Above: Army Special Forces jump into a river from an AFSOC 20th Special Operations Squadron MH-53 Pave Low III during joint exercises.

with a projected map display, enable the crew to follow terrain contours as low as 100ft and avoid obstacles even in adverse weather. It is a night, adverse-weather special operations weapon system that was designed to be a flight lead platform for less capable aircraft. The primary mission of the MH-53J is to conduct covert low-level, long-range undetected penetration into denied areas, day or night, in adverse weather for infiltration, exfiltration, or resupply of Special Operations Forces to include airdrops and heavy-lift sling operations. The aircraft can perform a variety of other missions including shipboard operations, radar vectoring, and CSAR.

Under the Air Force's Pave Low IIIE program, all Air Force H-53s were modified and designated MH-53Js. Their modifications include improved Pave Low avionics, satellite communications, shipboard modifications and structural improvements. All MH-53Js are modified for shipboard operations and feature automatic main rotor blade and tail rotor pylon fold. The MH-53J is also equipped with armor plating and a combination of three guns, 7.62mm miniguns or .50 caliber machine guns. It can be equipped with 27 troop seats or 14 litters. An external cargo hook has a 20,000lb capacity. This highly modified aircraft is equipped with a rack of navigation, communication, special/auxiliary equipment, and defensive systems.

Six of the older MH-53Js are being de-modified to TH-53Bs exclusively for use in training. Twenty-five aircraft are to be upgraded with interactive Defensive Avionics System/Multi-mission Advanced Tactical Terminal (IDAS/MATT) and redesignated as M models.

The MH-53J has three weapons stations: left

window, right door, and ramp. Each station can mount either an XM-218 .50 caliber machine gun or GAU-2 B/A 7.62mm minigun. A crewmember at each station manually operates the weapons. The weapons are used primarily for self-defense and enemy suppression. The helicopter was not designed for use as an attack gunship platform. However, the helicopter weapons are capable of providing suppressive fire support for teams on the ground. Crewmembers are trained to fly L attack, dogbone, racetrack, figure 8 and spooky gun patterns as per AFSOCI 11-208 for fire support missions. Weapons training, conducted during both day and night, is routine with an average of two missions per week per crewmember.

The typical gun configuration is a GAU-2 B/A 7.62 minigun at the left and right station with a GAU-18 .50 cal on the tail. The minigun is normally used for soft targets and troop suppression, which requires a high rate of fire (2,000-4,000 rounds per minute). The .50-cal allows the helicopter to engage light armor and reinforced positions at greater ranges. Each weapon system is capable of mounting an Infrared Aiming Device (IRAD) which enhances target acquisition. The type of threat and mission requirements will dictate the weapons configuration.

MH-60G Pave Hawk
Data: Essentially as MH-60J/M.

The MH-60G Pave Hawk is a modern, medium-lift, special operations helicopter for missions requiring medium-to-long-range infiltration, exfiltration, and resupply of Special Operations Forces on land or sea. In addition, the SOF-unique mission equipment allows this aircraft to be used for recovery of injured special operations personnel. The MH-60G is equipped with forward-looking infrared radar to better enable the crew to follow terrain contours and avoid obstacles at night. The Air Force has 55 Pave Hawks in the active component and 25 in the Reserves.

The MH-60G's primary wartime missions are infiltration, exfiltration and resupply of special operations forces in day, night, or marginal weather conditions. Other missions include combat search and rescue. The MH-60G, a highly modified variant of the UH-60A Black Hawk, offers increased capability in range (endurance), navigation, communications, and defensive systems. The MH-60G can be deployed to support a full range of special air warfare activities to include special operations, psychological operations, and civil affairs.

Defensive equipment includes ALQ-144 infrared countermeasures (IRCM) system, hover infrared suppression system, and improved flare and chaff dispensing systems. Defensive armaments include a forward cabin-mounted 7.62mm minigun firing either 2,000 or 4,000 rpm and cabin-mounted .50-cal machine guns. With the addition of the external stores support system (ESSS), the aircraft can carry fixed forward-firing armaments for use as a defensive and escort aircraft. Each ESSS wing can carry two 7- or 19-shot, 2.75-inch folding fin aerial rocket pods or dual 20mm cannons/.50-cal machine guns.

The MH-60G can be successfully employed in the low-to-medium threat environment. As the level of threat increases above this, the chance of detection will increase, decreasing the probability of success. The probability of success will also decrease as the total number of aircraft in the mission increases due to an additional possibility of detection (i.e., larger multi-ship or dissimilar type formations). The requirement to operate from a Forward Area Arming and Refueling Point (FAARP) will also decrease the probability of success due to the extended exposure time. The MH-60G operates at low altitudes over land and water. The aircraft will normally be employed as part of a larger vertical-lift package, which may require dissimilar multi-ship formations. The MH-60G can operate into unprepared, unlighted, uncontrolled landing zones 50 yards or larger in diameter.

The MH-60G can be deployed by airlift, sealift, or self-deployed. The preferred deployment option is airlift using a C-5, and is essential if rapid deployment is required. A C-5 can transport a maximum of five MH-60Gs. The aircraft can be broken down for shipment in less than one hour and off-loaded and rebuilt at the location in less than two hours. The optimum deployment package is four MH-60Gs via C-5. Due to the rapid tear down and buildup times, it is normally faster to air transport the aircraft rather than self-deploy when distances exceed 1,500nm using aerial refueling, or 1,000nm using ground refueling. Deployments can be worldwide using a main base or a limited/standby base with host support. Deployments can be conducted in a deceptive or low-visibility mode.

Air Mobility Command C-141 and C-5 SOLL II
The C-141/C-5/C-17 SOLL II forces from the Air Mobility Command (AMC) are capable of conducting clandestine formation or single-ship intrusion of hostile territory to provide highly reliable, self-contained, precision airdrop and airland of personnel and equipment. The assumed mission concept will be day/night, low-level, without the use of external aids. Mission success is enhanced by minimum lighting, minimum communications, deceptive course changes, and preplanned avoidance of enemy radar/air defenses and populated areas. Each aircraft is well-suited for many special operations applications due to their load-carrying capability, ability to operate into short austere runways, and their normal, known signature.

CV-22 Osprey
Dimensions: Fuselage length, 57ft 4in (stowed, wing fore and aft, 62ft 7in). Width, proprotors turning, 84ft 7in. Width, blades folded, 18ft 5in. Max height, 22ft 7in.
Weight: Max takeoff, 47,500lb for normal vertical takeoff; 55,000lb STOL; 60,500lb self-deployment.
Powerplant: Two Allison T406-AD-400 turboshafts, each 6,150shp.
Performance: Max speed, 377 knots; service ceiling, 26,000ft; range, 515nm amphibious assault; self-deployment range, 2,100nm.
Crew: 2 flight crew, 24 troops or 12 litters plus attendants, depending on role.

The missions of the new tilt-rotor CV-22 Osprey are to conduct long-range, night and adverse-weather infiltration, exfiltration, resupply, medical evacuation, and selected rescue and recovery. It is a variant of USMC MV-22 vertical/short takeoff or landing (V/STOL) aircraft with defensive suite upgrades. Capabilities include: aerial refueling; terrain following/terrain avoidance; precision navigation. It will self-deploy from U.S. bases.

Roll-out was in July 2000. Fifty aircraft are planned for procurement: initial operational capability (IOC) is scheduled for FY 2004.

Below: AFSOC has earmarked the tilt-rotor CV-22 for a quantum leap in long-range, adverse-weather covert-penetration missions from 2004 onwards.

ARMY SPECIAL OPERATIONS COMMAND

AH-6J Light Attack Helicopter

Dimensions: Length, 24ft 7in. Width, 4ft 7in. Height, 8ft 9in (9ft 9in with extended undercarriage); rotor diameter 27ft 5in.

Weights: Max takeoff 3,750lb with external load.

Powerplant: Allison 250-C30 turboshaft, 650shp.

Performance: Max speed, 152 knots at sea level; service ceiling, 16,000ft; range, 206nm at sea level.

Armament: see below.

The AH-6J is a highly modified version of the McDonnell Douglas 530 series commercial helicopter. The aircraft is a single turbine engine, dual flight control, light attack helicopter. It is primarily employed in close air support of ground troops, target destruction raids, and armed escort of other aircraft. The AH-6J normally is flown by two pilots. Overwater operations require two pilots.

The AH-6J is capable of mounting a variety of weapons systems. Normal aircraft configuration consists of two 7.62mm miniguns with 1,500 to 2,000 rounds per gun, and two seven-shot 2.75in rocket pods.

The following are additional configurations:

- The M134 7.62mm Minigun is a six-barrel, air-cooled, link-fed, electrically driven Gatling gun, with a 1,000 yard maximum effective range and a tracer burnout at 900 yards. The weapon has a rate of fire of 2,000 or 4,000 rounds per minute. The ammo can, two per aircraft, holds a maximum of 2,625 rounds of ball, tracer, low light tracer, or sabot launched armor piercing (SLAP) ammo.
- M261 seven-tube rocket launcher. This system fires a 2.75in folding fin aerial rocket (FFAR) with a variety of special purpose warheads, including: 10lb and 17lb high explosive

Below: A total of MH-6 Mission Enhancement Little Bird (MELB) are on order, fitted with aircraft survivability and avionics modifications.

(HE) warheads for light armor and bunker penetration (bursting radius of 8-10 yards for a 10lb warhead, 12-15 yards for the 17lb warhead), with either proximity or contact fuse; the anti-personnel flechette warhead, filled with 2,200 flechettes; white phosphorous; white and IR illumination warheads, providing up to 120 seconds of overt light or 180 seconds of IR light; the multi-purpose submunitions (MPSM) warhead, containing nine submunitions which are effective against light armor and personnel; and a warhead containing the CS riot control agent. The 2.75in FFAR can be used as a point target weapon at ranges from 100 to 750 yards and an area fire weapon at ranges up to 6,500 yards.

- M260 Rocket Launcher. 19-shot 2.75in FFAR rocket pod; all other data is the same as above.
- AGM-114 Hellfire. The Hellfire is a 100lb semi-active laser guided missile, capable of defeating any known armor. Missile launchers attach to the aircraft in pairs and are mounted on the outboard stores. Each launcher can hold two missiles, for a total of four missiles. The minimum engagement range is 550 yards to a maximum of 8,800 yards. The missile can be designated by any ground or air NATO standard laser designator, including the AESOP FLIR (if available).
- .50 cal machine gun or 40mm MK 19 automatic grenade launcher may be substituted for 7.62mm minigun in some configurations.

Mission equipment includes:

- Communications equipment capable of secure operations including UHF, VHF, and the Motorola Sabre VHF. SATCOM is installed on some aircraft and available as an option on all aircraft.
- Forward Looking Infrared (FLIR), a controllable, infrared surveillance system which provides a TV video-type infrared image of terrain features and ground or airborne objects of interest. The FLIR is a passive system and detects long wavelength radiant IR energy emitted, naturally or artificially, by any object in daylight

or darkness. Some aircraft may be equipped with the AESOP FLIR, which is a laser range finder/designator that allows the AH-6J to detect, acquire, identify, and engage targets at extended ranges with laser guided munitions.

MH-6J

Data: Essentially as AH-6J.

The MH-6J is the light utility helicopter modified to externally transport up to six combat troops and their equipment and is capable of conducting overt and covert infiltrations, exfiltrations, and combat assaults over a wide variety of terrain and environmental conditions. It is also used for command and control and reconnaissance missions. Its small size allows for rapid deployability in C-130, C-141, C-17 and C-5 transport aircraft. Aircraft modifications and aircrew training allow for extremely rapid upload and download times.

The basic MH-6 configuration consists of the External Personnel System mounted on each side of the aircraft, for a total of six external and two internal seating positions. The aircraft can be rapidly configured for fast-rope and STABO operations. Motorcycle racks provide the capability to insert and extract up to two motorcycles. Some aircraft are equipped with Forward Looking Infrared Radar (FLIR):, which is a passive system that provides an infrared image of terrain features and ground or airborne objects of interest. Defensive systems. Each aircraft is equipped with the APR 39 Radar Warning Receiver System, which detects and identifies hostile search/acquisition and fire control radars and provides audio and video alerts to the flight crew.

The MH-6 can be deployed by any Air Force transport aircraft. A C-141 is capable of transporting up to six MH-6s and a C-130 is able to transport up to three MH-6s, with a rapid upload/offload capability. MH-6s can offload, buildup, and depart within 15 minutes. Self-deployment is unlimited with refuel support at ground or surface vessel locations every 270nm.

A/MH-6 Mission Enhancement Little Bird (MELB)

Data: Essentially as AH-6J.

The MELB's mission is to conduct and support short-range, infiltration/ exfiltration, resupply operations in hostile areas, and selected personnel recovery missions; provide surgical-point and small-area target destruction/neutralization with provisions for close-air fire support; it also includes shipboard, platform, over-water, and urban operations. Production began in FY 2000, and a total of 40 MELBs will be supplied. Aircraft survivability equipment modifications and avionics upgrades are planned.

The maximum gross weight has been increased to 4,700lb. It has an upgraded six-bladed main and four-bladed tail rotor system; FLIR equipment; improved light-weight plank system; external conformal auxiliary fuel tanks. Weapons include minigun, Hellfire, Stinger, 2.75in rockets.

MH-60 Blackhawk

Dimensions: Length, rotors turning, 64ft 10in. Width, fuselage, 7ft 9in; rotor diameter, 53ft 8in; height, 16ft 10in.

Weight: Max takeoff 23,500lb with external load.

Powerplant: Two GE T700-GE-701C turboshafts, each 1,870shp max.

Performance: Max speed, 195 knots; service ceiling, 19,150ft; self-deployment range, 1,150nm.

Crew: 2 flight crew plus up to 14 fully equipped passengers.

The primary mission of the Army SOF's MH-60 is to conduct overt or covert infiltration, exfiltration, and resupply of SOF across a wide range of environmental conditions. An armed version, the Direct Action Penetrator (DAP), has the primary mission of armed escort and fire support. Secondary missions of the MH-60 include external load, CSAR and MEDEVAC operations. The MH-60 is capable of operating from fixed base facilities, remote sites, or ocean going vessels.

The 160th SOAR(A) operates three models of the Blackhawk:

• The MH-60K (Blackhawk) is a highly modified twin-engine utility helicopter based on the basic UH-60 airframe but developed specifically for the special operations mission. Improvements include aerial refueling capability, an advanced suite of aircraft survivability equipment, and improved navigation systems, including multi-mode radar to further improve pinpoint navigation in all environments and under the harshest conditions. Twenty-three MH-60Ks have been delivered to Army SOF, and upgrades of aircraft survivability and avionics are under way.

• The MH-60L is a highly modified version of the standard US Army Blackhawk, configured for special operations use.

• The MH-60L Direct Action Penetrator (DAP) is an MH-60L modified to mount a variety of offensive weapons systems. Its mission is to conduct attack helicopter operations utilizing area fire or precision guided munitions and armed infiltration or exfiltration of small units. It is capable of conducting direct action missions as an attack helicopter or has the capability to reconfigure for troop assault operations. In the direct action role, it would not normally be used as a primary transport for troops or supplies because of high gross weights. The DAP is capable of conducting all missions during day, night, or adverse weather conditions. It can provide armed escort for employment against threats to a helicopter formation. Using team tactics, the DAP is capable of providing suppression or close air support (CAS) for formations and teams on the ground.

The following are standard systems and equipment always on board the MH-60 during tactical missions:

• Communications: the MH-60 avionics package consists of FM, UHF (HAVE QUICK II capable), VHF, HF, Motorola Saber, and SATCOM. MH-60K includes SINCGARS. All are secure capable.

• FLIR.

• Door guns: six-barrel 7.62mm miniguns firing A165, 7.62mm ball, A257, 7.62mm low light ball, and SL66, armor piercing sabot. One gun each is mounted outside both the left and right gunner's windows and is normally operated by the crew chiefs. Sighting is by open steel sites, aimpoint, or AIM-1 laser.

• Ballistic armor subsystem: fabric-covered steel plating providing increased ballistic protection in the cockpit and cabin.

• Guardian auxiliary fuel tanks: two 172 gallon tanks providing range extension of approximately two hours (mains plus two auxiliary tanks: four hours total). Normal operational time without the Guardian tanks is approximately two hours ten minutes.

• Fast-rope Insertion/Extraction System (FRIES) bar, capable of supporting 1,500lb per side. MH-60 mission-flexible systems are systems that can be mounted on the MH-60L to support a primary mission or enhance the capabilities of aircraft performing assault or DAP missions:

• AN/AAQ-16D AESOP FLIR. The AESOP is a FLIR with a laser range finder/designator (LRF/D). The Q-16D allows the DAP to detect,

Below: **The Army Special Operations Command 160th Special Operations Aviation Regiment flies MH-60L, -60L DAP, and modified -60Ks.**

acquire, identify, and engage targets at extended ranges with laser guided munitions.

- Cargo hook. Mounted in the belly of the aircraft below the main rotor, the hook is capable of supporting external loads up to 9,000lb.
- External rescue hoist system. Eastern-Breeze hydraulic hoist capable of lifting 600lb with 200 feet of usable cable. Primary control is by the crew chief/hoist operator using a hand held pendant.
- Internal auxiliary fuel system (IAFS). The MH-60 has wiring provisions for four additional 150-gallon fuel cells which may be mounted in the cargo area. Each fuel cell would provide approximately 50 minutes flight endurance. The maximum number of additional fuel cells may be limited due to ambient conditions and weight limitations. Use of all four IAFS tanks with the Guardian tanks reduces usable cargo area space to near zero.
- External extended range fuel system (ERFS) (MH-60L only). This consists of either two 230-gallon, two 230- and two 450-gallon, or four 230-gallon jettisonable fuel tanks that can be mounted on the external stores support system for long range deployment of the aircraft. Use of the ERFS restricts usage of

Below: A six-barrel 7.62mm minigun being positioned in the left-hand side door of an MH-60, which has proven to be a versatile platform for SOF missions.

the M-134 miniguns and specific configuration may be limited by center-of-gravity or maximum gross weight limitations, and/or ambient conditions.

- External tank system (ETS) (MH-60K only): two 230-gallon jettisonable fuel tanks can be mounted on the external tank system for long range deployment of the aircraft. Restrictions are as for ERFS. The ETS is capable of fuel replenishment by air refueling.
- Air refueling: the MH-60K is equipped with an air refueling probe that allows extended range and endurance by refueling from MC/KC-130 tanker aircraft.
- Personnel locator system (PLS), AN/ARS-6(V). This locates personnel equipped with the AN/PRC-112(V) or equivalent survival radio.
- Command and control console. This provides four operator positions with access to the four AN/ARC-182(V) multi-band transceivers and FLIR display.

The MH-60 DAP has integrated fire control systems and a pilot's headsup display (HUD) that combine to make the DAP a highly accurate and effective weapons delivery platform both day and night. The DAP is capable of mounting two M-134 7.62mm miniguns, two 30mm chain-guns, two 19-shot 2.75in rocket pods, and Hellfire and Stinger missiles in a variety of combinations. The standard configuration of the DAP is one rocket pod, one 30mm cannon, and two miniguns. The 7.62 miniguns remain with the aircraft regardless of the mission.

MH-47D/E Chinook

Dimensions: Length, rotors turning, 99ft. Width, blades folded, 12ft 5in. Max height, 18ft 11in.
Weight: Max takeoff, 54,000lb.
Powerplant: Two AlliedSignal T55-L741s turboshafts, each 4,867shp max.
Performance: Max speed, 145knots; service ceiling, 10,150ft; self-deployment range, 1,260nm.
Crew: 2 pilots plus provision for combat commander, 33 to 55 troops or 24 litters and 2 attendants.

The MH-47 is a twin engine, tandem rotor, heavy assault helicopter based on the CH-47 airframe, and conducts overt and covert infiltrations, exfiltrations, air assault, resupply, and sling operations over a wide range of environmental conditions. The aircraft can perform a variety of other missions including shipboard operations, platform operations, urban operations, water operations, parachute operations, FARP operations, mass casualty, and combat search and rescue operations. The MH-47 is capable of operating at night during marginal weather conditions. With the use of special mission equipment and night vision devices, the air crew can operate in hostile mission environments over all types of terrain at low altitudes during periods of low visibility and low ambient lighting conditions with pinpoint navigation accuracy of plus/minus 30 seconds on target. MH-47s can be transported in C-5 and C-17 transport aircraft (two in each), or can self-deploy over extended distances using ground or aerial refuel. The 160th SOAR(A) currently operates two

models: the MH-47D Adverse Weather Cockpit (AWC), operated by 3/160; and the MH-47E, operated by 2/160.

MH-47D Adverse Weather Cockpit (AWC)
The MH-47D Chinook has been specifically modified for long range flights. It is equipped with weather avoidance/search radar; an aerial refueling probe for in flight refueling; a personnel locator system (PLS) used in conjunction with the PRC 112 for find-

ing downed aircrews; FLIR; a navigation system consisting of a mission computer utilizing GPS/INS/Doppler navigation sources for increased accuracy; secure voice communications, including FM, UHF with Have Quick II, VHF, HF, Saber and SAT-COM radios; a fast-rope insertion/etraction system (FRIES) for insertion of personnel/equipment and extraction of personnel; a defensive armament system consisting of two M-134 machine guns (left forward cabin window, right cabin door) and one M-

Above: The Army SOF's 25 MH-47E Chinooks are modified CH-47Ds with a range of enhancements, including avionics and survivability upgrades.

Below: U.S. Army Rangers rapidly exit the rear of an MH-47 Chinook helicopter aboard a Ranger Special Operations Vehicle (RSOV).

Above: With the use of special mission equipment and night vision devices the Chinook's crew can operate in hostile environments at night.

60D machine gun located on the ramp; and an internal rescue hoist with a 600lb capacity.

MH-47E

The MH-47E has been specifically designed and built for the special operations aviation mission. It has a totally integrated avionics subsystem which combines a redundant avionics architecture with dual mission processors, remote terminal units, multifunction displays and display generators, to improve combat survivability and mission reliability; an aerial refueling (A/R) probe for inflight refueling; external rescue hoist; and two L714 turbine engines with Full Authority Digital Electronic Control which provides more power during hot/high environmental conditions. Two integral aircraft fuel tanks replace the internal auxiliary fuel tanks commonly carried on the MH-47D AWC, providing 2,068 gallons of fuel with no reduction in cargo capacity.

MH-47D/E standard mission equipment includes:

- Aircraft communications equipment consisting of FM, UHF (with HAVE QUICK II capability), VHF, HF, SATCOM, and the Motorola Saber. The MH-47E is equipped with SINCGARS VHF-FM single channel ground and airborne radio system.
- Automatic Target Hand-off System (ATHS) providing the capability of data bursting pre-selected/ formatted information to other equipped aircraft or ground stations.
- A navigation system consisting of a mission computer utilizing GPS/INS/Doppler navigation sources for pinpoint navigation.
- Weapons systems, in three weapons stations: left forward window, right cabin door, and at the ramp. The forward stations mount a 7.62mm minigun and the ramp station mounts an M60D 7.62mm machine gun. A crew member at each station manually operates the weapon. The weapons are used primarily for self-defense and enemy suppression.

MH-47D/E mission-flexible equipment includes:

- FLIR: AN/AAQ-16.
- Map display generator (MDG) (MH-47E only): when used with the data transfer module (DTM) it displays aeronautical charts, photos, or digitized maps in the Plan and 3D modes of operation.
- Cargo compartment expanded range fuel system (CCERFS), consisting of one and up to three ballistic-tolerant, self-sealing tanks. Each tank holds 780 gallons of fuel. They are refillable during aerial refuel operations.
- Forward area refueling equipment, (FARE), consisting of fueling pumps, hoses, nozzles, and additional refueling equipment to set up a two-point refueling site. Amount of fuel dispensed is dependent upon range of operation required of the tanker aircraft.

Twenty-five MH-47Es are fielded by Army SOF, and planned upgrades include aircraft systems modifications, avionics system upgrades, and aircraft survivability enhancements.

Heavy Sniper Rifle (HSR)

HSR is a .50 caliber anti-materiel weapon that weighs less than 27.5lb, is effective out to 1,640 yards, fires a variety of specialized ammunition (including explosive incendiary rounds, and can cycle a minimum of six rounds in one minute. It is intended to provide the SOF sniper with a capability to engage materiel targets such as wheeled vehicles, light-armored vehicles, parked aircraft, ammunition and fuel storage facilities, radar and other equipment.

It is a joint USSOCOM-U.S. Army acquisition effort, and operational testing began in FY 2000 for follow-on fielding to USASOC and also NAVSPECWARCOM.

Lightweight Machine Gun (LMG)

This is a program to provide SOF with a reliable, belt-fed, man-portable system capable of addressing area targets at distances up to 655 yards using existing 5.56mm ammunition. It is a rugged, corrosion-resistant, lightweight (less than 13lb) weapon with a threshold barrel life of 10,000 rounds, and a threshold service life of 50,000 rounds. It will be supplied with a spare barrel, detachable/adjustable sling, bipod, blank-firing adapter, and cleaning kit. Safety and reliability testing was under way in early FY 2001, with first units planned to receive the weapon in late 2001.

NAVY SPECIAL OPERATIONS COMMAND

Patrol Coastal Class Ship

Dimensions: Length: 170ft. Beam: 25ft. Draft: 7.8ft.

Displacement: 328.5 tons (full load).

Fuel Capacity: 18,000 gallons.

Propulsion: Four Paxman diesels (3,350hp each). Generators: Two Caterpillar (155kW each).

Hull: Steel, with aluminum superstructure.

Performance: Max speed: 30+ knots. Cruising speed: 12 knots. Seaworthiness: survive through sea state 5. Max range: in excess of 3,000nm (two engines at 16 knots).

Armament: MK 38 25mm rapid fire gun; MK 96 25mm rapid fire gun; Stinger station; four pintles supporting any combination of: .50 caliber machine guns; M60 machine guns; MK 19 grenade launchers. Small arms. MK 52 Mod 0 chaff decoy launching system

Complement: 4 officers, 24 enlisted.

Detachment: Berthing for nine-man SOF/law enforcement detachment.

Naval Special Warfare Command has taken control of fourteen Patrol Coastal (PC) class ships. The PC class has a primary mission of coastal patrol and interdiction, with a secondary mission of Naval Special Warfare support. Primary employment missions will include forward presence, monitoring and detection operations, escort operations, non-combatant evacuation, and foreign internal defense.

The PC class operates in low intensity environments. Missions will include long range SEAL insertion/extractions, tactical swimmer operations, intelligence collection, operational deception, and

Below: **USS** *Tempest* **(PC2), one of 14 Cyclone-class Patrol Coastal craft, is assigned to Special Boat Squadron Two at Little Creek, Virginia.**

coastal/riverine support. The PC ships, used successfully by joint operational commanders during both wartime and peacetime operations, are particularly effective in counterdrug operations.

Since first being introduced, five Patrol Coastal ships have been reconfigured or built with a nine-foot hull extension. The new ramp enables the PC to launch and recover the 11-meter Rigid Inflatable Boat and SEAL Delivery Vehicle. The upgrade significantly increases NSW's ability to support surveillance and interdiction missions. PCs will normally operate as a two-boat detachment. This allows enhanced support and facilitates the assignment of one Mobile Support Team, every two ships.

MK V Special Operations Craft

Dimensions: Length: 81ft 2in. Beam: 17ft 6in. Draft: 5ft.

Displacement: 57 tons (full load).

Fuel capacity: 2,600 gallons.

Propulsion: Two MTU 12V396 diesels (2,285hp each); two KaMeWa waterjets

Hull: Aluminum hull with five watertight compartments.

Equipment: Radar, full suite communications (HF, UHF, HF, SATCOM), GPS, IFF.

Performance: Max speed: 45-48 knots for 250nm in sea state 2. Cruising speed: 25-40 knots in sea state 3. Seaworthiness: survive through sea state 5. Max range: 600+ nm (two engines at 45 knots).

Armament: Stinger station; five pintles supporting any combination of: .50 caliber machine guns; M60 machine guns; MK 19 grenade launchers. Small arms. Mounting stations for GAU-17 minigun, MK 95 twin .50 cal machine gun, MK 38 chaingun planned.

Complement: 1 officer, 5 enlisted.

Detachment: 16 SOF combat loaded operators with 4 CRRCs.

The MK V Special Operations Craft (SOC) is the newest craft in the Naval Special Warfare inventory. The MK V SOC primary mission is a medium range insertion and extraction platform for Special Operations Forces in a low to medium threat environment. The secondary mission is limited coastal patrol and interdiction (CP&I), specifically limited duration patrol, and low to medium threat coastal interdiction. The MK V SOC will normally operate in a two-craft detachment with a Mobile Support Team. Ten Mark V SOC detachments (20 craft) were delivered by March 1999.

The Mobile Support Team (MST) provides technical assistance and maintenance support during mission turnaround. The MK V SOC is fundamentally a single-sortie system with a 24-hour turnaround time. The typical MK V SOC mission duration is 12 hours. The MK V SOC is fully interoperable with the PC ships and NSW RIBs. As such, all could be employed from a forward operating base (FOB), in a synergistic effect. A MK V SOC detachment, consisting of two craft and support equipment, will be deployable on two USAF C-5 aircraft into the gaining theater within 48 hours of notification. A detachment is transportable over land on existing roadways. Detachments are not configured nor manned to provide their own security, messing, or berthing for personnel while forward deployed.

River Patrol Boat

Dimensions: Length: 32ft. Beam (including guard rails): 11ft 7in. Draft: 2ft.

Weight: 8.75 tons.

Propulsion: Two GM 6V53N Diesel Engines (215hp each); two Jacuzzi 14YJ water jet pumps.

Hull: Fiberglass-reinforced.

Equipment: Radar, VHF/UHF Radios.

Performance: Speed: 24 knots. Sea-worthiness: sea state 3. Max range: 300nm at full speed

Armament: (Standard) twin mount .50 cal machine gun, .50 cal machine gun; stand mounted MK19 40mm grenade launcher. (Options): 40mm/.50 cal machine gun, stand mounted 60mm mortar, M60 machine guns.
Complement: 4 crew and 6 passengers.

The River Patrol Boat (PBR) is designed for high speed riverine patrol operations in contested areas of operations, and insertion/extraction of SEAL Team elements. More than 500 units were built when first introduced in the Vietnam conflict in 1966 although the current inventory is 24 craft. They can be transported in C-5 aircraft on. skids. The PBR is heavily armed and vital crew areas are protected with ceramic armor. The unit can operate in shallow debris filled water. The craft is highly maneuverable and can turn 180 degrees and reverse course within the distance of its own length while operating at full power. Engine noise silencing techniques have been incorporated into the design and improved over the years. The combination of relatively quiet operation and its surface search radar system make this unit an excellent all-weather picket as well as a shallow water patrol and interdiction craft.

Mini-Armored Troop Carrier
Dimensions: Length: 36ft. Beam (including guard rails): 12ft 9in. Draft: 2ft.
Displacement: 12.5 tons.
Propulsion: Two GM 8V53N diesel engines (283hp each); two Jacuzzi 20YJ water jet pumps.
Hull: Aluminum, flat bottom.
Equipment: Radar, VHF/UHF radios.
Performance: Max speed: 25+ knots; seaworthiness: sea state 3; max range: 350nm.
Armament: Seven pintle-mounted weapons to include .50 caliber machine gun, M60 machine gun, MK 19 grenade launcher, 60mm mortar.

Complement: 4 crew and 8 passengers

The Mini-Armored Troop Carrier (MATC) is designed for high-speed patrol, interdiction, and combat assault missions in rivers, harbors, and protected coastal areas. It has a large well area for transporting combat equipped troops, carrying cargo, or for gunnery personnel operating the seven organic weapon stations. The propulsion system is similar to that of the PBR, with an internal jet pump, which moves the water on the same principle as the air breathing jet engine. This type of propulsion is especially appropriate for beaching operations. A hydraulic bow ramp is designed to aid the insertion and extraction of troops and equipment. The craft has a low silhouette which makes it difficult to detect in all speed ranges. The unit is extremely quiet, particularly at idle speeds. A high resolution radar and multiple communications suite provides a good all weather surveillance and command and control presence for interdiction and anti-smuggling operations. The overhead canopy can be removed or stowed below. Crew size is normally four but can be modified depending on the mission and mission duration.

Light Patrol Boat
Dimensions: Length: 25ft. Max beam: 8ft 7in. Draft: 18in.
Propulsion: Twin 155hp outboards.
Hull: Fiberglass.
Equipment: VHF, UHF, and SATCOM radios.
Performance: Speed, up to 40 knots; range, 150nm; seaworthiness, sea state 2.
Armament: Three weapons stations, one forward and two aft: combination of .50 cal, or M-60 mahine guns.
Complement: 4 to 5 operators and 6 passengers.

The Light Patrol Boat (PBL) is a lightly armed Boston Whaler type craft with no armor. This craft is con-

structed of fiberglass with reinforced transom and weapons mount areas. It is powered by dual outboard motors and is highly maneuverable. It is useful in interdicting a lightly armed adversary but not for engaging a heavily armed or well organized enemy. It functions effectively in policing actions, harbor control, diving and surveillance operations, riverine warfare, drug interdiction, and other offensive or defensive purposes. Sixteen PBLs are located at Special Boat Unit-22.

The weapon mountings can include .50 caliber heavy machine guns or 7.62mm machine guns mounted on 180-degree mounts, providing an effective weapon employment in any direction. Due to its unique hull design, the PBL is excellent for the riverine environment, allowing it to operate in virtually any water depth. Its two low-profile engines are capable of providing eight hours of continuous operation at a fast cruise speed of 25-plus knots. It displaces 6,500lb fully loaded and is transportable via its own trailer, helicopter sling, or C-130 aircraft.

Rigid Inflatable Boat (RIB) and NSW RIB
24-foot RIB/30-foot RIB:
Dimensions: Length: 24ft/ 30ft. Beam: 9ft/ 11ft. Draft: 2ft/ 3ft.
Weight: 9,300lb/14,700lb.
Propulsion: Single Volvo Penta Two Iveco Diesels with waterjets.
Equipment: Radar, HF, UHF, VHF Radar, HF, UHF, VHF, SATCOM radios.
Performance: Speed: 25+ knots/35+ knots; range: 170nm/200nm; seaworthiness: sea state 5.
Armament: M-60 or M-2 machine guns, or MK 19 grenade launchers.
Complement: 3 crew and 4 passengers/3 crew and 8 passengers.

Below: First of the PC class, USS *Cyclone* was designed for long-range, high-speed patrol/interdiction and to support SEALs and other SOF.

Left: Supporting a U.S. embargo policy in 1998, SEALs in a rigid hull inflatable boat (RHIB) race to board and inspect a vessel for unauthorized cargo.

Combat Rubber Raiding Craft
Dimensions: Length, 15ft 5in. Beam, 6ft 3in. Draft, 2ft.
Weight: 265lb without motor or fuel.
Propulsion: One 35-55hp engine.
Performance: Speed, 18 knots, no load; range: dependent on fuel carried.
Complement: 8 max.

The Combat Rubber Raiding Craft (CRRC) is used for clandestine surface insertion and extraction of lightly armed SOF forces, is employed to land and recover SOF forces from over-the-horizon, and is capable of surf passages. It may be launched by air (airdrop/helo-cast), or by craft (LCU, LCM). It may also be deck-launched or locked-out from submarines. It has a low visual electronic signature, and can be cached by its crew once ashore.

The Rigid Inflatable Boat (RIB) is a high speed, high buoyancy, extreme weather craft with the primary missions of insertion/extraction of SEAL tactical elements to and from enemy occupied beaches, and coastal surveillance. The RIB is constructed of glass reinforced plastic with an inflatable tube gunwale made of a new hypalon neoprene/nylon reinforced fabric. There are two types of RIBs currently in the inventory, a 24-foot RIB and a 30- foot RIB. The RIB has demonstrated the ability to operate in light-loaded condition in sea state six and winds of 45 knots. For other than heavy weather coxswain training, operations are limited to sea state five and winds of 34 knots or less. The 24-foot RIB carries a crew of three and a SEAL element. The RIB carries a crew of three and allows for a SEAL squad delivery capability.

The latest NSW RIB is deployed on USN amphibious ships. It has a 36ft Kevlar deep-vee hull with inflatable sponsons. It is powered by two 470hp Caterpillar iesels and two Kamewa FF280 waterjets. At full load max speed is 45 knots, cruise is 33 knots, range over 200nm. Thirty-six NSW RIBs were delivered to Special Boat Units (SBUs) in San Diego and Norfolk in October 199; forty more are being delivered through 2000. Each NSW RIB detachment consists of two NSW RIBs, detachment deployment packages, and prime movers (Ford F800 4x4 trucks (if land based), all of which are transportable on standard C-130 or larger military aircraft. In early 2000, Naval Special Warfare validated the Maritime Craft Air Delivery System (MCADS), which allows the RIB to be air-dropped. MCADS uses a 2,700lb platform measuring 21 feet long and 9 feet wide to deliver the craft to the water drop zone. Once the platform and the RIB exit the aircraft, they are rigged to separate and descend under their own parachutes.

SEAL Delivery Vehicle MK VIII
The SEAL Delivery Vehicle (SDV) MK VIII is a "wet" submersible, designed to carry combat swimmers and their cargo in fully flooded compartments. Submerged, operators and passengers are sustained by the individually worn underwater breathing apparatus (UBA). Operational scenarios for the vehicle include underwater mapping and terrain exploration, location and recovery of lost or downed objects, reconnaissance missions, and limited direct action missions.

The vehicle is propelled by an all-electric propulsion subsystem powered by re-chargeable silver-zinc batteries. Buoyancy and pitch attitude are controlled by a ballast and trim system; control in both the horizontal and vertical planes is provided through a manual control stick to the rudder, elevator, and bow planes. A computerized Doppler navigation sonar displays speed, distance, heading, depth, and other piloting functions. Instruments and other electronics units are housed in dry, watertight canisters. The special modular construction provides easy removal for maintenance.

Dry Deck Shelter
The Dry Deck Shelter (DDS) allows for the launch and recovery of an SDV or combat rubber raiding craft (CRRC) with personnel from a submerged submarine. It consists of three modules constructed as one integral unit. The first module is a hangar in which an SDV or CRRC is stowed. The second module is a transfer trunk to allow passage between the modules and the submarine. The third module is a hyperbaric recompression chamber. The DDS provides a dry working environment for mission preparations. In a typical operation the DDS hangar module will be flooded, pressurized to the surrounding sea pressure, and a large door is opened to allow for launch and recovery of the vehicle. A DDS can be transported by USAF C-5/C-17 aircraft, rail, highway, or sealift.

Left: An all-electric Mark 8 SEAL Delivery Vehicle (SDV) is piloted by members of NSW SEAL Team Two. It has an underwater intercom system.

Right: One of various types of SDV used by SEALs. New Advanced SEAL Delivery System (ASDS) submersibles with pressure hulls are being delivered.

The DDS is 40 feet long and weighs 65,000lb.

Current submarines capable of single DDS employment are USS *L. Mendel Rivers* and USS *Bates*. Current submarines capable of dual DDS employment are USS *Kamehameh* and USS *Polk*. There are five 688-class submarines being modified to be DDS host platforms in FY 2001. SSN 23 will be the sixth DDS host platform. Converting a submarine to function as a DDS host requires significant internal and external modifications to the submarine.

Advanced SEAL Delivery System

Dimensions: Length, 65ft. Beam, 6ft 9in. Height, 8ft 3in.
Displacement: 55 tons.
Propulsion: 67hp electric motor (Ag-Zn Battery).

The Advanced SEAL Delivery System (ASDS) is a dry, 1 ATM, mini-submersible that can transport a SEAL squad from a host platform, either surface ship or submarine, to an objective area. The ASDS has a lock-out chamber that is controlled by operators for lock-out from an anchored position. It will anchor above the bottom between 2-190 feet. The ASDS will be transportable by land, sea or C-5/17 aircraft. The first ASDS underwent tests in FY 2000.

Desert Patrol/Light Strike Vehicle

Dimensions: Length: 13ft 5in. Height: 6ft 7in. Width: 7ft 11in.
Gross vehicle weight: 2700lb.
Powerplant: 2,000cc gas engine.
Performance: Max speed, 60+mph; acceleration: 0-30mph in 4 sec; range: 200-plus miles; max grade, 75 percent; max side slope, 50 percent; ground clearance, 16in; payload, 1500lb.

The DPV, a joint program with USSOCOM and USMC, is a modified Chenowith off-road, three-man, 2x4 racing vehicle. The DPV was designed to provide greater mobility than the HMMWV and operate anywhere a four-wheel drive vehicle can, with additional speed and maneuverability. It is transportable in CV-22, MH-47D and fixed wing transport aircraft. The DPV can perform numerous combat roles including, but not limited to: special operations delivery vehicle, command and control vehicle, weapons platform, rear area combat operation vehicle, reconnaissance vehicle, forward observation/lasing team, military police vehicle, and artillery forward observer vehicle. The weapon systems used with the DPVs are: Mark 19 40mm grenade launcher, M2 .50 cal machine gun, M60 7.62 machine gun, AT-4 Missile, low recoil 30mm cannon, and TOW missile launcher. Due to enter service in FY 2004, USSOCOM plans to procure forty-four vehicles, although it may increase this to fifty to match CV-22 acquisition objective.

Right: A three-man desert patrol vehicle, which can be used for a variety of special operations, including reconnaissance, direct action, and personnel recovery.

PART THREE

SHAPING
TOMORROW'S
SPECIAL
OPERATIONS
FORCES

SHAPING TOMORROW'S SPECIAL OPERATIONS FORCES

As the Cold War came to a close in the early 1990s, few people predicted the degree to which the ancient problems of ethnic hatred, religious intolerance, and nationalist extremism would undermine the world's prospects for international stability. Though some observers argued that the changing political environment, combined with far-reaching advances in communications technology, would herald an era of unprecedented advancement and economic growth, it now appears that this prediction was overly optimistic.

Sweeping political, economic, demographic, and technological changes are shaping the international environment in ways that cannot be predicted, and since these changes are taking place at different rates around the world, they are exacerbating the already profound differences in the relative dispersion of economic and political power. Without doubt, those seeking power will attempt to exploit these disparities to their advantage – creating numerous challenges for the United States. The most difficult problems facing policymakers will be deciding whether and when political and military engagement will best support the nation's interests. In this rapidly changing international environment, it may be difficult to clearly picture the role of Special Operations Forces in support of U.S. national

security requirements. Indeed, many of the problems that the United States will face in the future will not be amenable to military solutions. However, it is inevitable that some international problems will require a military response. In these situations, SOF, because of their unique skills, regional expertise, cultural sensitivity, and operational experience, may be the force of choice for meeting the strategic requirements of the National Command Authorities or regional decision-makers. In the future, SOF will perform three important roles in support of the National Security Strategy.

Surgical Strike and Recovery

First, Special Operations Forces will be called upon to perform those "special missions" that can neither fail nor leave the perception of failure. These surgical strike and recovery missions, ranging from rescuing hostages to preventing terrorist use of WMD, are high-risk, high-payoff tasks no other force can accomplish – operations in which national decision-makers rely upon SOF's unique capabilities to carry out. Maintaining the ability to perform these missions will be SOF's highest priority; not because these missions will be frequent, but rather because no other forces at the NCA's disposal will be equipped and trained to perform these missions within an acceptable level of risk.

Special Reconnaissance

Second, SOF will be called upon to perform special reconnaissance to support the strategic and operational requirements of decision-makers and operational commanders. Because of the development of revolutionary reconnaissance and surveillance capabilities that appear to obviate the need for the "man on the ground," SOF have had to re-evaluate their role as the eyes and ears of the theater commander. Military commanders will be extremely reluctant to employ SOF or other ground forces to perform these kinds of missions when they can be adequately performed by unmanned reconnaissance platforms. Emerging reconnaissance equipment is indeed expected to reduce operational risk to SOF and allow U.S. Special Operations Command to concentrate on developing new concepts and capabilities that integrate advanced methods, personal judgment, and on-site analysis. This human/technological synergy can be expected to enhance SOF reconnaissance of enemy capabilities and, perhaps more importantly, the determination of enemy intentions.

Below: Terrorists blew a large hole in the hull of USS *Cole* as she moored at Aden, Yemen, on 12 October 2000, killing 17 seamen and injuring many more.

Political-Military Operations

Third, SOF will be called upon to perform missions that fall in the nexus between political and military operations. These missions, which include foreign internal defense, psychological operations, civil affairs, and humanitarian assistance, will provide a low-cost means of promoting the long-term strategic goals of the United States. At the same time, SOF will be called upon to support regional contingencies, including responding to natural disasters, assisting in the evacuation of U.S. and allied nationals in the event of regional hostilities, and operating as a vanguard for conventional military forces. Although these tasks are not very different from what SOF do today, the utility of SOF to the geographic C-in-Cs will be greatly enhanced by emerging transportation and communications capabilities.

Future Requirements

In the future, SOF must remain operationally unique and strategically relevant to retain their utility to national decision-makers. To accomplish this, SOF must maintain their technological edge and continue to invest in the quality and skills of their operators. These two absolutes have served SOF well in the past and must remain fundamental commitments in order to meet the security needs of the United States in the future.

People

The importance of having the right people in SOF will grow in the future as they are employed against difficult problems in increasingly hostile and challenging environments. Operating independently, SOF personnel will more than ever need to have exceptional character and integrity. Operating in arduous environments, SOF personnel will need to maintain the highest levels of fitness. Since they will be called upon to make critical on-scene decisions, they will need to be knowledgeable and self-disciplined. In addition to all of this, SOF personnel will need to be highly intelligent to operate increasingly sophisticated equipment and to perform operations in a technologically advanced threat environment, while remaining masters of the low- and no-technology environments.

Technology

Although people are undoubtedly SOF's most important asset, maintaining and improving material capabilities remains SOF's most difficult challenge. SOF must keep its equipment up to date, while keeping the costs for sustaining its war-fighting systems under control. Failing this, SOF will not have the resources required to be able to develop the truly revo-

lutionary hardware solutions needed to maintain SOF as an effective and readily useful instrument for supporting or implementing the nation's policy objectives.

SOF will depend on leading-edge technology to provide the critical advantage and to support participation in a growing number of technologically complex and challenging missions and operations. One of the cornerstones supporting all 21st century operations will be the effective use of information. SOF will also look to emerging, leading-edge technologies in such areas as mobility, sensing and identification, miniaturization, secure communications, advanced munitions, stealth, human enhancements, and robotics

Above: Advances in unmanned aerial vehicle (UAV) technology will assist in dangerous reconnaissance missions and save the lives of SOF personnel.

to increase the efficiency and effectiveness of its operators and platforms.

The Future Concepts Working Group

The challenges of preparing for the future require that USSOCOM develops a process that allows for purposeful change to be ready

Below: However many technological advances are introduced, the importance of selecting and training high quality SOF personnel is recognized by commanders.

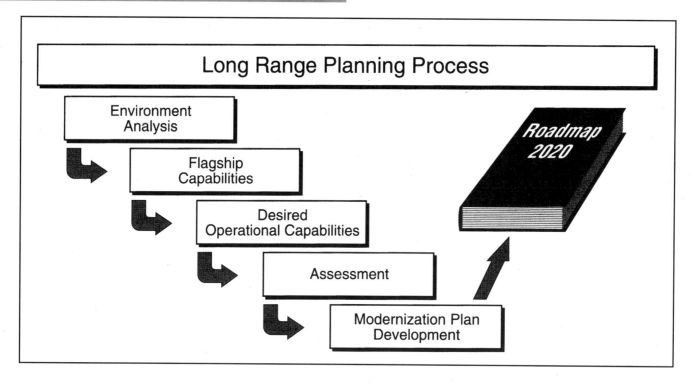

Long Range Planning Process

Environment Analysis

Flagship Capabilities

Desired Operational Capabilities

Assessment

Modernization Plan Development

Roadmap 2020

for an uncertain future. Therefore, USSOCOM is institutionalizing a process to implement the vision described in *SOF Vision 2020* and its supporting detailed guidance, *The Way Ahead*. To meet this challenge, USSOCOM has established a Future Concepts Working Group (FCWG) to develop a comprehensive process for new concept development, validation, and long-range planning. The FCWG uses a structured long-range planning process designed to facilitate development of new concepts into SOF future capabilities.

The Long-Range Planning Process

The Long-Range Planning Process is a disciplined and systematic approach to identify, refine, and present concepts and initiatives related to future capabilities and requirements. It provides USSOCOM with a vehicle to identify future desired operational capabilities and requirements for programmatic and resource consideration. This enables SOF to provide an array of enhanced options to the NCA and geographic C-in-Cs while maintaining the strategic economy of force that further defines the relevance of SOF. As the process develops sets of solutions, which define the road-map for 2020 and beyond, USSOCOM has emphasized that only SOF's core values (integrity, creativity, competence, and courage) are permanent and non-negotiable. Force structure, organizations, and legacy programs will be assessed. This five-phase approach will provide USSOCOM with a vehicle to analyze the future environment and identify future capabilities that will support SOF flagship capabilities. This capability-based approach is illustrated in the accompanying chart.

Evolving to Meet Future Challenges

USSOCOM has initially identified eight flagship capabilities for SOF that support operational concepts outlined in the Chairman, Joint Chiefs of Staff, *Joint Vision 2010* document. These flagship capabilities also provide the foundation for more detailed operational capabilities necessary for the development of sets of solutions designed to create the SOF of the future. These capabilities include strategic agility, global access, ubiquitous presence, regional expertise, information dominance, continuous secure connectivity, self-sufficiency in austere environments, and full-spectrum integrated operations.

Desired Operational Capabilities

USSOCOM perceives the next step in achieving the flagship capabilities as the development of Desired Operational Capabilities (DOCs). These are expected to provide the means to carry out the objectives of the flag-

Below: The performance, and survivability, of special operations personnel in hostile environments is a major consideration of USSOCOM.

Above: Technology will play an increasing part in SOF activities. Here an 8th Special Operations Squadron member works at an MC-130 control panel.

ship capabilities. They are operational level capabilities that will lead to the identification of specific initiatives and programs. The current DOCs are briefly described in the following bullet points.

- Personnel survivability – improve the survivability of personnel operating in hostile areas.
- Counter WMD – improve the capability to perform SOF counterproliferation missions.
- Mobility in denied areas – improve the capability to conduct undetectable ground, air, sea, and (possibly) space mobility operations in areas conventional forces are denied.
- Recruitment and leader development – improve the capability to recruit, select, assess, train, and retain SOF leaders with strong legal, ethical and moral foundations.
- Information avenues – improve effective use of information technologies across a wide range of SOF capabilities.
- Sensory enhancements – improve capability to augment human sensory systems to provide increased performance.

- Organizational design – improve the ability of the SOF organizational structure to integrate, operate, and sustain activities with DoD forces, and national and international agencies.
- Space and unmaned aerial vehicles (UAV) utilization – improve capability to fully interface and operate within the space surveillance network.
- Remote reconnaissance – improve the capability to utilize advances in technology for remote reconnaissance and mission situational awareness.
- Versatile weapons – improve multi-role/multi-purpose weapons with target discrimination and broader range of effects.

Relevance for the Future

For the future, USSOCOM emphasizes that SOF must be ready to deal equally with the demands of both their peacetime and warfighting roles. To prepare for this future, today's SOF are focusing on both traditional activities and emerging missions, while developing a strategy and structured process to build the integrated, combat-ready force necessary to face the challenges that lie ahead. To achieve this, USSOCOM is aiming at continuing its structured transformation, while maintaining readiness required to shape and respond to today's security challenges. The goal is to identify the changes

that will best enable SOF to achieve USSOCOM's Desired Operational Capabilities in support of *SOF Vision 2020*, the Chairman's *Joint Vision 2010*, and the geographic C-in-C and NCA requirements.

Budget and Manpower

To pay for USSOCOM's Special Operations Forces activities, and to achieve all of the above enhancements for the future, costs money. How much money, and in detail what USSOCOM is currently spending it on, and how much it anticipates it will need in the near future, are set out in the "United States Special Operations Forces Posture Statement 2000." The foreword to that document, prepared by Brian E. Sheridan, Assistant Secretary of Defense (Special Operations/ Low-Intensity Conflict), and then-Commander-in-Chief, U.S. Special Operations Command, General Peter J. Schoomaker, emphasizes:

"...as we prepare for an uncertain future, we must continue a robust modernization program, leveraging technology, to enhance the human dimension. We express the concept as 'equipping the man, not manning the equipment.' Merging technology with the human dimension will improve the SOF warrior's survivability, lethality, mobility, and ability to access and use all relevant information sources.

Above: Anywhere, anytime; all weathers, all terrains. These will continue to be the bywords of SOF personnel, who currently operate in about 150 countries.

"We look forward to meeting the security challenges of this new century as we work to ensure that America's SOF remain the most carefully selected, most fully prepared, and best-equipped and trained special operations fighting force in the world."

A summary of Year 2000 budget spend (estimated) compared with Year 2001 budget request is shown below. It will be the new adminsitration of George W. Bush that will determine if the U.S. Special Operations Command will be able to achieve its stated goals.

Background
The Nunn-Cohen Amendment to the legislation that created USSOCOM gave its Commander-in-Chief direct control over the majority of the fiscal resources necessary to pay, train, equip, and deploy SOF through the establishment of a separate major force program (MFP), MFP-11. USCINCSOC's control of SOF fiscal resources provides several significant benefits. First, SOF funding may now be debated solely on its own merits and not in relationship to the military departments' much larger programs. Second, a separate MFP for SOF also ensures visibility of the SOF program by the Department of Defense (DoD) and the Congress. Third, informed decisions are based on analyses of comprehensive, joint SOF data that balance the competing needs of all SOF instead of submitting separate justifications individually to each military department.

Although SOF resources constitute a small portion of the overall defense budget, direct management of SOF through MFP-11 is an extremely important means of ensuring

that the SOF are prepared to meet a myriad of operational requirements. At present, SOF stand ready to perform a host of missions spanning the entire spectrum of conflict. By dedicating approximately 46,000 personnel and 1.3 percent of the defense budget to MFP-11, decision-makers have provided the United States with a ready, highly capable and flexible joint SOF.

The FY 2001 President's budget request enables USSOCOM to support national interests worldwide. All DoD components contribute to meeting these requirements, but SOF are the single, near-term, joint force that can immediately provide an acceptable means of access, by regionally attuned forces, across the complete spectrum of military operations. SOF provide an array of options to the NCA which, despite a relatively static funding profile, are increasingly being exercised.

Above: Continuous training of Special Operations Forces, both assault and support, must continue to equip them for the harshest conditions.

The USSOCOM Strategic Planning Process drives decision-making related to resourcing, acquisition, sustainment, and modernization. It is a continuous process with a biennial cycle that facilitates the shaping of the strategic direction of SOF. It has four phases: guidance development, capability assessment, program assessment, and integration/resourcing. These phases contain activity related to the creation of guidance, the assessment of capabilities, and the prioritization of an integrated capabilities list to guide Program Objective Memorandum

Below: When attached to USSOCOM assets, Special Operations Capable Marines can be expected to increasingly operate in urban warfare environments.

Right: USSOCOM forces can expect to be involved in more Noncombatant Evacuation Operations, such as here, in Brazzaville, Congo, in 1997.

(POM) development. USSOCOM service component staff, theater SOC, and OASD(SO/LIC) participation is significant during all phases of the process. They serve as members of an integrated concept team and provide expert inputs prior to the completion of each phase of the process. Additionally, component commander participation, as members of the USSOCOM Board of Directors, which is co-chaired by the USCINCSOC and the ASD(SO/LIC), occurs throughout the process.

The starting point for the biennial cycle may be driven by actual or forecast changes in the planning environment or by DoD or USCINCSOC directive. The cycle ends with the approval of the next POM that includes the approved resource-constrained listing of capability-based programs. The POM serves as the basis for the development of the annual President's budget submission.

The USSOCOM Strategic Planning Process has been designed to provide a list of capability-based programs, over a range of constraints, that allows POM decision-makers to satisfy SOF mission needs and proactively guide development, acquisition, and employment of SOF resources in the future.

Military Department Support to SOF

The military departments also have a significant role in the resourcing of SOF. Title 10, Chapter 6, United States Code (U.S.C.), defines and apportions responsibilities between the military departments and the combatant commands, including USSOCOM. Title 10, U.S.C. Section 165, charges the military departments with the responsibility for providing administration and support for forces assigned by the respective military departments to the combatant commands, subject to the authority of the respective C-in-Cs.

DoD Directive 5100.1, "Functions of the Department of Defense and Its Major Components," requires the military departments to develop, garrison, supply, equip, and maintain bases and other installations, including lines of communications, and to provide administrative and logistics support for all forces and bases, unless otherwise directed by the Secretary of Defense. DoD Directive 5100.3, "Support of the Headquarters of Unified, Specified, and Subordinate Joint Commands," makes clear that this broad support responsibility also extends to USSOCOM and its subordinate headquarters.

Additional DoD guidance further defines military department support responsibilities. MFP-11-related programs funded in the appropriations accounts of the military departments (SOF Support Programs), but not identified as MFP-11, will consist of programs that support other users in addition to SOF. Programs in this category, such as base operating support, are programmed, budgeted, and executed by the military departments with input from USCINCSOC.

SOF Funding Profile

The SOF budget request for FY 2001 is approximately $3.7 billion, including military pay and allowances. The MFP-11 budget supports the SOF primary mission — maintaining the readiness and sustainability of current forces to support the geographic Commanders-in-Chief, U.S. ambassadors and their country teams, and other government agencies.

SOF Budget ($ Millions)

Appropriation	FY 2000	FY 2001
MILPERS*	$1,502.0	$1,540.4
O&M	1,295.9	1,356.6
Procurement	729.1	525.3
RDT&E	237.7	244.6
MILCON	54.8	74.5
Totals	**$3,819.5**	**$3,741.4**

* Funded in the MILPERS accounts of the military departments

Manpower End Strength

Category	FY 2000	FY 2001
Active Military		
Officer	5,353	5,389
Enlisted	23,867	23,775
Total Active	**29,220**	**29,164**
National Guard		
Officer	705	705
Enlisted	2,990	2,990
Total National Guard	**3,695**	**3,695**
Reserve		
Officer	2,737	2,735
Enlisted	7,308	7,308
Total Reserve	**10,045**	**10,043**
Civilian		
U.S. Direct Hire	2,781	2,788
Totals	**45,741**	**45,690**

Operation and Maintenance Budget ($ in Millions)		
Budget Activity	FY 2000	FY 2001
Operating Forces	$1,204.6	$1,263.6
Training	49.4	49.1
Administrative	41.9	43.9
Totals	**$1,295.9**	**$1,356.6**

Procurement Budget ($ in Millions)		
Program	FY 2000	FY 2001
Mobility	$272.8	$196.2
Ammunition	53.5	62.6
Comm Equip & Electronics	84.0	74.4
Intelligence	20.0	32.3
Miscellaneous	298.8	159.8
Totals	**$729.1**	**$525.3**

Personnel

Funding for military personnel is included in the military personnel accounts of the military departments. Military Personnel (MILPERS) includes the basic salaries for all active and reserve component (RC) military personnel assigned to USSOCOM, as well as the RC military pay necessary for additional schools and training days necessary for RC SOF.

As the Manpower End Strength table shows, the SOF total end strength for FY 2001 is about 46,000 with approximately one-third of their military personnel in reserve component units. Although the active force is largely responsible for meeting the demands of regional crises and conflicts and providing overseas presence, USSOCOM relies on reserve component units to augment and reinforce the active force. U.S. Army Reserve SOF personnel, for example, provide a variety of essential skills, particularly in the areas of CA and PSYOP. Additionally, about 2,800 civilians join SOF active and reserve military personnel as partners in defense.

Operation and Maintenance (O&M)

This is the heart of maintaining SOF operational readiness. O&M includes: civilian pay; services for maintenance of equipment, real property, and facilities; fuel; consumable supplies; spares; and repair parts for weapons and equipment. The table above left details the FY 2001 funding request for O&M budget activity (BA) areas.

Operating Forces

BA 1 includes necessary resources for SOF tactical units and organizations, including costs directly associated with unit training, deployments, and participation in contingency operations. Resources support civilian and military manpower, SOF-peculiar and support equipment, fielding of SOF equipment, routine operating expenses, and necessary facilities. BA 1 is divided into two activity groups: special operations operational forces and special operations operational support.

Training

BA 3 includes resources for O&M costs directly attributable to supporting the component special operations schools. USSOCOM operates the John F. Kennedy Special Warfare Center and School at Fort Bragg, North Carolina; the Naval Special Warfare Center at Coronado, California; and the Air Force Special Operations School at Hurlburt Field, Florida. Also included are training development and support activities. The schools and centers provide mobile training teams to support the operational forces as required. SOF

Below: About one-third of USSOCOM's military personnel are in reserve component units. Here, SEAL reserves undergo para-insertion training.

aircrew training and training at the joint readiness training center (JRTC) are directly related to SOF Operational Forces. The SOF medical training center at Fort Bragg, North Carolina, provides modularized qualification, advanced enhancement, and limited sustainment medical training for joint SOF.

Administrative

BA 4 provides resources for O&M costs supporting SOF-peculiar acquisition programs being developed or procured. Funding is executed by the Special Operations Acquisition and Logistics (SOAL) Center. It funds acquisition program management, engineering, and logistical support for SOF tactical acquisition programs. Support includes funding for travel, operational testing and evaluation support, and related supplies and equipment. It funds civilian program management and general contractor support for SOAL to include support equipment, necessary facilities, SOAL civilians, and costs associated with the management of SOAL.

Procurement

Procurement provides vital modernization and recapitalization in areas such as mobility, weapons and munitions, communications, intelligence equipment, and miscellaneous programs, as shown in the table above left.

Mobility Programs

The largest mission area within the procurement budget is for mobility programs, and includes funds for completion of major aircraft and maritime procurement programs, as shown in the table. Major programs included are as follows.

- Rotary-Wing Upgrades and Sustainment funding provides for a variety of critical improvements to the A/MH-6, MH-60L/K, MH-53J, and MH-47D/E aircraft. These aircraft must be capable of operating at extended ranges under adverse weather conditions to infiltrate, provide logistics for, reinforce, and exfiltrate SOF. This program provides ongoing survivability, reliability, maintainability, and operational upgrades as well as procurement appropriation sustainment costs for fielded rotary-wing aircraft and subsystems to include forward basing of MH-47E helicopters.
- Funds for the SOF Training Systems will integrate and support MH-47E/MH-60K aircraft simulator with upgrades, including avionics, aircraft survivability equipment, and integrated aircraft systems.
- The MC-130H Combat Talon II is a production and sustainment program in

Above: Recent history has shown that USSOCOM's Civil Affairs operations, often involving reserves, have increased, and will to continue to do so in future.

Below: U.S. Army Special Forces Group member guards the perimeter of a limited-duration, but maximum-effect combined services reserves training exercise.

which a specialized avionics suite has been integrated into a C-130H airframe. Its mission is to conduct night, adverse-weather, low-level, long-range operations in hostile, politically denied/sensitive, defended areas to infiltrate, resupply, or exfiltrate SOF and equipment. The funds allocated in the budget forecast below reflect the focus of ongoing efforts on meeting operational requirements in the System Operational Requirements Document by establishing organic inter-mediate- and depot-level maintenance capability on the APQ-170 Radar, Nose Radome, and AP-102A Mission Computer.

- The CV-22 SOF Modification program provides for SOF modifications to the V-22 vertical-lift, multi-mission aircraft. The Navy is the lead service for the joint V-22 program and is responsible for managing and funding the development of all V-22 variants, including the CV-22. The Air Force will procure and field 50 CV-22 aircraft and support equipment for USSOCOM, conduct Initial Operational Test and Evaluation, and provide Type I training. USSOCOM funds the procurement of SOF-peculiar systems, e.g., terrain-following radar, electronic warfare suite, etc. The Air Force will fund 85 percent of the procure-ment cost for CV-22 training systems; USSOCOM funds 15 percent. In addition, FY 2001 funds incorporate Pre-planned Product Improvements into the first CV-22 production lot.
- The FY 2001 AC-130U Gunship program

provides a reduced level of interim con-tractor support and piece part spares procurement, completes procurement of depot-level-peculiar support equipment, and begins a reliability and maintainabili-ty assessment of system line-replaceable and shop-replaceable units. The program also continues software integration labo-ratory support, post-production support, and test program set modifications.

- The C-130 Modification program pro-vides for numerous modifications to vari-ous models of the C-130 aircraft. The FY 2001 program includes: completion of interim contractor support (ICS) on the 85-185L(A); auxiliary power unit upgrade on the MC-130H and AC-130U aircraft; procurement of final data and ICS for AC-130H Low Light Level TV (LLLTV) program; completion of communications system upgrade for AC-130U; comple-tion of the AC-130U radar upgrade for higher resolution and improved projectile impact prediction; procurement of pro-duction installs for the Gas Turbine Compressor; installation of the first four ALE-47s; upgrade of AC-130U All Light Level TV laser illuminator; complete retrofit of AC-130U fleet with the ALR-69 radar warning receiver; and funding of field-requested minor modifications required to maintain operational capabil-ities of SOF C-130 aircraft.
- The Aircraft Support program continues procurement of avionics to enhance C-17 capabilities for USSOCOM special opera-tions low-level missions and the continu-

ation of EC-137 communications upgrades and other airworthiness requirements as directed by the Federal Aviation Administration.

- Funding for the Advanced SEAL Delivery System (ASDS) provides engineering and planning yard support, government-fur-nished equipment, host submarine con-version and support equipment, peculiar support equipment, ASDS alterations, and long lead-time material for major subcomponents of Vehicle No. 2. The ASDS is a manned combatant mini-sub-marine used for the clandestine delivery of SEAL personnel and weapons and will provide the requisite range, endurance, payload, and other capabilities for opera-tions in a full range of threat environ-ments.
- The Submarine Conversion program modifies Submarine Ship Nuclear (SSN) 688 class submarines to host dry deck shelters (DDS) and ASDS. FY 2001 fund-ing completes the fit-up of one SSN-688 class submarine and updates logistics support.
- The SOF Combatant Craft Systems pro-gram provides a short-range surface mobility platform for SOF insertion and exfiltration. The program supports the procurement of craft, trailers, prime movers, deployment packages, contrac-tor logistics, and engineering support.

Below: The Naval Special Warfare Advanced SEAL Delivery System (ASDS), for which USSOCOM is seeking $48 million in funding in 2001.

Mobility Programs ($ in Millions)

Program	FY 2000	FY 2001
Rotary-Wing Upgrades	$81.6	$68.5
SOF Training Systems	2.1	2.4
MC-130H Combat Talon II	16.8	10.4
CV-22 SOF Modifications	3.6	8.5
AC-130U Gunship Acquisition	26.6	13.9
C-130 Modifications	103.1	26.2
Aircraft Support	1.7	2.2
Advanced SEAL Delivery System	15.4	48.0
Submarine Conversion	3.3	1.6
SOF Combatant Craft Systems	18.6	14.5
Totals	**$272.8**	**$196.2**

Ammunition Programs ($ in Millions)

Program	FY 2000	FY 2001
Ordnance Replenishment	$37.6	$36.6
Ordnance Acquisition	15.9	26.0
Totals	**$53.5**	**$62.6**

Intelligence Programs ($ in Millions)		
Program	FY 2000	FY 2001
MATT	$ 2.1	$ 0.0
Silent Shield	1.8	11.0
PRIVATEER	0.5	2.5
SOTVS	0.6	7.0
JDISS/SOCRATES	11.4	11.8
JTWS	1.0	0.0
SOF IV	2.6	0.0
Totals	$20.0	$32.3

Communications Programs ($ in Millions)		
Program	FY 2000	FY 2001
SMRS	$4.2	$3.9
NSW Tactical Radio	0.9	0.0
MBMMR	5.7	16.5
MBITR	11.7	3.4
CONDOR	0.3	0.0
Miniature Multiband Beacon	0.0	1.0
SOFTACS	14.6	22.3
Joint Base Station	19.9	4.0
SO Comm Assemblage IMP	3.5	2.9
SOF C4IAS	17.0	10.7
SCAMPI	4.7	8.8
VTC	1.2	0.3
HQ C4I Systems	0.3	0.3
MPARE	0.0	0.3
Totals	$84.0	$74.4

Ammunition

Funds within this budget will be used primarily to procure munitions for training, operations, and war reserve stocks. Programs include:

- Funding for Ordnance Replenishment, providing replenishment munitions to support Navy SOF peacetime expenditures, combat reserve quantities, and training ammunition required to maintain AC-130 Gunship crew mission-related readiness skills.
- The Ordnance Acquisition program, which includes funds to meet the inventory objectives for war reserve and training on a variety of items developed and modified for SOF. This includes selectable lightweight attack munition (SLAM), SOF demolition kit, 40mm refuze, remote activated munitions system (RAMS), IMP 105, multi-purpose anti-armor/anti-personnel weapons system (MAAWS), and improved limpet mine (ILM).

Communications Equipment and Electronics

Special Operations Forces units require communications equipment that will improve their warfighting capability without degrading their mobility. As budgeted, the SOF Communications Program represents a continuing effort to procure lightweight and efficient SOF C4 capabilities. USSOCOM has developed an overall strategy to ensure that C4 systems continue to provide SOF with the required capabilities into the 21st century. This integrated network of systems provides positive C2 and the timely exchange of intelligence and threat warning to all organizational echelons. The C4 systems that support this new architecture will employ the latest standards and technology by transitioning from separate systems to full integration with a multitude of existing and projected national C4 assets.

Intelligence Programs

USSOCOM consolidates Intelligence programs in one budget line item to emphasize the importance of effective management in an area that is critical and essential to special operations. The table shows the distribution of funds for these programs.

Funds for Silent Shield, the airborne subset of an evolutionary Joint Threat Warning System (JTWS), will provide twenty-seven communications surveillance systems, twenty-one tactical

data receivers, engineering change orders, and initial spares. Funds for PRIVATEER, the maritime subset of JTWS, will procure the standards compliance evolutionary technology insertion (ETI) for twenty MK-Vs and seven PCs, the modern-modes exploitation ETI for twenty MK-Vs and seven PCs, and the SATCOM antenna ETI for seven PCs. The SOTVS program, which will provide a capability to forward digital/video imagery near-real time via current or future communication systems, will procure four low-rate, initial production, splashproof, single-frame video grab (SVIB) cameras; 101 splashproof, still digital (SVIA) cameras; 35 splashproof, single-frame video grab cameras; 46 SV2s; software and data controllers; initial cadre training; and initial spares. The Joint Deployable Intelligence Support System/SOC Research, Analysis, and Threat Evaluation System (JDISS/SOCRATES) program will provide enhancements to intelligence preparation of the battlefield, joint intelligence fusion, collection asset management, automated language translation, and meteorological and oceanographic system capabilities.

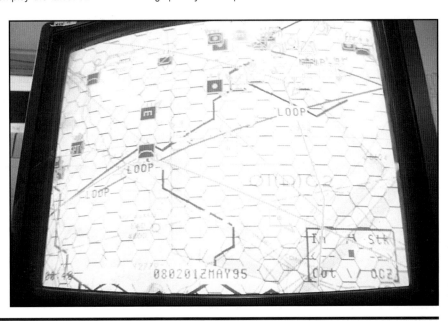

Right: Technology advancements, such as this computer monitor used in a SOF joint-services, multinational exercise, figure high in USSOCOM's budget.

Weapons Systems Advanced Development

This program includes development and testing of specialized, lightweight individual weapons, and combat equipment to meet the unique requirements of SOF. FY 2001 funding provides M4 modifications kits to increase lethality and enhance target acquisition and fire control, both day and night, in close quarters combat, and out to 550 yards range. In addition, the Lightweight Environmental Protection provides SOF operators with wet-weather handwear, headgear, and footwear.

SOF Training Systems

Funds for this program are for analysis, development, testing, and integration of SOF training and mission rehearsal systems and upgrades. Funding is provided for the AC-130U gunship aircrew training device/testbed, the Light Assault Attack Reconfigurable Simulator (LASAR for the MELB), and High-Level Architecture (HLA) development.

Communications Advanced Development

This project includes several important communications items, such as improved radios, message entry devices, and antennas. FY 2001 funds will be used for initial testing and evaluation of a special mission radio system vehicle kit; continued test and evaluation of

Above: Much of USSOCOM's budget request is for direct-action operations training, and the technical development of weapons for Special Operations Forces.

Below: An AC-130U Gunship fires counter-measures flares to thwart potential attack. Its aircrew benefit from latest training devices/testbeds.

Above: Funds have been requested for ongoing improvements to the terrain-following capability and enhanced situational awareness on the MC-130H.

Below: Army Rangers get the "go-ahead" and begin to storm their objective during an exercise at one of USSOCOM's sophisticated training centers.

new technologies in support of evolutionary technology insertions (ETIs) for all variants of the joint base station; test-bed operations for block 3ETIs and market research for block 4ETIs for SOF tactical-assured connectivity; and continued development and integration of the mission planning, analysis, rehearsal, and execution system.

Munitions Advanced Development

These projects provide specialized munitions for unique SOF requirements. For FY 2001, these include the improved limpet mine, the SOF demolition kit, and time-delay firing device.

Miscellaneous Equipment Advanced Development

This program provides development and testing of miscellaneous equipment items.

Above: The EC-130E Volant Solo epitomises development of specialized equipment required to meet unique SOF aviation requirements.

Below: A Selectable Lightweight Attack Munition (SLAM) developed for Special Operations Forces, displayed during a "Modern Day Marine Corps Expo."

Above: When the CV-22 finally reaches Air Force Special Operations Command, it will do more than simply replace some aging aircraft. It promises to transform the way AFSOC operates and how it thinks about its mission.

Aviation Systems Advanced Development

This research program investigates the applicability of already developed and maturing technologies that have great potential for direct application to the development and procurement of specialized equipment to meet unique SOF aviation requirements. The FY 2001 program begins development of AC-130U P3I, and continues aviation engineering analysis, MC-130H air refueling ground and flight testing, and the common avionics architecture for penetration.

CV-22

This acquisition program delays the incorporation of some operational capabilities until the completion of block 10 improvements. Block 10 consists of integrating directional infrared countermeasures, troop commander situational awareness connections, ALE-47 control relocation, second forward-firing chaff and flare dispenser, AVR-2A laser detection, AAR-54 warning sensor upgrade, hover couple altitude to five feet, and dual digital map. The FY 2001 program continues development of RAA block 10 changes; begins development of post-initial operational capability block 10 changes; begins risk reduction for Suite of Integrated Radio Frequency Countermeasures and CV-22 JASS software integration; and continues program office support for the block 10 program.

RDT&E Budget ($ in Millions)

Program	FY 2000	FY 2001
Sml Bus Innovative R&D	$ 4.9	$ 0.0
Tech Base Development	6.9	7.3
Adv Tech Development	7.7	7.8
Intelligence Systems	5.1	3.0
Medical Technology	3.9	2.1
SOF Oper Enhancements	61.8	87.1
Tactical Sys Development	147.4	133.5
Spec Recon Capability	0.0	3.8
Totals	$237.7	$244.6

Tactical Systems Programs ($ Millions)

Program	FY 2000	FY 2001
Aircraft Defensive System	$ 11.6	$ 19.0
AC-130U	1.3	1.3
PSYOP Adv Dev	0.8	0.3
SOF Aviation	7.2	13.4
Underwater Sys Adv Dev	43.3	10.4
SOF Surface Craft Adv Sys	4.6	1.8
SOFPARS	3.1	3.3
Wpns Sys Adv Dev	0.9	0.9
SOF Training Systems	9.2	8.7
Comm Adv Dev	2.7	3.6
Munitions Adv Dev	4.7	11.8
SOF Misc Equip Adv Dev	0.3	0.5
Aviation Sys Adv Dev	17.4	18.0
CV-22	32.2	40.5
SOF Oper Enhancements	8.1	0.0
Totals	**$147.4**	**$133.5**

Above: A Naval Special Warfare SEAL undergoing submarine training. USSOCOM's 2001 budget request includes over $43 million projected for "Underwater Advanced Development" systems.

Miscellaneous Programs

Within the procurement area of the budget is planned expenditure on miscellaneous programs, which include the following.

- Small Arms and Weapons, providing small arms and combat equipment in support of SOF and procuring a variety of weapons and equipment to include: MK93 tri-purpose M60/40mm/.50 caliber boat gun mounts; SOF-peculiar modification to the M4 carbine (SOPMODM-4) accessory kit items; lightweight, environmental protective handwear and headgear to meet the inventory objectives and additional body armor/load carriage systems; improved night/day observation/fire control devices; heavy sniper rifles to meet war reserve and training inventory objectives; and

Above: Members of NAVSPECWAR Unit One-SEAL Team Five with M-91 .308-cal sniper rifle. Funding for a new Heavy Sniper Rifle (HSR) is budgeted.

Below: The FY 2001 budget applies funding for continued service entry of Mark V Special Operations Craft (SOC) and Rigid Inflatable Boats (RIB).

5.56 lightweight machine guns to meet inventory objectives.

- Maritime Equipment Modifications, providing for PC and MK V maritime modifications. The FY 2001 program includes the PC upgrade of existing integrated bridge system (IBS) to incorporate evolving technologies including a complete electronic chart display information system, visual line of bearing integration, radar overlay capability, operator interface improvements and hardware upgrades for faster processing, display, and dissemination of IBS data, as well as installation of main propulsion diesel engine noise reduction.

- The Spares/Repair Parts program finances both initial weapon system and aircraft modification spares for SOF fixed- and rotary-wing aircraft. Initial weapon system spares include new production spares, peculiar support equipment spares, and updates to existing spares required to support initial operations of new aircraft and increases in the inventory of additional end items. Aircraft modification spares include new spare parts required during the initial operations of modified airborne systems. These funds reimburse the Air Force Stock fund for SOF initial spares provisioned with Air Force Stock fund obligation authority.

- SOF Maritime Equipment, providing necessary equipment to enable NAVSPECWARCOM to meet specific requirements for the execution of special operations and fleet support missions as the Naval Component of USSOCOM. Numerous items of equipment, such as small craft, open- and closed-circuit scuba equipment, and mine countermeasure equipment are required for the NSW component to execute their unique, special operations missions.

- Miscellaneous Equipment, providing for various types of low-cost procurement equipment that do not reasonably fit in other USSOCOM procurement line categories. Examples include: joint operational stocks, a USSOCOM managed stock of materiel designed to provide joint SOF access to immediately available equipment, such as night vision devices and optics, weapons, communications, personnel protection, and bare base support; civil engineering support equipment; and NSW sustainment equipment.

- The SOF Planning and Rehearsal System (SOFPARS), an integrated family of mission planning systems supported by intelligence databases and imagery that will

MILCON Budget ($ Millions)		
Location - Project	**FY 2000**	**FY 2001**
NAB CORONADO, CALIFORNIA		
SOF NSW Command and Control Addition	$ 6.0	
SOF Applied Instruction Facility		$ 4.3
NAS NORTH ISLAND, CALIFORNIA		
SOF Small Craft Berthing Facility		1.3
EGLIN AUXILIARY FIELD 9, FLORIDA		
SOF Airfield Readiness Improvements		3.0
SOF Hot Cargo Pad		7.3
SOF Corrosion Control Facility		8.1
SOF AGE Maintenance/Dispatch Complex		4.8
FORT BENNING, GEORGIA		
SOF Regimental Command and Control Facility	8.9	
FORT CAMPBELL, KENTUCKY		
SOF Flight Simulator Facility		5.4
SOF Tactical Equipment Complex		6.4
SOF Equipment Maintenance Complex		4.5
MS ARMY AMMUNITION PLANT, MISSISSIPPI		
SOF Small Craft Training Complex	9.0	
FT. BRAGG, NORTH CAROLINA		
SOF Battalion Operations Complex	16.7	
SOF Deployable Equipment Facility	1.5	
SOF Media Operations Complex		8.6
FLEET COMBAT TRAINING CENTER-ATLANTIC, DAM NECK, VIRGINIA		
SOF Mission Support Facility	4.7	
SOF Operations Support Facility		5.5
NAVAL AIR STATION, OCEANA, VIRGINIA		
SOS Operations Support Facility		3.4
NAVAL AMPHIBIOUS BASE, LITTLE CREEK, VIRGINIA		
SOF Air Operations Facility		5.4
NAVAL STATION, ROOSEVELT ROADS, PUERTO RICO		
SOF Boat Maintenance Facility		1.2
TAEGU AIR BASE, KOREA		
SOF Tactical Equipment Maintenance Complex		1.5
PLANNING AND DESIGN	5.7	3.8
MINOR CONSTRUCTION	2.3	
Totals	**$54.8**	**$74.5**

be used by planners within the SOF command structure worldwide to plan and preview SOF missions. FY 2001 funds procure 193 laptop mission planning systems, four deployable planning cells, and continue life-cycle replacement.

- PSYOP Equipment, the budget for which procures equipment designed to induce or reinforce foreign or hostile attitudes and behavior favorable to U.S. national objectives. The FY 2001 program will procure seven wind-supported air delivery systems, continued evolutionary technology insertions for the mobile radio broadcast system and the mobile television broadcast system, and various components of the PSYOP broadcasting system.

Military Construction (MILCON)
Budgeted funds for the military construction program allow USSOCOM to provide unique facilities necessary for the training, housing, or deployment of SOF. Projects are shown above.

INDEX